CU00793474

THE
DUST
OF
URUZGAN

FRED SMITH

THE DUST OF URUZGAN

Dedicated to Maryanne, who bore all my absences,
and then Olympia

Supported by

First published in 2016

Copyright © Iain 'Fred' Smith 2016

All rights reserved. No part of this book may be reproduced or transmitted in
any form or by any means, electronic or mechanical, including photocopying,
recording or by any information storage and retrieval system, without prior
permission in writing from the publisher. The Australian *Copyright Act 1968*
(the Act) allows a maximum of one chapter or 10 per cent of this book, whichever
is the greater, to be photocopied by any educational institution for its educational
purposes provided that the educational institution (or body that administers it) has
given a remuneration notice to the Copyright Agency (Australia) under the Act.

Allen & Unwin
83 Alexander Street
Crows Nest NSW 2065
Australia
Phone: (61 2) 8425 0100
Email: info@allenandunwin.com
Web: www.allenandunwin.com

Cataloguing-in-Publication details are available
from the National Library of Australia
www.trove.nla.gov.au

ISBN 978 1 76029 221 8

Map by Darian Causby
Set in 11.75/16.5 pt Dante MT Pro by Bookhouse, Sydney
Printed and bound in Australia by Griffin Press

10 9 8 7 6 5 4 3 2

MIX
Paper from
responsible sources
FSC® C009448

The paper in this book is FSC® certified.
FSC® promotes environmentally responsible,
socially beneficial and economically viable
management of the world's forests.

CONTENTS

Contents

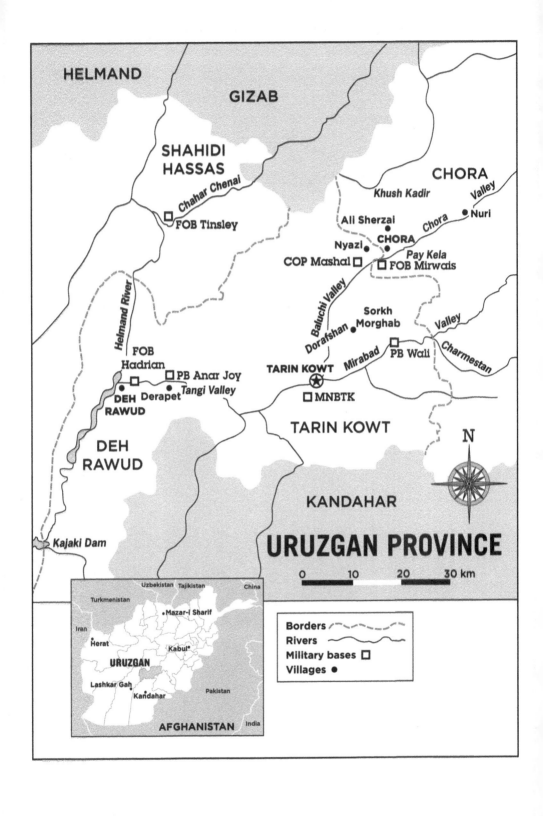

ACRONYMS

AFTER ARRIVING AT THE MNBTK VIA AMAB AND KAF, I QUICKLY CAME
to the conclusion that the ADF had turned the MEAO into an
ARE (acronym-rich environment). There were TLAs coming out of
everyone's ARSES. It took me months to sort through the barrage
of acronyms, so to save you time and vexation . . .

2 Shop	intelligence cell (military)
ADF	Australian Defence Force
AMA	Amir Mohammad Akhundzada
AMAB	Al Minhad Air Base (home of Australian HQ in the Middle East)
ANA	Afghan National Army
ANP	Afghan National Police
ANSF	Afghan National Security Forces (ANA and ANP)
AP	antipersonnel mine
ASG	Afghan Security Guards
ASLAVs	Australian Light Armoured Vehicles
BDA	battle damage assessment

BUB	battle update brief
CER	combat engineer regiments
COP	combat outpost
CO TAC	commanding officer's tactical support officer
CP	command post
CPP	Close Personal Protection
CTU	Combined Team Uruzgan (2010–2013)
DBIED	donkey-borne improvised explosive device
DC	district chief
DCU	daily commander's update
DFAC	dining facility
DFAT	Department of Foreign Affairs and Trade
ECM	electronic countermeasures
ECP	entry control point
FACE	Forces Entertainment Unit
FAM	fighting-age male
FOB	forward operating base
IDF	indirect fire (rockets)
IED	improvised explosive device
IO	information operations
ISAF	International Security Assistance Force
JMK	Jan Mohammad Khan (Popalzai tribal leader)
KAF	Kandahar airfield
KAU	Kandak Amiante Uruzgan (Uruzgan Road Police)
KIA	killed in action
LN	local nationals
LZ	landing zone
MAK	Mohammad Akbar Khan (Barakzai tribal leader from Chora)
MDK	Mohammad Daoud Khan (Chora district chief/ provincial Barakzai tribal leader)
MEAO	Middle East Area of Operations

MK	Matiullah Khan (Popalzai tribal leader and provincial Chief of Police, 2011–15)
MNBTK	Multinational Base Tarin Kowt
MNKT	Mohammad Nabi Khan Tokhi (Ghilzai tribal leader)
MP	Military Police
MRAP	Mine Resistant Ambush Protected (vehicle)
MRTF	Mentoring and Reconstruction Task Force
MT-C	Mentoring Team Charlie
MTF	Mentoring Task Force
OEF	Operation Enduring Freedom
OMLT	Operational Mentoring and Liaison Team
OTW	outside the wire
PKMs	general purpose machine gun (Russian design)
PMT	Police Mentoring Team
PPIED	pressure-plate initiated IED
PRT	Provincial Reconstruction Team
PsyOps	psychological operations
PUC	person under custody
RAR	Royal Australian Regiment
RIP	relief in place
RPG	rocket-propelled grenade
RSM	regimental sergeant major
RSO&I	reception, staging and onward movement, and integration
RTF	Reconstruction Task Force
SAS	Special Air Service
SF	special forces
SMA	Sher Mohammad Akhundzada
SOP	standard operating procedure
TBLS	Taliban's Last Stand (Kandahar air terminal)
TIC	troops in contact
TK	Tarin Kowt

TLO   The Liaison Office
TLSR   Transfer of Lead Security Responsibility
TTP   tactics, training and procedures
UMEP Uruzgan Monitoring and Evaluation Program
VBIED vehicle-borne IED
YPOC   yellow palm oil container

CHAPTER 1

CHRISTMAS IN KANDAHAR

Paint that you may see, see that you may paint.
EDGAR DEGAS

I am writing tonight, from the lines here in Kandahar . . .
FRED SMITH, 'CHRISTMAS IN KANDAHAR'

I WENT DOWN THE FIRE ESCAPE STAIRS TO THE THIRD FLOOR, looking for Al Sweetman. I found him sitting behind a desk in an office near the Afghanistan section, with the lights switched off for some reason. Resembling a yeti more than a diplomat, his tie only just made it around his neck and hung there reluctantly, as if it would rather be elsewhere.

'What do you reckon, Al?'

Al had a habit of taking unaccompanied postings to inhospitable places. He was back in Canberra on leave from the most recent of these, as deputy ambassador in Afghanistan. This was why I'd come looking for him.

It was May 2009 and the NATO-led coalition strategy in Afghanistan had shifted to 'counterinsurgency', an approach concerned more with protecting the population than smiting the enemy. It had become clear that killing Taliban was a necessary but not sufficient way to solve the problems of the country, that we needed to build the Afghan security forces, and that political and economic solutions were also required. Thus diplomats like myself were being sent by participating nations to work alongside their soldiers as part of a 'civilian surge'.

So it was that on 29 April of that year, Prime Minister Kevin Rudd announced Australia would be upgrading its involvement in Afghanistan. An additional company of soldiers would be sent to Uruzgan Province, while on the diplomatic side, a special envoy would be appointed to handle the high-level stuff, AusAID would take over the development work, and two Department of Foreign Affairs and Trade (DFAT) advisers would be sent to military bases in southern Afghanistan.

As a junior officer, I was exactly six pay grades too low to be in the running for the special envoy position, which in any case had already been filled by my father, a former Secretary of the defence department, hauled out of retirement for one last bout. But the adviser positions were at my level and had just been advertised on the DFAT intranet.

'Should I apply?' I asked Sweetman.

'Yeah, mate, it's the biggest rock show on earth,' he said. 'You'll find it interesting – too interesting at times. Plenty of material and inspiration for your songs. Not to mention a captive audience; there's not much else happening on a Saturday night at those bases – you'll have them cornered!'

'Gee, thanks, Al,' I said.

'And who knows?' he added. 'Someone like you might even be able to make a difference with the locals.'

I had been involved in protests against the invasion of Iraq back in March 2003, but I was in two minds about the Afghanistan intervention. I was in two minds about most things, actually. I was born in two minds and had lived that way ever since. My family moved to India when I was six weeks old and I was raised in the kitchen by the staff. At age three, I spoke better Hindi than English. My parents would try to practise their Hindi on me and I'd look at them like they were taking the piss, because for me there were two worlds: the world of brown people who did useful, important things around the house, and the world of whitish/pinkish people who seemed to spend their time chasing balls across fields and tennis courts.

At eleven, with my parents now in Manila, I was enrolled in boarding school in Canberra under the name on my birth certificate, Iain Smith. But the rough rugby-centric Riverina country boys I shared the dorm with struggled to make sense of me, this dreamy little ranga with sticky-up hair and an accent from nowhere. So they just called me 'Fred'. The name stuck, and by the time I finished school I had two names.

I went to university and emerged a few years later with, yes, two degrees, then won a graduate position at the Department of Foreign Affairs and Trade (DFAT). So there I was, in Canberra, in 1996 – with my two minds, two names and two degrees, and a good job – and life was going swimmingly. Then I decided I needed to write songs. So I embarked on a parallel career, writing, recording and performing. Bingo – two careers. That's when life got complicated.

In the years that followed I managed to maintain both careers through a sophisticated process of indecision. At various points, the situation seemed to call for me to throw my lot in with one or the other, if only to resolve the tension. But whenever I reached a fork in the road, I just kept on going – over the rail and onto the nature strip, where I would improvise my way back to some semi-viable path.

While neither career skyrocketed, both endured. So by mid-2009, I had recorded seven albums and, according to critics, none of them sucked. And I hadn't died or gone insolvent. I was working during the week in the Indonesia section of the DFAT main office in Canberra and spending most weekends gigging in remote corners of the country.

This lifestyle and its attendant distractions, it's fair to say, was putting strain on my marriage. It was putting strain on me too, being a full-time public servant during the week, running the business aspects of my music career in the evenings after work, heading out on a Friday afternoon to some gig or other, crawling back home on a Sunday night, then getting up on a Monday morning and doing it all again. I needed a bit of peace and quiet, and Afghanistan seemed just the ticket.

So I went back to my desk and knocked out a one-page application for the advertised positions, emphasising my experience on civil military missions in Bougainville in the late 1990s and early norties – where, if you believed my application, I had single-handedly brought peace to the war-torn island armed only with pen and guitar.

Three weeks later I was getting lunch in a cafe when I took a call from Staffing Branch.

'Congratulations, we're offering you the Afghanistan job. Please confirm acceptance by Monday.'

I got in the car and the radio came on with a news report from Afghanistan. Violence was up 82 per cent on the previous year and international forces were being targeted more than ever. I started to have second thoughts.

I consulted my shrink. Sceptical about the therapeutic possibilities of attending a war, he advised me to decline the position. I almost did.

I spoke to my wife Maryanne. She wasn't ecstatic about me going to a war zone. But aside from that, she knew me well, and had my interests at heart: 'Jobs like this have been good for you in the past,' she said. 'They get you out of your shell.'

So I accepted the position, and was scheduled to leave on 19 July.

DFAT enrolled me in a hostile-environment first-aid course and the ADF Force Preparation Course at Randwick Barracks. I also did what diplomats do before any posting and went around the Canberra bureaucracy and academic circles, talking to anyone I could learn from. I started with the head of DFAT's Afghanistan branch.

'We're interested in how the provincial government works, and any insights into what the Dutch will do in August 2010,' he told me. The mandate of the Dutch mission in Uruzgan was due to expire at that time.

Then he gave me some broad marching orders: go to the Regional Command in Kandahar, try to get to Uruzgan, figure out where you think the job is, and let me know. In short, suck it and see. These instructions might seem a little vague, but DFAT is an organisation that prizes ground truth and flexibility, and I appreciated the room to move.

'Either way, you'll report to the ambassador in Kabul. You are effectively part of the embassy.'

AusAID already had an officer, Kate Elliott, on the multinational base in the Uruzgan provincial capital, Tarin Kowt. She was home on leave and we arranged to meet. She was a forthright Tasmanian with a friendly face and a confident gait. I noticed this as she sauntered into the Phoenix pub for a chat after work.

'The job is in TK, for sure,' she said, leaning on the bar. 'We need a political officer there to talk with the provincial government and pick up on Dutch knowledge and contacts. And you'll need a good working relationship with the ADF to get things done. You'll have to manage that.'

'Okay, that sounds reasonable,' I said. 'Any other tips?'

'A hat – you'll need a really good hat. It's hot there. And when you pass through Kandahar airfield, go to the German PX store and get a little green torch to get around the base at night. Green light is harder for snipers to see, so they say.'

I went to Seears Workwear and bought a brown canvas hat in the shape of an Akubra and some smart but reasonably rugged shirts and pants.

❖

As I was thrashing around town absorbing wisdom and buying kit, things were intensifying on the home front. There was the usual mounting low-level anxiety of an imminent deployment, and more, between Maryanne and me. In late June, we attempted to buy a house but failed through mismanagement and lack of conviction. We were still smarting from that in early July when Maryanne discovered she was pregnant. I could see it would be a lonely pregnancy with me away for the next year, but it was too late to pull out.

On 18 July, the day before I was due to leave, we had arranged lunch with my parents. Driving over to their place, news came on the radio of the death of an Australian soldier; he had been killed by an improvised explosive device in Baluchi Valley, twenty-four kilometres north of Tarin Kowt. I switched it off – but too late to avoid alarming Maryanne.

When we arrived, my folks had also heard this news; we stood in the kitchen in a sober frame of mind. My father sought to rectify this by offering Maryanne a glass of wine. She declined, which was out of character. Eyebrows rose.

'She's not drinking at the moment because she is pregnant,' I said with all the nonchalance I could muster.

Dad seemed pleased. Mum was overjoyed. She had been lobbying for us to make babies for a decade or so.

Mum talked to Maryanne in the kitchen while I went to the living room for a yarn with Dad. He had instincts for working with soldiers after a long career in DFAT and Defence.

'Show them all your reporting; it'll build trust. And if security turns bad, just do what they say,' he advised. 'It's the right time for DFAT to get involved. The prime minister wants it, other ministers want it. You'll have support back here.'

I was in a melancholy mood as we drove away, but my mother waved goodbye with her usual cheerfulness. My diary from that night reflects that I was still ambivalent.

> I'm about to set off to a war that I'm not convinced is a worthwhile enterprise. My strength is also my weakness: open-mindedness.

It occurred to me that while open-mindedness was something soldiers could ill afford when going to war, it might actually be useful for a diplomat. In my preparations I had read a journal article by the British ambassador to Kabul, Sherard Cowper-Coles. In it, he wrote: 'War-winning armies need to be unflaggingly optimistic, unquestionably enthusiastic, institutionally loyal, and to some extent susceptible to groupthink.' But at the same time, he argued, political leaders needed access to an objective opinion to inform policy making, and that was where diplomats came in.

❖

With all this going on, it was a relief to get on the plane the following morning with my mate Hugh, who'd been selected for the second position assigned to go to Kandahar.

A diarist by habit, I often addressed myself in the second person, particularly when struck by a thought that needed to be brought to my own attention. I was growing a beard too, in order to fit in with Pashtun culture and to save the trouble of shaving. Stroking that stubble probably added to my philosophical disposition, and my diary from the plane trip suggests that I spent much of the flight organising my thoughts for what was to come.

This, on the professional side:

> Spend first couple of months building relationships, figuring out lay of the land, and learning. Become more useful as you have more to offer.

On the artistic front, paraphrasing Degas, I had written a little manifesto for myself:

> Write that you may see, see that you may write.

We landed in Kuwait after a fourteen-hour flight and made our way to a hotel in Kuwait City. There were glass cabinets on the ground floor with memorabilia from the First Gulf War: gasmasks, machine guns and busted-up encryption devices.

The following morning, we were collected by Australian soldiers in a minivan and driven out into the middle of the Kuwaiti desert to attend the mandatory RSO&I (reception, staging and onward movement, and integration) course on an American base in a place called Ali Al Salem. It was seriously hot. When the temperature rose above 50 degrees Celsius, Base Command would raise black flags to remind soldiers not to go jogging.

The ADF had a little enclave called Billabong Flats, some prefab buildings arrayed around a patch of astroturf. The ensuing PowerPoint briefing highlighted the dangers in theatre, prime among those being Improvised Explosive Devices (IEDs). They showed us footage of horrific IED attacks set to an MP3 of REM's 'Everybody Hurts'.

Hugh and I had time off the following morning and I filled in the 'DIY Will Kit' I had bought off the shelf at the post office before leaving and posted it to my brother.

The next day we flew to Dubai and another minivan took us from the airport into the desert to Al Minhad Air Base, the Australian military headquarters and logistical hub for the Middle East Area of Operations (known as the MEAO).

We arrived to find flags at half-mast. At the induction brief, they let us know there would be a ceremony the following morning, as the casket containing the remains of Ben Ranaudo, the Australian soldier killed in Uruzgan on 18 July, passed through the airbase en route to Australia for burial.

The following morning, the entire Australian contingent was up at dawn to attend the service. The ceremony took place in the Australian compound around a stone monument erected on a rectangular patch of grass. Engraved plaques listed the names of the ten Australian soldiers who had been killed in southern Afghanistan by July 2009. A photo of Ben rested against the monument: a baby-faced soldier with an eager smile who had died too young, killed by a mine he could not have seen, laid by a man he did not know. It was the first such ceremony I attended, and I was pretty affected by it. It sank in for me that the dangers ahead were serious and real, and it got me curious about what exactly had happened to Ben.

Later that morning we were briefed by the senior staff, who were good enough to open the session with an apology, acknowledging we'd already been subjected to months of 'death by PowerPoint'. My notes from the session are fragmentary: *ADF responsible for your life support and security . . . Afghanistan a fear-dominated society . . . whole of government – we know it's important, we don't know how to do it . . .*

The following morning, Hugh and I were fitted out with helmets, body armour and ballistic goggles. We boarded a Royal Canadian Air Force plane and three hours later were walking across the Kandahar airfield (KAF) on a blisteringly hot summer's day. It was said to be the busiest airstrip in the world. Civilian flights, fighter jets on bombing raids, CH-47 Chinook helicopters medivacing wounded coalition and Afghan forces, Hercules C-130s, C-17 Globemasters and massive Antonov-124 cargo planes were all landing and taking off 24/7 from what had become the supply hub of the massive multinational war machine that was pouring into southern Afghanistan in the summer of 2009.

Hugh and I headed for what passed for an arrivals lounge, a curved concrete structure built by American contractors in the 1950s, which was referred to as TBLS – Taliban's Last Stand. In November 2001, international forces combined with the Northern Alliance militia to drive the Taliban out of Kabul. They fled southwards to their ethnic stronghold in Kandahar. But Kandahar couldn't save them, and remnants of the Taliban forces were chased into the air terminal building by an element of the 15th Marine Expeditionary Unit. There they made an Alamo-style stand. They were routed, and the terminal still bore the scars of that battle.

TBLS was jam-packed with uniforms from thirty different nations, their occupants queueing up, milling around or just sitting there waiting. Soldiers on bases in Afghanistan were required to carry weapons at all times, and the full spectrum of national standard issues was on display. There were tidy American M4s (an M16 variant), green, plastic Steyrs in the hands of Australians, and those nasty-looking guns the Romanians carry, with fat barrels and wooden stocks.

Harried-looking 'movers' from each nation were buzzing around with clipboards, wrangling their nationals on or off flights that were constantly delayed or cancelled according to the whims of the war. Incoming travellers were ferried into minibuses and driven to the various national enclaves that had sprung up around the base, sitting side by side like pieces of a jigsaw puzzle.

Hugh and I were driven out to the Australian enclave, Camp Baker. There, ADF engineers had constructed three two-storey, baby-shit-coloured buildings, using double-reinforced concrete due to the frequent rocket attacks on KAF. Camp Baker had a gym, a welfare centre, an aviary, a volleyball court and a bar where only 'near beers' were served. Adjacent to the bar was an immaculately tended thirty-metre-square patch of grass – the only grass on KAF. Australians must have grass.

We were taken to a room on the ground floor of the second building and subjected to the mandatory induction brief. The major explained there were around 25,000 soldiers on KAF, but this was projected to rise to 50,000 by the height of the surge next summer. Alas, the sanitation was only built to accommodate 5000 bums. The septic pit in the middle of the base was about the size of three Olympic swimming pools. With daytime temperatures reaching 45 degrees Celsius, the base had a smell that could kindly be described as 'faecal'.

Accommodation was tight. Officers were living two to a room while non-commissioned officers were sharing bunkrooms with eight to ten others. The construction was rough and ready: painted concrete walls, linoleum floors and cold neon lighting. The room Hugh and I were to share was about three metres wide, with a single bed pushed against each side wall, and less than half a metre separating them. We felt more like Bert and Ernie than serious combat diplomats.

We had an appointment to meet a Dutch major named Rob, who was to work with Hugh in the office of the Civilian Representative on Kandahar. He was smart, spoke great English and had a nice wry sense of humour.

'Sorry I'm late,' he said. 'Another ramp ceremony.'

With the summer 'fighting season' in full swing, casualties were being repatriated through the airfield daily.

Rob took us for a spin around the base in an air-conditioned SUV. We encountered traffic jams at the intersections of dusty streets arrayed on a grid around KAF.

'This place is huge,' said Hugh.

'Fourteen miles in circumference,' said Rob, empirical as the Dutch often are. 'We know because some people go jogging around the base.'

We drove past a single-storey structure, about 100 metres long, with a corrugated-iron roof.

'The Boardwalk,' Rob informed us. 'It's famous. Lots of stores. You can get whatever you want in there.'

A further 200 metres down the road we passed the septic pit. Rob had a story.

'One afternoon two weeks ago, a Slovak soldier took a dare to swim across. He made it but they sent him home with reduced rank – and a staph infection! People get bored here.'

Rob dropped us back at Camp Baker and I went to find the 'welfare' phones. There were four of them in little wooden booths. Late afternoon in Kandahar, it was just before bedtime in Australia, and there was a queue of soldiers lined up to call their kids and partners before nigh-nighs.

I rang Maryanne. It's not in her nature to hide her feelings; I could always tell within a few seconds what state of mind she was in. She was distressed.

'I'm having a miscarriage.'

She had looked up the symptoms on the internet.

I did what I could to console her before vacating the booth after my allocated fifteen minutes.

I walked out into the warm, dusty evening air with a heavy heart and a sense of shame for being on another one of my cowboy missions in her hour of need. Soldiers and civilians deployed to these places get praised for their sacrifices, but there's something selfish about it too. They're like artists that way.

I wandered aimlessly along the streets of KAF. Groups of soldiers jogged by in grey, standard-issue army T-shirts and black shorts. Across their chests were fluorescent bands, compulsory for anyone moving around the base on foot at night. Traffic accidents were a problem; pedestrians had been killed.

As I was walking, a message came over the loudspeaker system that the Role 3 base hospital was in urgent need of AB positive blood. I wondered what tragedy might have led to the shortage.

I stumbled upon the Boardwalk and into a Tim Hortons, the Canadian equivalent of a Starbucks. There I saw a poster on the wall, which read: AFGHANISTAN – EXPERIENCES MAY VARY! Above this text were two photos: one of a patrol hunkering down in a dusty ditch taking cover against heavy fire, the other of soldiers lined up for morning coffee and doughnuts at that self-same Tim Hortons.

As Rob had said, the Kandahar airfield Boardwalk was famous, perhaps infamous. War correspondents in multi-pocketed vests seeking metaphors for the wastefulness and indulgences of the war effort had lampooned it often. It was an easy target that way, and one that got even harder to miss every time the Hooters Girls showed up there to put on a show.

The Boardwalk is not easy to describe. Picture a parade ground the size of a football field, surrounded on four sides by a raised wooden walkway, on the outer perimeter of which are shops of all kinds: a US Post Office, DHL, a German PX store, KFC, Burger King, Subway and Pizza Hut, interspersed with Afghan tailors and merchants selling carpets, novelties, souvenirs and hookah pipes, even an outlet taking pre-orders for Harley-Davidsons. Between the shops on each side of the rectangle were AT&T phone booths, where soldiers lined up to call home.

I came out of Tim Hortons and leaned on the railing of the walkway. I watched female soldiers dressed in beige sumo 'fat suits' wrestling awkwardly in the dust, while a ring of onlookers whooped and cheered. For those with more conventional tastes, there were volleyball matches, badminton and horseshoe competitions.

In one corner of the parade ground was what looked like an ice hockey rink under stadium lights, except it was too hot for ice, so the skating surface was made of white-painted boards. Canadians must have hockey. So from seven every evening, teams of Canadians with sticks and rollerblades went at each other with the feverish aggression this otherwise chronically polite race (thankfully) saves for the rink.

At the other end of the Boardwalk, a laptop-powered karaoke rig had been set up. US soldiers of all ages, races and genders took turns stepping up to the microphone in full uniform, rifles slung over shoulders. There was a surprising depth of vocal talent in the US military, but much of the repertoire jarred with my sensibilities. I heard 'Coward of the County', followed by 'Daytime Friends'. Then the DJ on the laptop started the backing track for what turned out to be a Christian rock song. I could take it no longer and went off in search of the British dining facility, or DFAC, as they are known across Afghanistan.

I found the Cambridge Mess halfway back to Camp Baker, and followed a group of British squaddies through the door. There was a counter where you signed in, then a hand-washing station comprising a line of taps over a stainless steel trough. I grabbed a brown plastic tray and walked into a large, neon-lit canteen with tables and plastic chairs. I filed past a twenty-metre-long bain-marie, piling all sorts of tucker on my tray.

All-you-can-eat buffets are a problem for me. My diary entries from the years to come often began with: *Ate too much last night, slept badly.* An abundance of free food was partly to blame, but also, far from home and loved ones, certain emotional appetites are not sated, and one compensates by overeating. I'd find myself lying in bed wide awake, filled with discomfort, gas and self-reproach.

Sitting there alone under the neon lights of the British chow hall with 200 of my new closest friends, I got thinking about Maryanne, hoping she was asleep by now. It occurred to me that Kandahar airfield would be a lonely place to spend Christmas.

I ploughed through the food, cleared my tray at the exit, and made my way to the Aussie movers office to sign up for the next bird to Tarin Kowt.

Christmas in Kandahar

I am writing tonight, from the lines here in Kandahar
Bunks beneath neon lights, hear the other guys snore and fart
Planes take off in the night, on missions unknown
While the rest of us turn away and face the night all alone

Fighting season is through, and the winter seems here to stay
Not like it was in June, ramp ceremonies every day
Put the flag on the box, and fly the boy home
We salute and then turn away to face the night all alone

Out on the Boardwalk tonight karaoke from 8 pm
Hockey under the lights, you just can't help those Canadians
While the Yanks and the Brits, line up for the phone
Make their calls and then turn away to face the night all alone

Instrumental

Could do much worse, I guess, than a Christmas in Kandahar
Ate too much at the mess, stumbled home to this cold guitar
Someone turns out the lights, but I sit like a stone
Then I lay down and turn away and face the night all alone

I can't remember writing this song, but I know I finished it sometime between July and Christmas of 2009. The melody and guitar pickings, along with the refrain 'turn away and face the night all alone', actually came to me in 2005 when I was touring in the United States.

In the intervening years, I had been trying to write the lyrics around events in the town of Galveston, Texas, when a massive hurricane caused a sea swell that drowned the burgeoning port city in September 1900, the deadliest natural disaster ever to strike the US, killing between 6000 and 12,000 people. I wasn't there at the time, so was finding it difficult to finish the song.

I recorded the guitar, vocals and harmonica with Peter Kennard in his studio in the Blue Mountains in early January 2010. Hamish Stuart and Leon Gaer added drums and bass at Megaphon Studios in Sydney a week later.

The song has not garnered a whole lot of attention from listeners or critics, with a couple of notable exceptions. A pilot named Peter Douglas, who spent time in Kandahar, made a video of the song and put it on YouTube. Also, Melbourne *Age* journalist Martin Flanagan wrote a piece on the *Dust of Uruzgan* album in 2013, and he focused on 'Christmas in Kandahar' as the highlight of the recording.

It seems to be a hard song to fit into the live set list, which is a shame because I like it.

CHAPTER 2

WOMAN IN A WAR

A painting is a series of corrected mistakes.

ROBERT BISSETT

There's nothing like the hunger for some softness in the night
When you wake up every morning with a war to fight

FRED SMITH, 'WOMAN IN A WAR'

SONGWRITING IS A MESSY BUSINESS. YOU HEAR A MELODY IN YOUR head then start scribbling words in its general direction. Then the phone rings and you're grateful for the distraction. A week later you scribble some more words. You read the words you scribbled the previous week. They look dumb, they feel dumb, they are dumb, and the whole project seems to be going nowhere. You feel like a fraud for calling yourself a songwriter, but you keep scribbling and eventually it becomes clear what the song is and isn't about. You scratch out the dumb and irrelevant words and look at what's left – there's your song, as if it had been there all along.

Was the time spent writing the discarded words wasted? No. You look back on those early scribbles and see a series of mistakes that led to revelations that led to clarity. This is how I moved forward in that first month in Tarin Kowt: by making mistakes.

The next bird to Tarin Kowt was a Dutch bird, and like most Dutch birds, it was an early bird. The Aussie 'movers' had told me 'bag drag' was at 0530 hours. I managed to drag my arse and my bags onto the loading pallet by 0531, which, by musician's standards, was positively punctual. But I was reprimanded by the Dutch loadmaster: 'On time is too late!' he said.

After that, things got more relaxed – surprisingly so. The TBLS departure lounge was full of Dutch soldiers, men and women, tall, blond and beautiful, lying about languidly – sleeping with their heads on one another's shoulders, joking and poking each other, or sitting, legs crossed, reading. I guessed a lot of those Dutchies had been in and out of theatre a few times – and in any case, they are a social species and the martial spirit is seldom glorified in Dutch culture.

The flight was smooth, except for the last minute of it, when the plane banked and descended steeply to avoid any surface-to-air pot shots. The rear hatch opened, the ramp dropped and I got my first glimpse of the austere brown mountain ranges that surrounded the Tarin Kowt 'bowl'. We piled on the back of a people-moving truck that conveyed us along a dusty road through a dusty security gate manned by Slovak soldiers in dusty-coloured uniforms.

The truck dropped us at the movers' shed for yet another induction briefing. As it was ending, AusAID Kate arrived. She took me up to the accommodation lines. Most of the office and living quarters on Kamp Holland were assembled from faded yellow shipping containers made by the German Drehtainer company with six-inch thick steel to protect the contents – mostly us – from incoming rockets. Modular like Lego, they were bunched into clusters of twenty-four Drehtainers, arranged in a rectangle on a concrete slab, a dozen containers lined up on each side of a corridor. Each of these clusters, known as a 'chalet', was surrounded completely by Hesco barriers – steel mesh cages one metre thick and two metres high, filled with rocks and earth. Overhead was a 'det roof', a corrugated-iron covering was suspended above the roof of each chalet by triangular roofing frames. These were designed to cause incoming rockets to detonate before hitting the surface of the container.

Twenty-four chalets were arrayed in a grid on the south side of the camp, and a dozen or so chalets were clumped together on the north side, designated as headquarters and general offices. In between were a parade ground/volleyball court, a DFAC, a chapel, gym and laundry, a Dutch cafe called Echoes and an Aussie rec area called Poppy's.

As we walked to the office chalets, Kate apprised me of the political geography of the base, pointing in the direction of the various 'camps' within the grounds of the Multinational Base Tarin Kowt (MNBTK). The base had evolved on the northern edge of a gravel airstrip the Russians built in the early 1980s, two kilometres away from the provincial capital Tarin Kowt. The perimeter of MNBTK – about the same circumference as an international airport – was guarded by four-metre-high rammed-earth walls with guard towers every couple of hundred metres manned by Afghan Security Guards (ASG).

Since 2001, half a dozen separate camps had sprung up within this perimeter, each within their own high walls, razor wire and entry checkpoints. It all started with Forward Operating Base (FOB) Ripley, an operating platform for detachments of US special forces that had been working in Uruzgan since late 2001. Next to FOB Ripley was Camp Cole, occupied by a squadron of attack helicopters and related support called Task Force Wolfpack.

'They've got great ice-cream in the Camp Cole DFAC,' Kate confided.

On the east side of the base, Australian Special Forces had set up Camp Russell in 2006, naming it for Sergeant Andrew Russell, the first Australian soldier killed in Afghanistan four years before. Beyond Camp Russell was the Afghan National Army camp, a burn pit for garbage disposal, and a weapons range used for live fire practice.

In the centre of the base, where we were standing, was Kamp Holland, built by the Dutch with the help of Australian military engineers when both arrived in 2006. The surface of Kamp Holland was all dust roads or walkways carpeted with rocks the size of golf balls. No grass. My calves were already aggrieved.

At the Dutch headquarters chalet, Kate introduced me to the new Dutch political advisers, Eric and Arjan, who had arrived a week beforehand. Both were tall, at least six foot four; they clasped my hand heartily, patted me on the back from a great height and invited me into their office container, pulling out a chair.

'You will sit here. We want to have an integrated PRT.'

Eric was a blond, athletic-looking guy with a quirky, friendly manner. His accent was mild and his English fluent. Arjan was sporting a newly grown beard he kept fiddling with.

They introduced me to Michel, the new Civilian Representative (CivRep) and head Dutch diplomat on base. The three of them led me to a room where I was briefed within an inch of my life. That was the first time I experienced the infamous 'Three D' brief, a set piece PowerPoint barrage that the Dutch leadership inflicted on visitors and innocent bystanders.

The Dutch, as I came to understand, have didactic tendencies. But to be fair, they had a good story to tell about their work in Afghanistan. The three Ds were defence, diplomacy and development. It was essentially the counterinsurgency approach that had recently become fashionable, only they'd been doing it since 2006.

On the defence side, the Dutch were the lead nation in Uruzgan and had 2000 soldiers on the base, including a large battlegroup with infantry, artillery and engineers, as well as a special forces contingent called Task Force 55.

'They do the "kinetic" stuff, but the PRT is in the lead,' said the outgoing CivRep.

The PRT was the Provincial Reconstruction Team. There were PRTs of various shapes and sizes right across Afghanistan and Iraq, doing development and diplomacy work. The Dutch had given the PRT primacy and their CivRep shared an office, and leadership of a diarchy, with the Task Force Uruzgan commander, Brigadier Marc van Uhm. Whenever the two men reached a door together, there was an 'after you', 'no, after you' moment, but on the whole it worked well.

On the diplomacy front, they explained that the focus was on managing tribal relations and supporting the provincial administration, lobbying in Kabul through their embassy to have good Afghan staff and leaders sent to the provincial government. There was also a certain amount of crisis management, handling relationships with Afghans whenever there was a civilian casualty incident or when one of the various task forces accidentally killed the wrong guy.

In terms of development work, the Dutch were into everything: rule-of-law programs focused on courts and prisons, schools and hospitals. They had a saffron program to try to displace the opium industry – the main source of cash income for farmers in the province and 50 per cent of Afghanistan's GDP. They subsidised flights to Uruzgan by an Afghan airline called KamAir in an attempt to mitigate the province's main curse, its isolation.

There were also big projects for the Dutch home audience –
'eye-catching deliverables', as they called them – including their
flagship project, the 'Road to Chora', a paved road which was
slated to run north up the guts of the province, from Tarin Kowt
through Dorafshan and the Baluchi Valley to Chora. They were
having some difficulties with security and contractors for the
project, but hoped to get it done by the middle of 2010.

Which begged my first question.

'What happens after 2010?'

To which I got the sanctioned answer: '2011.'

Fair enough, I thought; it was a decision for their political masters.

'In the meantime, we should create a fully integrated PRT
with you Aussies and the Americans,' said Michel.

This was a sensible enough aspiration, but as always with the
Dutch, there was an angle. A narrative of the Dutch graciously
handing over the baton would 'play' better back home than images
of bewildered and unprepared Australians left holding the baby.
Political support for the mission in the Netherlands was tenuous,
so home-front politics influenced a lot of what they did on the
ground, with the 3000-mile screwdriver ever present.

'You should work in here with us,' said Michel, 'and join
us when we go outside the wire for meetings. We can provide
mobility and, of course, security.'

I ventured a second dumb question: 'Are we civilians a target
out there?'

There was an awkward pause. They all turned to the Dutch
intelligence major sitting in the corner.

'Big time!' he said.

Two hours later, 3D brief over, and Eric and I headed to the
quartermaster's store to see if I could pick up some office shelving.

'You know,' he said, 'with all this dust and the big sheds, I guess
this place feels like the Australian outback.'

'Yeah, like something out of *Mad Max*. Have you seen *Mad Max*?'

'All three of them,' he said.

❖

Later that afternoon, Kate took me across to the headquarters chalet of the Australian Mentoring and Reconstruction Task Force 2. MRTF 2 had 'RIPped' (relief in placed) with MRTF 1 back in May, which in turn had replaced four rotations of the Reconstruction Task Force (RTF), who were the first contingent of Australian regular forces sent to Uruzgan, in 2006, comprising around 400 soldiers, mostly ADF engineers building schools, roads and hospitals.

The 'M' in 'MRTF' had been added in October 2008 to reflect the new focus of the Australian mission – to build the capacity of the Fourth Brigade of the Afghan National Army, the 'ANA' as we called them. The strategy was that at some point we could all go home and leave the fight to them.

MRTF's mission was narrowly defined to mentoring the ANA. Nonetheless, they were beginning to broaden their horizons.

Outside the MRTF headquarters, a couple of guys were sitting at a wooden picnic table. Kate introduced me first to Tristan, a tall civilian. His sidekick and military minder, Anton, was a compact moustachioed Aussie major with a subtle air of mirth about him.

I explained that I thought my role would be to liaise with the provincial government and learn a bit about the politics of the province.

'Oh, cool, we should talk,' said Tristan. 'We're mapping the white space.'

In military parlance, there are the good guys – us, the 'blue team' – and the enemy – them, the 'red team'. Then there is the partnering force, in this case the ANA, the 'green team'. Everyone else – i.e. the human beings occupying the province – is the 'white space'.

Anton explained that recent strategic directives had identified that the centre of gravity for all operations was now the white space. 'So mapping the white space has become a priority. Tristan here is a mathematician. We're working with a methodology called social networking analysis.

'It's difficult, though,' he continued, 'trying to keep track of all the players in the civilian space. Everyone seems to have the same names, like Mohammad Akhtar, or Akhtar Mohammad. And then the reports from the patrol teams are messy. The same bloke might have four different names. Or he might be listed as "possibly insurgent", "possibly a mullah", "possibly murdered his brother", and so on.'

'Sounds complicated,' I said.

'You should come and have a look some time – in fact, we're briefing S2 on it tonight.'

Kate took me in to the headquarters chalet to meet the Aussie S2. By NATO convention, the various departments within military headquarters are designated numbers: one is for personnel, two is for intelligence, three for current operations, four for logistics, five for plans etc. So the intelligence cell is referred to as the '2 Shop' and the head of the 2 Shop is the S2, G2 or J2, depending on the size and nature of the headquarters.

We found S2 sitting behind her desk in an office container, maps all over the wall. She spoke quickly and directly and meant business, but she had a certain warmth about her, and was good mates with Kate. The operational tempo had been fierce through the summer, and she had been working fourteen-hour days, fuelled by Diet Coke and adrenaline. She said her resources were stretched and it would be good to have someone keeping an eye on the political space.

I told her I intended to run all my reporting by her before sending it outwards. She agreed this would be good practice.

In DFAT we have a saying: 'I report therefore I am.' It's partly self-parody – most of us like to write and be recognised for our reporting – but there is a purpose to this habit. Policies and policy-makers need to be informed by a ground truth. A key mechanism for this is 'cables', carefully crafted reports distributed widely and deliberately around government agencies – the minister's office, Defence, AusAID, the Office of National Assessments, the PM's department, Immigration and whoever else needs to know. DFAT officers take great pride in their cables, and each embassy develops a house style under the guidance of the editor-in-chief, the ambassador.

Up until 2009, the only reporting the Australian government had on Uruzgan came from our military. It was, naturally, focused on the military contest and was not disseminated widely. So there was a gap in the government's visibility of the politics of the province, which needed to be filled.

I spent my first few nights in TK sleeping in the Officers' Transit Container, where I learned that the higher the rank of the officer the more likely he is to snore. Then the Force Support Unit told me there was a bed for me in Chalet 6, so I went there and found an empty double shipping container with the number 14 on the door. Next door, containers 16 and 18 were designated for a dozen officers from the Australian Federal Police, also outsiders in this sea of green, so this seemed the right neighbourhood for me. I moved in and put sheets on the bottom mattress of a bunk in the corner, chucking my stuff on the top bunk for want of anything resembling a cupboard. Soon, a guy who introduced himself as Shorty moved in to Container 14 (anyone in the ADF under five foot ten is at risk of being called 'Shorty'). A couple of nights later, I came home after working late and the lights were out. Not wishing to wake Shorty, I felt my way to my bed and got a rude shock when I sat on something hard and lumpy. During the day, it seemed, six others had moved in and dumped my stuff from the top bunk onto my bed.

Soldiers get good at managing their stuff in tight accommodation, whereas when I occupy a hotel room, within fifteen minutes I can make it look like a thief has ransacked the place. I knew I was going to need help to keep my gear in order. Some furniture would be a good start; apart from the bunks, the container had none.

Fortunately, the following Tuesday night was 'Bunnings Night'. Hosted by the chippies in the maintenance yard, you rocked up at 1600 hours with ideas for furniture and they supplied everything you needed to make your dream come true. Dressed in a blue King Gee work shirt and my hat from Seears Workwear, I walked up to a weathered old warrant officer who directed me to a bloke named Red at the other side of the workshop.

Red was one of life's happy campers. He welcomed me with a broad grin and a 'What can I do you for?' I outlined to him in ballpoint a representation of my wildest dreams: a double cupboard for me and the private who had just moved in upstairs. Red sent me back to Chalet 6 to verify the dimensions of the desired object.

There I got lucky again; Shorty revealed that he was once a chippy, and knocked out a very tidy technical design. I took it back down to the maintenance yard.

'Want us to make this for you, mate?' Red asked, after glancing down at my soft musician's hands.

'Yes, please,' I conceded.

'That'll cost you a carton – of Coke.'

Three days and a carton of Coke later, a robust rectangular cupboard was delivered to Chalet 6, Container 14. It was not the sort of piece my wife would let anywhere near the house, but this far from home, it felt like a luxury.

❖

The embassy in Kabul sent me an old Nokia that ran on the local Roshan network. Afghanistan is a country where simple, durable things with interchangeable parts prevail: like Toyota Corollas, AK-47s and Nokias. Everyone you met, down to the poorest farmer, had a Nokia – they're a conversational bunch the Afghans, and everyone had the same ringtone!

So I had an Afghan cell phone, but no Australian landline phone at my desk in the Dutch PRT. Whenever I needed to call home or DFAT, I trudged over to the 'welfare centre' in the middle of the base. This was a room with sixteen small pinewood booths; in each was a phone that went direct through a Sydney switch to anywhere in Australia. In the daytime, it was bloody hot in those booths, but mostly you didn't notice that as you entered a portal to another world – the one you had left behind. With the thin partitions, though, you also entered into the world your colleagues had left behind, more so than you really wanted.

My diary records:

> The welfare centre is a place of all kinds of chaos.
> The ADF includes a two-page SOP [standard operating
> procedure] in their pre-deployment psychology manual
> on how to handle phone calls home: Keep it light, make
> a list of ordinary things to talk about etc. Good
> counsel but hard to put into practice.
>   Yesterday afternoon there was a young digger
> reeling off a string of nasty vitriol in the direction
> of, presumably, his girlfriend back home. It went on
> for about ten minutes, while I was having a fairly

difficult conversation myself with Maryanne, who
had been troubled by a news article that showed
a map of Uruzgan surrounded by red ink denoting
Taliban dominance.

Sometimes you overhear a young father obviously
copping it from his wife back home, stressed by the
rigours of single parenting. He starts to feel responsible,
then guilty, then lashes out with 'Yeah, well I'm
fighting a fuckin' war here!' The older dogs, warrant
officers and the like, have been doing this all their lives
and seem to know how to keep things on an even keel.

Today there was a young female soldier in the
phone booth behind me evidently talking to her
boyfriend at home. Things weren't going well, and she
was sniffling quietly. As her call finished, out of the
corner of my eye I saw her pick up her backpack, put
on some dark sunglasses and walk out, chin up, chest
pressed forward. It can't be easy being a woman in
the army.

For internet access, I used my own laptop in the office I shared
with the Dutch political advisers, Eric and Arjan. I learned a lot
from spending time with them. I could keep my finger on the
pulse of what was going on for the Dutch, and they were tapped
in to the political space of the province.

But at times the constant flow of people coming in and out
of that office with questions and taskings made it hard to get
written work done. And the Dutch had a full-time historian on
staff, Sebastian, who enjoyed pushing people's buttons.

'I have been to Canberra,' he said of my hometown when we
first met, 'and I think it is a pitiful, tragic place.'

One evening, as I was trying to write up a meeting report, Sebastian came into the office to ask Eric something. He saw me there and pounced.

'What do you call a guy with no dog?'

'Dunno.'

'Douglas.'

And so on.

I left, and came back five minutes later. Sebastian was still there.

'Hey, Iain, do you like dingoes?'

'I prefer women.'

'I hate dingoes. I went to Fraser Island and they stole all my food.'

I could take it no longer and resolved to get myself a second desk in the Aussie MRTF headquarters, where Sebastian couldn't find me. I also needed to be closer to the Australian leadership and 2 Shop, and have access to my own Defence Secure Network and Defence Restricted Network laptops for drafting and sending cables to the embassy, but I was sensing resistance somewhere in the system, probably relating to the ambiguity of my status in TK.

When working with the military, some problems are best solved by going straight to the top and letting the chain of command do its thing. As luck would have it, Major General Mark Kelly, Commander of Australian Forces in the Middle East, came to town for a visit from his headquarters in the United Arab Emirates. Over lunch, I explained what I thought I should be doing and how I proposed to operate. Late that afternoon a buckled old trestle table with a couple of laptops appeared for me in the office of the CO's tactical officer, right next door to S2.

The tactical officer himself, Andrew Hastie, was a tall, young, square-shouldered lieutenant. He read more broadly than other lieutenants; we often conversed about the bigger picture of the war. His job was to organise and lead outings for the commanding officer and he always travelled in the lead Bushmaster. Over the two weeks after I moved in, his vehicle got hit three times by IEDs. He seemed to handle it with equanimity, although he did go a little quiet for a while there.

The CO TAC's office also doubled as the transit office for colonels coming in and out of theatre. On 14 August, a Colonel Mark Frendin joined us for a few days before heading up to Combat Outpost Mashal to investigate the incident in which Ben Ranaudo was killed.

I spent those early weeks in TK settling into the 'battle rhythm' of the base. Each day, bar Sunday, work began at 0730 with the daily commander's update (DCU) in the Task Force Uruzgan conference room. The senior Dutch staff sat around trestle tables set up in a U-shape facing a screen. Up the back of the room were some folding chairs.

One morning I arrived at 0730 just as the Dutch sergeant major was closing the door.

'On time is too late!' he growled at me.

I sat beside Michel and Brigadier van Uhm, who were still sitting in the rows of 'back seats' as their predecessors had not yet left. Although there were only two or three Australians in the room, in accordance with NATO regulations, the Dutch conducted the briefing in English.

The Dutch G2 was explaining a rocket attack on the base that had happened the night before. He had a map on the screen and, pointing to a red X marked about three kilometres to the west of MNBTK, he said: 'This is the POO site, sir!'

I whispered to Michel, 'What's a poo site?'

Michel asked Brigadier van Uhm, who in turn whispered the same question to his adjutant.

'Point of origin, sir.'

Van Uhm whispered to Michel, 'Point of origin.'

Michel turned to me and whispered, 'Point of origin.'

'Got it,' I said.

G2 went on to cite reports that two men in turbans, not known to locals, had been seen working furtively on something in the vicinity of the POO site before the attack, then fled on a motorcycle.

He said, 'We can't tell for certain what they were doing, but we're pretty sure they weren't out there *swaffelen.*'

The staff all sniggered. I didn't get it. I wrote down the word 'swaffelen' with an asterisk in the adjacent margin as a reminder to make inquiries.

After the DCU, I went back to the office I shared with Eric. The outgoing political adviser, Alex Oosterwick, dropped in for a final handover.

'*Swaffelen?*' I asked him.

'Ah yes, *swaffelen,*' he said after an awkward silence. 'Every year in Netherlands we have a New Word of the Year competition. *Swaffelen* was the New Word of the Year in 2008.'

'Yes, but what does it mean?'

'Well, um, it's a Dutch cultural practice. It means to swing your penis back and forth and bump it up against something.'

'Is this practice popular in Holland?'

'More so among the men than the women.'

Alex explained that in the 2008 competition, two Dutch tourists filmed one another *swaffelen* the Taj Mahal. They put the footage on YouTube and it went viral. *Swaffelen* won the word competition by a mile, and this triggered a whole craze of Dutch tourists travelling around the world *swaffelen* national monuments – the Sphinx, the Eiffel Tower, the Washington Monument etc.

'This was a problem for me,' he said. 'My ambassador in Delhi was summoned by the Indian foreign ministry to "please explain". I had to write defensive talking points for him with background notes explaining the *swaffelen* pandemic.'

All this was very troubling. It occurred to me that the Australian government was spending large amounts of money on counterterrorism, but doing nothing to counter the *swaffelen* threat. I couldn't sleep that night, so I got up and drafted an email to a number of people around DFAT, highlighting the *swaffelen* risk and recommending a range of countermeasures – biometric testing for Dutch tourists at Australian borders, and passing an electric current through the Sydney Harbour Bridge.

Sleep-deprived, and breathless at my own prescience and eloquence, I pressed send.

Big mistake.

Foreign policy is a serious business. But every now and then I see something so funny I can't stop myself. Or maybe the line between performer and government official gets blurred.

Kate was the first to see the email and gently suggested that, while she found it pretty funny, it might not be a good idea to distribute this sort of thing too widely. The embassy sent a short sharp email: 'Save this stuff for the memoirs.' Sound advice, though I have since lost the email. Fortunately, it went no further.

❖

On the morning of 8 August, I was due to make my first trip OTW – outside the wire. The night before I was pretty nervous and didn't sleep well. Having been briefed rigid about the IED threat, I was pretty certain I was going to die. I woke early and swept through my office to pick up my body armour then went out the back of the PRT to join the convoy.

An interpreter named Farid had been lined up for me. I was waiting inside the secure area at 0756 but Farid was not there. One of the Dutch soldiers suggested I look outside the secure area gate near the Dixis.

Dixis were blue plastic portaloos that proliferated around the base. There was a cluster of them out behind the gate of the headquarters which served as a key rendezvous point for any convoy, and for meeting up with interpreters who were not allowed into the secure area unescorted. In the years to come, I must have said, 'Meet you out by the Dixis,' a hundred times.

Sure enough, I opened the gate and there was a young Afghan male, with neatly combed hair and soft brown eyes, squatting in a little rectangle of shade created by the Dixis.

'You must be Farid.'

'No, Farid is not coming. My name is Iamatullah. But you can call me Ian.'

'Hi, I am Iain, but please call me Farid.'

'Ah, "Farid",' he said. 'In Arabic that means "he who walks alone".'

'I'll take it,' I said, and thereafter introduced myself to Afghans as Farid, a variation on 'Fred' which I figured they could pronounce and relate to.

We joined the considerable Dutch security contingent to receive our orders. I was wearing the ballistic ski mask some card in the Force Support Unit had given me, and this set the Dutch soldiers to laughing so hard that the young special forces captain had to quieten them down.

'Okay,' he barked with a casual authority. 'Mission: to escort VIPs into Tarin Kowt for a meeting at the governor's compound and then to the prison and bring them back without incident. Dangers: there is known to be a Pakistani suicide bomber with a missing finger in the area. Actions on: in the event of signs of threat, use escalation of force, if this does not work, take him down. Mission will commence in sixty seconds.'

I saw a Bushmaster, tapped Iamatullah on the shoulder, and we were away.

The ADF insisted that all Australian personnel travel by Bushmasters. In seventy IED strikes, they had a 100 per cent survival rate. A couple of weeks before, a Bushmaster had hit a victim-initiated mine – one front wheel was found 120 metres to the west, the other 130 metres to the east, but the driver survived. The Dutch had taken to buying Bushmasters from us, hence our ride for the day.

We were greeted by a skinny Dutch driver with a thick accent, close-cropped hair and a crazed grin, his haphazard teeth stained with nicotine. This was Dennis.

'Welcome to Dutch Air,' he announced, 'we hope you enjoy the ride.'

Dennis had a pistol and a bayonet in the webbing of his body armour vest. 'What do you do?' I asked the other Dutch soldier in the Bushy.

I thought he had said 'surgeon', and gulped at the notion that it had come to this.

'Searchin',' he clarified. 'We are combat engineers – sappers. We try to detect the IEDs.' He pointed to the metal detector in the corner of the vehicle. 'This one is for finding the general location of the mine.' He gestured to another tool of trade. 'And this one is for finding the exact location and the size of the mine.'

I noticed a paintbrush attached to his body armour. 'You like to paint?'

He pulled the paintbrush out of his webbing and made a flicking motion. 'For moving the dirt,' he said.

I watched Dennis pour a Red Bull down his neck, and observed that he looked a little tired.

'Yes, I've been here six months already. Every time we go out, you know, it is stressful. But still, we are a little bit the thrill seekers.'

The mission went well; I didn't die on the way there or the way back.

❖

Although I was spending most of my time with the Dutch, I was, of course, working for the Australian government, and at 1800 every day attended the battle update brief, the BUB, held in the Aussie MRTF headquarters chalet. The room was always chocka with forty-odd staff; officers took it in turns to brief the commanding officer, Lieutenant Colonel Peter Connolly, on the day's events: patrols, IED strikes, TICs (troops in contacts) and the environmental challenges soldiers were wrestling with out at the FOBs, the forward operating bases.

I had been going to the BUB every day, often presenting points. I was getting the hang of it: the level of detail required and the language, what was appropriate to talk about and what wasn't. But again it was a process of learning from my mistakes. A couple of days beforehand I had overstepped a line I did not see.

The new US Department of State officer, Russ, had buttonholed me in the corridor of the Dutch PRT. He had showed up on base the week before – in a pink short-sleeved shirt. He had a sharp and faintly camp wit and an air of self-assurance, having served with the State Department in these kinds of places before, Iraq and Syria in particular. He didn't seem too fazed by anything.

'There's something I need to talk to you about,' he told me. 'Apparently TF66' – this was the Australian special forces task force – 'called in Wolfpack on an airstrike in Chora that killed three kids aged ten, twelve and fifteen. Michel is pissed off. He's saying the Aussies have gone too far again!'

I had heard the outline of this story in the BUB the previous night and Governor of Uruzgan Province, Asadullah Hamdam, had raised his concerns about the incident at a meeting that morning.

The Chora district chief, Mohammad Daoud Khan (known as MDK) had called him about it. Pretty soon the term 'civilian casualties' was going around and things were threatening to escalate back to Regional Command South in Kandahar.

I found Julian Thirkill, an Aussie major who managed public relations – 'IO' or 'information operations' as the military call it – with the Afghans through the local media. He said there were two stories going around on the question of who had called the strike, perhaps TF66 or the MRTF. But both were wrong. The Wolfpack Apache attack helicopter had been flying in the area and spotted what looked like four men burying a square container on the side of a road known to be a travel route for coalition forces. Acting within their rules of engagement, they fired on the assembled group with 'hellfire' rounds.

An Aussie MRTF company based at FOB Mirwais had gone in shortly afterwards, picked up the pieces (literally) and given them to the new district police chief. According to the Aussies' subsequent report, the remains appeared to be those of boys in their late teens and there was one survivor who was sent back to the US FOB Ripley medical facility.

Meanwhile, Julian continued, the local Taliban had seized the opportunity to instigate an IO campaign, starting rumours around Chora District that the boys had simply been going up the hill on their motorbikes to get better phone reception.

I went back and found Russ and Michel, both smoking cigarettes out the back of the Dutch headquarters chalet.

'What sources of information are there?' Russ asked.

I said that the MRTF report from the scene suggested there were no children killed.

'There should be video footage from the helicopter gun turret,' said Michel. 'Have you asked Wolfpack to see it?'

'Apparently it's been passed to RC South already,' said Russ.

'They always pass it up the line too quickly,' snapped Michel.

'Wait,' I said, 'there's another source of info here. There was a fourth guy who was only injured. Where is he?'

'He's in the US hospital down at FOB Ripley; I'd better go talk to him,' said Russ, and he headed out the back gate.

Later that evening, I met Russ outside the Dixis and we went into the office compound.

'Okay,' he said, 'I talked to the so-called child. We asked how old he was and he said ten. He had a beard! We asked his name, he was evasive, then he gave us a false one. He pretended to be semiconscious but he had no head injuries and was under no sedatives. Conclusion – the dude was totally bogus!'

I went into the BUB feeling a bit full of myself for having unravelled this mystery, and keen to tell everyone what I had discovered. But as soon as I got up to speak, the executive officer shut me down; he'd heard it already. I felt like I had stuffed up. The executive officer pulled me aside afterwards and explained that this was a very sensitive issue. Wolfpack's choppers were a great resource, he explained; the relationship with them needed to be handled carefully to keep them on side.

I later ran into Michel. He seemed a little contrite about blaming the Aussies for calling the strike. He'd asked Hamdam to advise MDK that the story about children being killed was false. I appreciated that. Turned out he was fallible too. This was an important early lesson for me: no one had a monopoly on the truth here in Uruzgan.

❖

I went to see S2 in her office and told her I was feeling like I had overstepped the boundaries that evening at the BUB, but at the same time I felt I had done my job. She confirmed that my only mistake was to raise it in the BUB, reassuring me that I was adding value, and in this job I would always be stepping into other people's lanes. For the first time I had the sense that I might be barking up the right tree.

The following morning, I sat down next to Russ at the DCU.

'Just quietly,' I said, 'I think we did well yesterday.'

'Yeah,' he replied, 'but it took me yelling at a wounded man in a hospital bed. Is this what my life has come to?'

'All in the service of your nation,' I said.

'Sure. My mom would be so proud!'

After my first trip outside the wire, I reported to the BUB on discussions at the Provincial Security Council meeting, which had been all about the presidential election scheduled for 20 August. With Eric and Arjan, I'd met several times with the Independent Electoral Commission representative, a worried-looking guy named Osmani. His bosses in Kabul wanted him to deliver a plausible election result in the province. The Taliban wanted to kill him, and the local warlords were putting the screws on him to distort polling centre locations to suit their favoured candidate and patron in chief, President Hamid Karzai.

In the lead-up to the election, the Taliban were doing all they could to create fear and insecurity. On 15 August, a huge truck bomb detonated outside the NATO-led International Security Assistance Force (ISAF) headquarters in Kabul. On 18 August, a suicide bomber detonated in the bazaar in the Chora District, forty kilometres north of Tarin Kowt; four Afghan soldiers were killed. Reports were coming in of Taliban leaving 'night letters' under doors in the villages, threatening to cut off the ink-marked finger of anyone who voted.

Coalition forces were on standby to provide a quick response if things went bad at a particular polling centre, but security on the ground was in the hands of the Afghan National Army and police. I spent election day at the provincial Operational Command and Control Centre, located within the outer security perimeter of MNBTK, from which the local security leaders monitored proceedings.

Juma Gul, the provincial chief of police, was straight out of central casting. Think the prison warden from *Midnight Express*, only charismatic. Wide of girth with piercing green eyes and dark permanent stubble, he had big meaty hands which he often used to slap his men into shape.

Juma held court, keeping his coterie of minions in stitches with his jokes, and taunting the Dutch general for his inability to get helicopter support from Regional Command South, who were tapped out responding to 647 incidents that day, mostly in Kandahar and Helmand. In Uruzgan, insurgents fired twenty-three rockets in the vicinity of polling centres, but they failed to show up in person, while a respectable number of voters did. At first blush, the day seemed a success.

I have a mind that tends to organise events into stories, and wrote this up for the Australian Embassy in an anecdotal style augmented with comments.

'Interesting content,' replied the embassy, 'but the style doesn't translate to cables. Suggest you get yourself on the next plane to Kabul.'

By now the embassy had me intimidated. And the matter of where I would be stationed was still unresolved. I felt like I was getting some traction in TK, and was getting good feedback from Canberra on my reporting, but there was talk of basing me out of Kandahar. So I set out for Kabul on 25 August ready to argue the case, armed with a list of reasons why I should remain in Tarin Kowt.

Alighting from the plane in Kabul, I clapped eyes on the astonishing mountains that surrounded the city. I was met in the terminal by a burly Close Personal Protection (CPP) guy who introduced himself as John, then picked up all my bags and chucked them, and me, in the back of an armoured SUV. The driver had an M4 rifle beside his leg. There was a second vehicle with a couple of blokes in work shirts, fat watches and big arms – ex-Aussie military now working as security contractors.

'If we stop for any reason,' John said, 'just follow our instructions, and stay where you are until we tell you to move.'

The streets of Kabul were mayhem – dusty, busy and full of potholes. There were people everywhere – walking, on motorbikes, or in cars. There were rundown little shops beside the roads – barber shops, bike shops and lots of butchers, with animal carcasses hanging out on the street.

The two CPP vehicles worked their way through the chaos with assertive dual vehicle manoeuvring, accelerating into any gap in the traffic to make their way through the city.

Then suddenly the chaos ended and we came to the diplomatic zone: high concrete 'T-walls', Hesco barriers and checkpoints every 200 metres. We went past the entrance to ISAF headquarters. John pointed out where the car bomb had exploded on 15 August; the adjacent wall was pockmarked with shrapnel.

The vehicles turned a corner and we arrived at the gates of the US Embassy, which, after a month scrambling around in the provincial dust, struck me as a vision splendid. The main building was a big white square structure about six storeys high with pillars and glass and nicely tended grass out front. To the right were several apartment buildings, and to the left were rows of prefabricated containers. The Americans called them 'hooches'; we called them 'dongas'.

The Australian Embassy, as of mid-2009, was temporarily located in three adjoining dongas in the little hooch village there on the US Embassy compound. It was a sensible and secure stopgap arrangement while preparations were under way to upgrade our diplomatic footprint to a level proportionate to our military commitment.

After making my way through the Gurkha-manned security booth at the front gate of the US Embassy, I entered the 'Australian Embassy' and dropped my body armour on a wooden frame by the door. Al Sweetman appeared from behind a partition; I said hi. We sat down on the vinyl couch in the corridor outside his tiny office which seemed to pass for a meeting facility.

'You will be based out of Kandahar from now on,' he said.

I could see there was no point arguing and remained silent. He went on to admonish me for the looseness of my emails; any slip-ups could undermine the project – not everyone in government was comfortable having DFAT officers in the south. As for my reporting style, he said we would discuss this later.

That evening we went for dinner. The conversation was convivial and interesting but I felt green in my ignorance of the bigger picture of Afghan politics. After dinner I was driven to the CPP quarters, where I slept in a room containing a bunk bed, first-aid kits and ammunition. Ammunition doesn't snore, and after a month sharing a container with seven guys I was happy to have my own space. I slept well.

I spent the next two weeks working from the embassy, writing up meeting reports, kicking around the grounds of the US compound and attending meetings around Kabul with Al.

The embassy donga was a small space for four grown men. There was a consistently grumpy discourse that was not uncomfortable since it was honest. Like most people working in Afghanistan, the staff were often tired, and in any case the conversation was entertaining. Al had a passion for the classics, and conversations between him and the Ambassador about political developments in the snakepit of Afghan politics often drew analogies from Thucydides or the Peloponnesian War.

The US Embassy itself was a wonderland. With 800 staff, it was the largest US embassy in the world. There was a tennis court, swimming pool, bottle shop and a bar called the Duck and Cover that pumped on a Thursday night. The embassy was designated as an unaccompanied posting, so the bar was full of late twenties/ mid-thirties/early forties types off the leash from family, spouse and mundane suburban lives, and in need of release. And the need for release was palpable, because the prevailing atmosphere was one of frustration. Lots of A-type personalities thrashing around with emails and synchronisation meetings trying to achieve KPIs in a country that seemed immune to our KPIs.

At the same time, fiercely contested political deliberations back in Washington were delaying the emergence of a clear strategy. Not that it was clear to anyone what a winning strategy would look like. Afghanistan was all contest and complexity. There is a legendary PowerPoint slide from an ISAF briefing attempting to explain the various interrelationships in Afghanistan – the government, the tribal leaders, the various insurgent factions, the drug lords, the population, the Afghan National Security Forces and, somewhere in the corner, us, the international community. The diagram looks like a bowl of spaghetti.

The US Embassy shared a high razor-wire wall with the ISAF headquarters and there was a gate between the two compounds. The International Security Assistance Force was technically a distinct operation from the original but ongoing special forces intervention called Operation Enduring Freedom (OEF). ISAF

HQ was also fascinating. Military contingents from twenty or so nations, all mashed together behind high stone walls, trying to make sense of the world beyond the wire. PowerPoint was ubiquitous. I sat in on a briefing one day at ISAF headquarters in which a colonel delivered a PowerPoint presentation on the development of the ANSF's capacity for 'kinetic' (violent) operations. He finished a very tidy and convincing little brief then, after a pause, one of the generals probed with a further question. The colonel responded, 'I'm sorry, sir, my knowledge on this matter is only PowerPoint deep.' An honest answer, but reflective of the difficulty of grasping ground truth in a country where it was impossible for soldiers to walk the streets without a dozen of their closest friends.

Even more interesting were the meetings around Kabul. An eloquent Indian diplomat explained how Pakistan and China could turn the Taliban tap off at will. It was a predictable line from an Indian diplomat but plausible in the case of Pakistan.

A leading Afghan intellectual told us the main problem was unemployment, which created a pool of willing recruits for the Taliban. Apart from that basic economic need, he explained, most Taliban were driven by combinations and permutations of five impulses: there were the rabid, ideologically-driven types under the influence of Al Qaeda; those who wanted power, just like the old days; those who hated foreigners and wanted to drive them out; and others disappointed with the government. And finally there were those who had had family killed by the US or ISAF and wanted revenge.

One night we went for dinner with an intense former ADF sapper named Craig Coleman. He'd received an OAM in the 1990s for his work clearing mines in Cambodia, but had since left the army and was in business. His current focus was road projects in Afghanistan and 'culvert protection'. These culverts were a great spot for Taliban to hide IEDs, so Craig developed metal grilles to fasten to the entrance of culverts to slow down insurgents long enough to give soldiers the opportunity to spot them laying mines.

Craig's approach to security hinged on building relationships with the local community. If they wanted the road, had an economic stake in building it and were satisfied with the distribution of work and wages, security would not be a problem. This made sense to me. Craig was a practical man to the core. After beers, he loved to play guitar and sing, but his sensibilities were not those of an artist: as we jammed that night, he sang Leonard Cohen's 'Famous Blue Raincoat' with the same snarl and aggression as Dylan's 'All Along the Watchtower'. Craig had one gear: balls out, full speed ahead.

In contrast to Craig was Martine van Biljert, who we visited the following morning. She had been working as an analyst in Kabul since 2001. There was a Nordic fineness to her facial features, and she spoke softly and carefully. Sitting with Al out there on the patio of her leafy compound, I could have listened to her soft voice for hours. She had seen a lot, had a weariness about her and was worried about the way things were going.

'Since 2001 we have made the powerbrokers stronger. We see them as good partners against the Taliban but forget they are the reason the Taliban became popular in the first place.

'In every province there are high-powered spoilers, and high-value cooperators. The role of the PRT is to build a bridge to the cooperators and contain the spoilers.

'Everyone is looking for a solution, but it may be there is no solution. Governments like to believe there are solutions, and careers are not made from describing complexity.'

At the time, ISAF commander General Stanley McChrystal was in Washington trying to do just that. He had released his famous strategic review in a large briefing session attended by ambassadors and others at ISAF headquarters. According to his assessment, the Taliban were not popular and most Afghans did not want them to return to power. Killing the enemy was not the right approach, he asserted; we needed to protect the population.

Concurrently, President Obama announced there would be a surge in troop numbers but famously said it would be followed by a withdrawal in 2014. This announcement was designed to play favourably with a US domestic constituency tired of the war, but it sent a clear message to the Taliban that they only needed to survive a few more years and the pressure would be off.

The evening before I was to leave Kabul, I had dinner with Al followed by a drink down at the Duck and Cover. There were attractive young women dancing to the music played by a band that had been put together from around the diplomatic circuit. As Russ put it, 'When you've been deployed for two months even *The Economist* starts to look like porn,' so Al made some interesting conversation to distract us both from this unhelpful spectacle.

Al had worked in East Timor and felt, in retrospect, the objectivity of his judgements and reporting might have been compromised by his love of the people.

'When someone is telling you something, ask yourself who they are and why they are giving you this message,' he advised.

He was naturally curious about people – listened to them and sought to understand their world view while retaining a level of professional scepticism. I recorded various fragments of wisdom in my diary.

On the orientation of an embassy around its ambassador, he quoted Machiavelli: 'Gentlemen, protect your prince.' On assassination as a strategy in Afghan politics, Stalin: 'No man, no problem.'

On the perennial trade-off between young men's blood and the pursuit of strategic objectives: 'The political calculus of war is always ugly if you look at it too closely.'

When I said I was enjoying myself in Uruzgan, he observed: 'War is fun, until it isn't.'

Al was a fan of the folk genre I work in, and observed that some of his favourite songwriters had, in their senior years, lapsed into telling the audience what to think and feel rather than simply relating the story. It was a view on songwriting I shared passionately, and it led to his final advice on reporting.

'There is enough headquarters spin and opinion passing itself as expert judgement in reporting coming out of Afghanistan already – let's not be part of this. Short sentences, stick to the known facts, no gratuitous commentary – this is the house style. Let the readers come to their own conclusions. The smart ones will anyway.'

The trip to Kabul had been an unwelcome distraction just as I was gaining momentum in Tarin Kowt. But it had been useful. I was ready to return to the south with grounding in the bigger picture of Afghanistan, a sober view of the interdepartmental politics around my position, and a sense that I now knew how to go about my reporting.

And Kabul had been an exciting place to visit. Full of bustling military officers, brilliant diplomats and buffed security contractors, it was a sexy combination of brass, biceps, brains and booze. The latter, of course, was not available out in the provinces, and as I walked out of the Duck and Cover and made my way through the hooches to the armoured SUVs, I realised that this was the kind of place where a boy from the provinces could get into trouble.

Back in the austere little room I shared with the bandages and ammunition in the CPP compound, I started writing this song.

Woman in a war

I was working up in Kabul in the last years of the war
Karzai had decided he didn't love us anymore
The town was full of checkpoints and security companies
And everyone with money had an exit strategy

She came in in December to work for State
On her second posting straight across from Kuwait
I met her at a briefing down at ISAF HQ
Some colonel was pretending that he knew what to do

There's nothing quite as sexy as a woman in a war
A delicate reminder of what we're all fighting for
Says the word 'kinetic', like she'd seen it for real
She was her daddy's daughter with her daddy's ideals

But she said:
Pay no heed what people say, notice only what they do

There's no one quite as horny as a woman in a war
The sugared instant coffee, the adrenaline and more
There's nothing like the hunger for some softness in the night
When you wake up every morning with a war to fight

Still she'd say:
Pay no heed what people say, notice only what they do

Couple of weeks later in the Duck and Cover bar
We'd been on a trip together with the general in Mazar
We got talking 'bout the problems with the ANSF
It was getting late, and the others all had left

I came a little closer and to her I said:
'We could die tomorrow, tonight I need you for my bed

Back in my hooch I've got a bottle of Jack'
My dick was claiming victory, like Bush did in Iraq!

But she said:
'I've enjoyed our conversation and your offer is as bold
As your loquacious admiration of the problems you can't solve
But these are not your problems, this is not your war
You only really came here because you were bored

'So get back to your family and your ordinary life
Your ordinary children and your ordinary wife
I am not your mother, your virgin or your whore
Only a survivor, I am a woman in a war'

I recorded this song as a duet. The female part is sung by Carola van Houwert, a Dutch nurse who worked in the Kamp Holland Role 2 hospital in 2010, and sang in the band I had going at the time. I posted the backing track to her as an MP3 and she recorded the vocal in a studio in The Hague.

The song begins in the first person, but this person is not necessarily me. Nor is he likeable. I'm working here with a poetic device called the 'dubious narrator'; i.e. you are not supposed to like the storyteller, but it might take you a few verses to reach that conclusion. It's not a device used often and for good reason – it can get you into trouble, as I was to find out four years later.

CHAPTER 3

NIET SWAFFELEN OP DE DIXI

I respect your Lowlands culture and I love you very much
But there is one important thing I say to all you Dutch . . .

FRED SMITH, *'NIET SWAFFELEN OP DE DIXI'*

A LOT OF GREAT SONGS HAVE BEEN CO-WRITES, BUT I CAN'T WORK that way. I need to be alone, in the safety of my head, where a state of dreamy revelry kicks in and words flow. It's not the state of mind you want to be in when crossing a busy street or prosecuting a war in southern Afghanistan.

Artists are notorious for having a vexed relationship with reality. It's not necessarily their fault, it's just the way their minds work, and everyone's mind works differently. That's why Lord Byron took to writing poems, while Craig Coleman removed landmines and built culverts.

I have wrestled with this all my life. I struggled to pay attention at school and was pretty average academically until year eleven, when a maths teacher with a mean streak tricked me into getting focused and organised. I value reality and realise that when participating in a war it is important to pay attention.

With one's head in a cloud, one could easily stub one's toe on an IED.

Though not something I'm proud of, this state of dreamy revelry is my default setting; it's where I go when I am safe from practical concerns. It's the state of mind I get into in a motel room, or on an aeroplane. You are pretty safe up there, barring anti-aircraft fire, and there's not much you can do about that except sit on your body armour. I write a lot on planes.

And so it was that on my flight out of Kabul, verses for a song called 'Niet Swaffelen op de Dixi' began to come to me. The lyrics – scrawled, semi-legibly on account of turbulence, in a pocket-sized military field notebook – urgently entreat Dutch soldiers not to swing their dicks in the portaloos. The song didn't come from nowhere; the problem was serious. Apart from the sanitation blocks among the accommodation chalets, the Dixis were the only place on base to go when you needed to go. They were 'the dunnies', a sacred place for the Australian soldier; this was where your modern day digger writes his best poetry. In short, the future of Australian war poetry was at stake; I had to do something about it.

More generally, the Dutch were on my mind. The meetings in Kabul had got me thinking about why things were the way they were in Uruzgan: the interplay of tribes, warlords and political economy. The Dutch, as lead nation in the province, took responsibility for understanding and influencing these dynamics, whereas US and Australian elements in Uruzgan at the time were focused on much more narrowly defined missions. It was important for me to understand the Dutch approach, because if and when they departed, Australia would be left holding this troublesome baby.

As with everything in Afghanistan, none of the theories of how things worked were straightforward; all were contested.

My diary from my last night in Kabul shows that my head was spinning with the complexity.

Too many narratives to sort through ... might be a good idea to wait a few months before having an opinion again.

Barbara Stapleton, a political adviser to the office of the EU Special Representative, famously described working in Afghanistan as a process of 'removing layers of blindfolds'. As I headed south in early September 2009, I resolved to do so.

❖

Tolerance for ambiguity is a key skill for a diplomat. There are times when you can't see the whole picture and can only muddle forward by instinct. This was how I resolved the question of where I would be located. While in Kabul, I booked myself on a flight back to TK, and no one objected. When I got there, I stayed, and all conjecture on the matter faded.

After landing in TK, I dropped off my body armour in Chalet 6, and went to the office in the Dutch headquarters. There I found a huge watermelon sitting on the desk. Curious.

I went out the back to visit the Dixi. I opened the security gate and looked towards the mountains in the east but couldn't see them, only the valleys. Dust. Early September and it hadn't rained for six months; there was nothing to keep the dust down. Then a wind picked up from Kandahar and the air was brown. You couldn't see more than a hundred metres in any direction.

When I returned, the office door in the Dutch headquarters was locked from the inside. I knocked; Eric opened the door slightly and looked anxiously to the left and right before letting me in. He said Sebastian was trying to place a watermelon in his custody, but since he didn't want to eat the watermelon a war had developed between them, each trying to sneak the melon into the other's office.

Not wishing to get caught up in this, I made my way towards my office in the MRTF headquarters and found Anton and Tristan sitting on the picnic table out the front, mapping the white space while smoking their cigarettes.

'How goes the white space?' I asked.

'Not bad,' said Anton.

'I'm in favour of the white space,' I said.

'So am I,' said Anton, 'but there's a problem.'

'Yeah?'

'But I think I've worked it out.'

'Yeah?'

'Counterinsurgency theory requires troops-to-population ratio of one soldier per thirty civilians. The problem is that we don't have enough troop numbers per head of population . . .'

'Right.'

'And we can't get any more troops out of the coalition partners . . .'

'Right.'

'So if we can't increase troop number, then there's only one thing to do to get the ratio right.'

'What?!'

'REDUCE THE WHITE SPACE!'

'REDUCE THE WHITE SPACE?'

'REDUCE THE WHITE SPACE!'

'Great work, crack on,' I said, and was about to walk away when a remarkable thing happened. Without breaking eye contact with me, Anton flicked his cigarette butt four metres over the picnic table and straight into the narrow entrance of the fire bin. Two points! I bowed my head in newfound respect, then made my way into the Aussie headquarters chalet.

I got back to my desk in the CO TAC office to find my phone and laptop caked in dust. This was what happened in Uruzgan; the dust was all-pervasive, as if to remind you that dust was the natural order of things and you were just a temporary aberration.

My office mate, Lieutenant Hastie, suggested I go down to the quartermaster's store and get some 'air in a can' – compressed air for blowing dust out of laptops and other orifices.

I always enjoyed going down to the Q store. It was a shed about the size of a tennis court. There were shelves and shelves of cool stuff, from body armour to cricket bats. There was said to be a PA system in there somewhere. The headquarters could be a bit intense, but for the boys in the Q store, every day was Groundhog Day. They got up to all sorts of hijinks to keep one another amused.

The quartermaster was an Aussie Pacific Islander whose full name was deemed unpronounceable. Everyone just called him H.

'What can I do for you?' H asked.

'Got any air in a can?'

'What?'

'Air in a can. You know, compressed air for cleaning the dust out of computers.'

'Oh, you mean canned air.'

'Yeah, canned air. Actually, while you're at it, do you have any cloths? There's dust all over my desk and I don't want to have to clean it with my old undies.'

'This is getting untidy,' he said as he started ferreting around the three-metre-high shelves.

'Does anyone know where the canned air is?' he shouted to no one in particular.

'Yes, sir,' called a voice from behind the shelves.

'Where is it?' asked H.

'It's in a can, sir.'

'No one likes a smartarse!' H responded, and eventually emerged with a can of air and a bag labelled: *Yellow dusting cloths: lemon-scented anti-bacterial anti-static impregnated with unique dust-trapping emulsion to effectively attract, capture and remove dust.*

What chance did the Taliban have against this sort of technology? I wondered.

H was a musician and had played professionally before joining the army. He had a band going with some Dutchies on base. Until then I had kept my guitar stashed under my bed because I wanted people to think I was a serious diplomat, not a flaky folk singer. But I was beginning to earn some professional respect on the base and was yearning to play some music. I mentioned to H that I played a bit of guitar.

He looked at me with suspicion. 'You're a folky, aren't you?'

I guess the beard and hat gave it away.

'Yes,' I confessed. 'I have been known to strike a chord or two in sorrow.'

'Hmm. Well, come along on Sunday and I'll introduce you to the guys.'

❖

Walking to the DFAC that evening, the sun setting through the dust, I felt at peace with the world. I was looking forward to another month with my new friends here in Uruzgan, plus maybe a little music.

But then things got bad. That night, at 3 am, the sirens went off and I heard a dull thud – *crump!* – and the earth shook as a rocket hit the ground nearby. With the dusty conditions preventing aerial surveillance, Rocket Man had felt safe to ply his trade. The rockets missed, and no one was hurt.

My sleep disrupted, I missed the DCU and came in late to my office in the Dutch headquarters. Arjan and I were typing away at reports when an officer opened the door and said, 'Confirmed.'

Arjan's head bowed just slightly, and he fell silent. I wasn't sure what to do. I left him alone and went to the MRTF office. A friend from the 2 Shop walked in and told me another Dutch guy had been killed.

'Another one?' I asked.

'Yes, a TF55 guy was killed yesterday. There'll be a rollcall at 1700 to announce the death.'

Things were going nuts. There had been a bomb in TK that morning that had killed two children, and wounded twelve others and seven adults. Chora was becoming dangerous following the dismissal of checkpoint commander Toor Abdullah. On top of that, a delegation of Dutch officials was in TK, and there was to be an AusAid delegation on Friday. Kate was frenetic and exhausted; she could hardly string sentences together.

❖

9 September

It was a busy morning for the bagpiper. All hands in the camp lined the dirt roads to the airstrip for the ramp ceremony for the two Dutch boys. For some reason, they held the memorial services last night, separate from the ramp ceremonies this morning, so all that remained today was to convey the caskets to the Hercules for repatriation.

Dutch and Australian soldiers started lining up along the side of the road from about 0715 onwards. The route ran from the Role 2 medical facility, where the corpses lay, to the airfield. They dealt with the Task Force 55 special forces guy first. The bagpiper was in front. That's not quite right. The photographer and cameraman were out front of the bagpiper. They like to send footage to the families back home. The bagpiper was followed by an open-top wagon carrying the casket. Then fifty or so guys from TFSS marched behind up the dirt road, out through the gate and to the airfield. Sharp-looking lads in green berets. Soldiers lined up along the side of the road saluted as the party went by and de-saluted when the party was eight metres past, creating a kind of salute-ripple along the line broken only by we civilians, who don't salute as a matter of protocol.

Then there was the procession for the OMLT [Operational Mentoring and Liaison Team] soldier. The bagpiper and cameraman returned quickly in vehicles to hook up with the second party and lead it out to the aircraft. After they went past, we waited in silence along the side of the road. The party rounded the corner towards the front gate, someone said the word and we all dispersed back to work.

Last night there were separate memorial services for the two men. At 7 pm they began the service for Sergeant Major Mark Leijsen from the OMLT. About 300 of us shuffled silently into the Apache hangar near the airstrip. There was an illuminated podium against the back wall; the rest of the hangar was dark. I sat in the last row of seats next to a couple of guys from the visiting Dutch delegation. There was a two-metre-high image of Mark mounted on one side of the podium, and other pictures of him flickering on a screen. The first image projected was of Mark patting a white dog.

The program read: Sergeant Major Mark Leijsen,
15 Oktober 1964–7 September 2009. Short cropped grey
hair and stubble; he looked to be about six foot two.
An engineer working on IED safety on the IED
training lane. He was driving in the seventh vehicle of
an eight-vehicle convoy at about 1400 on 7 Sept. They
had their ECM [electronic countermeasures] switched
off in order to enable them to call the vehicle in
front. A remote-control-initiated IED exploded beneath
their vehicle. Mark was evidently thrown from the
vehicle, then it landed on top of him. He was survived
by his wife Lucy and a daughter.
> There were some interesting music choices in the
ceremony. It started with 'Brothers in Arms'. Then
Brigadier van Uhm spoke, initially in English before
he said, 'Please excuse me, but we are going to speak
Dutch now.' Other music included Coldplay's 'Clocks'
and a song called 'If Everyone Cared' by Nickelback
right at the end of the ceremony, which seemed to
make sense to those around me. Then we all shuffled
out silently.

After the first memorial service, I went to Echoes, the Dutch cafe,
with Eric and Arjan and the Dutch delegation for tea and coffee.
I got yarning with the Dutch ambassador, who had just finished
serving in Pakistan. We got talking about Pakistan, which had
been one of the few nations to recognise the Taliban regime in
1996 but was now finding the Taliban in their own country a
big problem.

An hour later we filed back into the aircraft hangar for the
ceremony for Korporaal Kevin van de Rijdt, 22 March 1983–6

September 2009. A young special forces guy, handsome and muscular, with brown hair slicked back and a confident smile. The photos had him looking fabulous on motorcycles and water skis, in uniform stalking enemy and getting out of choppers – a young lad still in Superman phase. Again 'Brothers in Arms' was played and Brigadier van Uhm gave his introductory speech. Then Phil Collins's 'In the Air Tonight', followed by some Dutch instrumental tune. Then one of his comrades spoke. As he finished his speech, he grabbed the green beret off his head, thrust it in the air and shouted something defiant in Dutch before bursting into tears and leaving the podium.

I had positioned myself up the back of the hangar with the intention of leaving, but, in the end, didn't have the heart to go. The ceremony drew to a close with a minute's silence. I watched as Kevin's friends, all strapping lads, filed out, deep in grief, comforting each other. I hadn't seen these Dutch giants emotional before and was struck by the sight of their long ghostlike silhouettes, their heads bowed, passing through the dim light of the hangar's door.

I spoke to Russ later. Apparently Kevin was travelling north up the Helmand River Valley in a ten-man patrol, chasing the bad guys into the hills north of Deh Rahwud – solid Taliban country. They were engaged intensely with small arms fire. Russ spoke to the American medic who came to collect Kevin's body. The medic had to shoot three insurgents just to get out of the chopper and collect the body.

❖

I settled back into the battle rhythm of the base. Within the Dutch-run PRT, immediately after each morning's daily commander's update, there was a second meeting in the PRT briefing room, the 'PRT synch'. Synch is military shorthand for synchronisation; it means 'meeting'. The Dutch loved meetings and prescribed them for all ailments. There'd be synch after synch all day long. Whenever they sensed discord among Australian elements, they would look at me with pity and concern and ask: 'Are you guys synching enough?'

People are the way they are for a reason. Seventeen million Dutch share a landmass half the size of Tasmania. When you're packed in that tight, collective values prevail; punctuality is the prince of virtues and internal cohesion essential. On the base in Uruzgan they socialised regularly and joined in heartily in party games and singalongs. They were well organised – everyone in the mission sang from the same hymn sheet.

Yet with all this internal cohesion, they could seem inflexible to outsiders. It's fair to say the relationship between the Dutch and US elements was not always easy. Stylistic issues aside, they had differing views on the fundamental question of how to manage the two main warlords in the province: Jan Mohammad Khan and Matiullah Khan. In the ARE (acronym-rich environment) that was the MEAO (Middle East Area of Operations), not even the Afghans were spared; these two were referred to as JMK and MK, respectively – if not respectfully. Both were from a Pashtun sub-tribe called the Popalzai, which, although comprising only 10 per cent of the Uruzgan population, dominated local politics and business due to their numerical dominance around the provincial capital, their support from President Karzai (also Popalzai), and the effectiveness and aggression of JMK and MK.

For those with charisma and a talent for marshalling aggression, conflict makes for social mobility. When the Mujahedin (meaning 'one engaged in jihad') were fighting the Russians, JMK had risen from school janitor to prominent 'commander', then to landowner and drug baron. He was imprisoned when the Taliban took over and was due to be executed on the day that Hamid Karzai liberated the south. Karzai was a good friend of JMK, who had saved Karzai's life on a couple of occasions. So when the Taliban came to Karzai begging for a ceasefire, Karzai insisted JMK be released immediately.

On that November morning in 2001, Taliban jailers hauled an emaciated JMK out of his cell. JMK was ready to line up against the wall and meet his maker. But instead they opened the prison gate and said, 'Go!'

When Karzai became president in 2002, he appointed JMK governor of Uruzgan. An old school thug and patriarch by instinct, JMK used and abused the position to inflict hurt on competing tribes in the province, particularly the Ghilzai and Barakzai.

His chief henchman in this was Matiullah Khan. MK started life as a taxi driver in TK but had built a militia as client and bully boy for JMK. He parlayed this militia into the semi-official Kandak Amiante Uruzgan (which translates to 'Uruzgan Road Police'). Dominating roads is a good way to make money. You can request 'protection money' from business users and get a slice of everything that moves. MK grew rich, particularly from the huge volume of traffic created by the international forces stationed at MNBTK. The richer he got, the more militia he could pay and the stronger his monopoly on everything that moved. He built a home and compound outside the front entrance of the MNBTK and cemented his relationship with the US Special Forces.

In 2009, MK's status within government was somewhat ambiguous. He was a wealthy powerbroker with extensive 'business interests' but he was also head of the semi-official KAU; some 600 of his 2000-strong militia were on the government *tashkeel* (payroll). A tall, skinny guy with a proud nose, most of the time he dressed traditionally. But sometimes he would appear in a police uniform, pants worn unnaturally high, a habit Afghan military leaders picked up from the Russians and meant to be a sign of status. It was as if there was a competition among them to see who could wear their pants the highest.

Conjecture was ripe as to what MK's future would be in government. US elements said it was inevitable that he would be chief of police, and that this would be a good thing. For the Dutch this would have been a very bad outcome.

I spent a lot of time analysing the MK phenomenon, writing reports with such titles as 'The Rise and Rise of Matiullah Khan'. Half of these reports argued MK was the problem, the other half that he was the solution. In the end, he was both; that's the way he'd set things up, that's the way he liked it. As one Australian officer put it: 'You can try working around Matiullah, but in the end you run into him.'

The warlord problem was not unique to Uruzgan. They tend to emerge wherever government is weak, as it was all over Afghanistan by the end of 2001. So coalition forces stationed around Afghanistan faced a basic dilemma as to what to do with the friendly neighbourhood warlord in their respective provinces – did you work with him, against him or around him? Most chose to work with him, partly because 'it is hard for thee to kick against the pricks', but also because the warlords were the natural enemy of the Taliban. Monopolists by nature and trade, the warlords did not want to share power with anyone, let alone these anti-business, anti-modern God-botherers. The enemy of my enemy is my friend, and so the warlords became our natural allies in what was perceived to be the central task of smiting the Taliban.

But there was a catch: while the warlords were the natural enemies of the Taliban, they also effectively created the Taliban. It worked like this: if you were a leader in a village and were fortunate enough to be within the local warlord's patronage network – one of his mates or a fellow tribesman, perhaps – life was good. If you were not, he would be out to get you. You would need protection. Who you gonna call but the local Taliban sales representative?

This created a wicked dilemma for coalition forces, for which the only long-term solution was to try to create that virtuous nexus between power and accountability that you get when government works as it should. And this was, in part, why the international mission in Afghanistan, which began as a narrowly defined exercise in regime change and counterterrorism, evolved into a project to build a nation state.

When the US Special Forces set up shop in Uruzgan in 2002, JMK was the governor; it was natural for them to work with him. Then, in 2006, it was mandated that all coalition force elements were to link up with Afghan military partners. The US Special Forces found MK's boys good to work with. They were disciplined, well paid, well fed and more motivated than the Afghan National Army guys, who, because they came from outside the province, had less stake in the fight. And so the US Special Forces in Uruzgan developed a close relationship with the Popalzai powerbrokers and, Afghans being the persuasive people they are, tended to see the province exclusively through their eyes.

The Dutch, on the other hand, had a policy of eschewing any contact with JMK and MK. This was partly about managing political risk in the Netherlands. On one page of my diary I found scrawled, apropos of nothing else, a random observation: *The Dutch desire to be good people.* And so they avoided contact with these two warlords in order, as one Dutch official explained to me, to remain 'holier than the Pope'.

But the Dutch approach to the warlords had a purpose that went deeper than managing home front 'optics'. When they arrived in Uruzgan in 2006, they did some research into the province, commissioning a study by a group called the The Liaison Office (TLO) to seek some understanding of the problems in the province.

The TLO came to the conclusion that the Taliban was gaining support among non-Popalzai tribes in Uruzgan because they feared and loathed the Popalzai warlords, felt unloved by the provincial government and needed protection.

So proactively supporting Barakzai, Ghilzai and Noorzai tribal leaders became a cornerstone of the Dutch approach in Uruzgan. It set them at odds not only with the US elements but also with Australian special forces Task Force 66, who were partnered with a group of 100 or so of MK's men, on the government payroll in a unit called the Provincial Police Reserve.

The Dutch called their approach the 'tribal balance policy'. It permeated everything they did and played out in all sorts of ways.

Sometimes it was a matter of protecting the districts from interference by the Popalzai warlords. Juma Gul, the chief of police, had gained his position as a result of JMK lobbying Karzai. JMK had a broad agenda to unsettle security in the Barakzai areas up in Chora, so in mid-September 2009 he prompted Juma to sack Toor Abdullah, a viable Chora checkpoint commander, and replace him with an unlikeable figure named Pay Mohammad.

The Dutch swung into action and the next ten pages of my diary followed the intricacies of this case, which I'll spare you. Suffice to say, the Dutch lobbied in Kabul and the provincial capital, while encouraging the local leaders in Chora to make it clear to Juma that the appointment of Pay Mohammad would not be accepted. In the end, Juma had to back down.

Projects were another battleground for the tribal balance policy. The contracts for their flagship Road to Chora project stipulated that MK was to play no role in construction or security.

Resupply convoys were another expression of this policy. For a fee, MK had the connections to ensure the Taliban didn't touch convoys to Kandahar. But if you tried to use that road without paying him, you'd get hammered, whether you were a twenty-vehicle military convoy or a lone Pakistani 'jingle truck' with bells and mirrors and 'Boom Boom Afridi' painted on the door. Russ's predecessor told me of an occasion when the Dutch resolved to send a convoy to Kandahar without paying off MK. The five-hour trip took three days, with IED strikes followed by ambushes. Regional Command South had to launch a rescue mission. They cleared out twenty-two IEDs on the way; nine soldiers were wounded.

Another expression of the Dutch strategy was their support for Chora District chief Mohammad Daoud Khan. MDK had been a party boy enjoying the high life until his father, respected warrior and provincial Barakzai tribal leader Rozi Khan, was shot dead. It was an accident. A TF66 element was in Rozi's neck of the woods late one night in October 2008. Rozi heard something moving not far from his house. He shot at it, which, in Afghanistan, is usually a reasonable response. But the guys from TF66 didn't know who was shooting at them and fired back, killing Rozi.

So it was that MDK, then in his mid-twenties, was thrust into the role of provincial Barakzai leader. Afghan leaders are almost invariably warriors, but MDK was a 'make love not war' kind of guy. With a small frame and squeaky voice, he didn't quite have the gravitas for the role. But he was charismatic in his own way and intelligent; his people skills were good. A networker, he was constantly talking on one of the several phones he carried. The Dutch did what they could to support, mentor and protect him.

❖

Towards the end of September, things started to quieten down. The weather was cooling and the locals were getting ready to celebrate Little Eid, marking the end of Ramadan, the month of fasting. There were queues outside MK's compound. People lined up to pay tribute to the khan (landowner) and receive gifts. A capacity to wield violence is one side of being a big man in Afghanistan. The obligation for largesse is another, and MK provided housing for widows, computers for schoolboys, food for beggars – he also ran a radio station. Afghans are accustomed to the notion that their predators may also be their protectors and providers, and for many in Uruzgan, MK was 'a river unto his people'.

The province settled down for Eid. Government officials returned to their home provinces, and the PRT also took on a lazier feel. In the weekly battle rhythm, Sundays were 'low ops' mornings – the base took the morning off to sleep late, get laundry done and generally catch their breath. Some took the opportunity for personal grooming and on that front there were two Afghan hairdressers on base to choose from. On the Australian payroll was a guy who cut hair in a little room next to the laundromat. We all called him 'Two', because when you sat down in his chair he'd ask, 'One or two?' This was the only English he spoke, and the only two haircuts he could deliver, i.e. a buzz cut with either a number one comb or a number two. Then there was a guy on a Dutch contract who operated out of a shipping container near Poppy's. He was a highly skilled coiffeuse who could style your hair any way you wanted. But there was a price to pay – suffice to say, the diggers didn't call him 'Dick on Arm' for nothing. His sense of personal space was a little more intimate than most Australian soldiers were comfortable with.

At 1200 hours sharp, every Sunday, the weekly battle rhythm began anew, with the DCU followed by the PRT brief. After that there was a PRT social. The Dutch would gather out the back of their headquarters. Cake would appear, and coffee – they took coffee seriously. Michel would speak, pinning medals on soldiers and announcing joke awards. If it was someone's birthday, they'd sing a jocular Dutch variation on 'Happy Birthday' which ended with them all shouting 'huppity-hup-hup-hup!' in unison.

This was where I contrived to debut 'Niet Swaffelen op de Dixi'. The night before, I played it to Eric and Sebastian in the office. They told Michel about it. Himself a connoisseur of music and the arts, Michel invited me to play at the PRT social, and gave me a lavish and theatrical introduction.

The song was an instant hit. More than that, it seemed to render me explicable to the Dutch, this curious red-headed Aussie who'd wandered into their world without a clear role in the ecosystem. 'You are like Vincent van Gogh!' one said. The Dutch development adviser, Marc, was president of the Eric Clapton fan club back home. He suggested we make a video of the song and post it on the site he hosted. Michel put the kibosh on this, fearing political blowback, but subsequent performances were uploaded to YouTube by their amateur cameraman. And there were many subsequent performances.

A few of the Dutch elements were by now rotating out. Every second night there seemed to be a farewell party, and I was frequently called from my office to play the 'Dixi song'. I joined forces with H's Dutch band, No Synch – military speak for no more meetings!

I became a minor celebrity among the Dutch on base. Like Australians, the Dutch prefer their humour dry, so it was never gushy or uncomfortable. Sometimes I would be lining up in the DFAC and a Dutch soldier would whisper to me, 'Niet Swaffelen,' and shake his head in feigned sternness. Other times I'd walk past a group of Dutch soldiers and one would yell out, 'Hey, Dixi man!'

The Dutch had built a meeting facility called PRT House on the outskirts of Kamp Holland. There were couches on one side of the room and on the other a big Afghan rug with cushions on the floor in the traditional Afghan style. It was a place to meet with Afghans, but was also used for internal functions.

The last of the farewells was held down there at PRT House. They had shown a homemade video of my first performance of 'Niet Swaffelen' at the PRT brief that morning, but this was a more intimate affair with Dutch foreign ministry colleagues, Russ, Kate and a handful of Australian soldiers. I played a few other songs from my repertoire. They were surprised – I wasn't some one-hit wonder. It was a really pleasant night with people I liked, respected and understood. The next day, half the PRT rotated out and a few days later I went home on leave myself.

Reflecting on the Dutch, a couple of surveys by The Liaison Office identified that the Afghans appreciated the Dutch sensitivity to their culture and tribal dynamics, but also thought they could have been more aggressive towards the Taliban. On that latter count, perhaps the Dutch military in Uruzgan was constrained by their home politics – a body politic generally ambivalent about prosecuting a hot war.

Still, the Dutch deserve respect for their work in Uruzgan. Their approach was a comprehensive, considered and sincere attempt to improve the lives of local Afghans. They chucked a lot of money at the province and lost twenty-six men, including the son of their Chief of Defence Force, General Peter van Uhm (Marc's brother). And they didn't take the easy road with the warlords.

Moreover, I liked the Dutch. They were fun social people who took the piss out of everyone, themselves included. I suppose that's why I got away with the 'Dixi song'.

Niet Swaffelen op de Dixi

I've heard that when the Taliban held power in Kabul
They messed up people's lives with lots of really silly rules
Women were illegal and so was flying kites
And God defend the kind of men who like to dress in tights

I wouldn't want to be like Taliban and tell you what to do
I'm fighting here for freedom, after all, just like you
I respect your Lowlands culture and I love you very much
But there is one important thing I say to all you Dutch:

NIET SWAFFELEN OP DE DIXI, it is against the law
NIET SWAFFELEN OP DE DIXI we're tryn'a fight a war
And if you're swaffelen in the Dixi like a Dixi swaffelen man
How the hell are we supposed to defeat the Taliban?
So *NIET SWAFFELEN OP DE DIXI, NIET, NIET, NIET*

NIET SWAFFELEN OP DE DIXI, there isn't enough room
If I catch you swaffelen in the Dixi I'll tell Brigadier van Uhm
And he will have you court-martialled and sent back to The Hague
Where they'll put your dick on a table and whack it with a spade
So *NIET SWAFFELEN OP DE DIXI, NIET, NIET, NIET*

NIET SWAFFELEN OP DE DIXI, it really isn't fair
People need to use the Dixi and you could swaffel anywhere
You can swaffel in Paris you can swaffel in Rome
You can swaffel in the Taj Mahal or swaffel at home
You can swaffel in the shower block with shampoo and soap
You can swaffel with the RSM OR WITH THE BLOODY POPE
But *NIET SWAFFELEN OP DE DIXI, NIET, NIET, NIET*

NIET SWAFFELEN OP DE DIXI, did you hear me or are you deaf?
If I hear you have been swaffelen in the Dixi I will call in the SF
Task Force 55 and the boys from 66
Go swaffelen at night with black paint on their dicks
And they will find you swaffelen in that Dixi, my friend
They'll 'hard knock' on the Dixi door in which case I
     would recommend
That you immediately bend over, place your chest upon
     your thighs

68

Stick your head between your knees and KISS YOUR
  ARSE GOODBYE
So *NIET SWAFFELEN OP DE DIXI, NIET, NIET, NIET*

NIET NIET NIET NIET NIET NIET . . .

NIET SWAFFELEN OP DE DIXI, it really is quite gross
Once a week they clean the Dixi with a great big vacuum hose
If you're swaffelen in the Dixi on a lazy Saturday
You may find yourself fellatioed in a most unpleasant way
It will grab and suck until there is nothing left
What's the BDA [battle damage assessment] gonna say about
  your cause of death?
THAT YOU DIED SWAFFELEN IN THE DIXI, *NIET, NIET, NIET*

I recorded this song in Megaphon Studios in January 2010 with Leon Gaer and Hamish Stuart as rhythm section. Then I sent the MP3 over to Perth to get renowned tuba player Wayne Freer to double the baseline for a bit of extra oom-pah-pah. It's a polka, after all.

There are a couple of additional verses that didn't make the recording. More on these below . . .

CHAPTER 4

A THOUSAND SPLENDID SUNS

Ah! How beautiful is Kabul encircled by her arid mountains
One could not count the moons that shimmer on her roofs
Nor the thousand splendid suns that hide behind her walls.

SAIB-E-TABRIZI, 'KABUL'

'Why did this struggle begin? When will this war ever end?
A time of triumph of sin, a time of dangerous men'

FRED SMITH, 'A THOUSAND SPLENDID SUNS'

ON MY WAY BACK IN TO URUZGAN FROM LEAVE, I WALKED THROUGH the retail wonderland that is Terminal 3 in Dubai International Airport at five o'clock in the morning. From there I took a taxi to the less salubrious Terminal 2, where I'd catch my flight to Afghanistan.

Once you reached Terminal 2, you knew you were heading back to the war. You started to notice middle-aged men with beefy biceps and lots of pockets in their pants, quietly grieving the transition they were making from home and holidays to another rotation with one of the many private security companies that proliferated in Afghanistan and Iraq to protect embassies and expatriate businesses. The TV screen in that grey terminal building was running CNN News. The Taliban had attacked the UN mission in Kabul, killing three expat workers. There was footage of an explosion and a burning building. The UN was reconsidering its staffing profile in Afghanistan in light of the attacks. Meanwhile, fifty-five coalition soldiers had been killed to date in October, the worst month since the war began.

Arriving in Tarin Kowt, I chucked my stuff back into Chalet 6, Container 14, and went to find Eric and Arjan.

'Abdullah has pulled out,' said Eric, referring to the ongoing saga that was the elections. President Hamid Karzai had won more votes than any other presidential candidate, but less than 50 per cent – which, according to the post-2001 Afghan constitution, required a run-off election with Abdullah Abdullah, the second-placed candidate.

Few in the international community or Afghan armed forces wanted this second ballot – elections were a security and logistical nightmare. Fortunately, Abdullah wasn't keen either. Realising he wouldn't win, he withdrew. Theoretically, this posed a constitutional crisis, but everybody ignored it and it went away.

'What's the fallout?' I asked.

'No fallout, just a sigh of relief,' said Eric.

Sebastian poked his head in and shouted something in Dutch before slamming it shut.

'He has run out of English expressions,' said Eric, 'now he's using Dutch ones!'

'And that one means?' I asked.

'Um, it means to take somebody a cabbage up his arse!'

'Right, and speaking of such, any clarity on next year?'

'Not yet. It's frustrating.'

Whereas the Australian mission in Afghanistan enjoyed bipartisan political support, each of the six parties in the Dutch parliament had a different angle on the Uruzgan mission. So it was taking a long time to get a decision from The Hague on the future of the Dutch mission. Officials on the ground were left trying to read the tea-leaves, which by September 2009, seemed to be spelling out a message.

'I think we're looking at *finito* for the Uruzgan mission,' said Arjan.

This forecast had the Dutch on the ground fixated on two objectives. First, they redoubled their efforts to finish the Road to Chora. The contract had initially been given to a contractor, who contracted another contractor, who subcontracted MK, whose involvement in the project was explicitly prohibited by the terms of the original contract. The Dutch said this wasn't on, and withheld funds from the subcontractor. The subcontractor couldn't pay MK, MK got cross, the subcontractor got scared and left the province with the project dangling in the air. The Dutch began referring to the project as the 'Road *Towards* Chora' just to hedge their bets. Russ found this funny.

The second Dutch fixation was TLSR, an acronym no one had heard before. It stood for Transfer of Lead Security Responsibility; in short, the Dutch were seeking to formally transfer security leadership to the Afghan military at a number of the FOBs, particularly out west in Deh Rahwud, in order to claim some level of 'mission accomplished' with the Dutch public. The Australian view was that since the Afghan army was not ready to assume full responsibility, Australian and US soldiers were likely to have to take over those FOBs. The narrative that the Afghans were fully trained and ready to go it alone was inaccurate and would set us up for failure.

Not surprisingly, the Dutch pursued these two agendas by calling a meeting. The 'Big Four' was the brand they assigned to meetings of the province's four main government leaders: the governor, the chief of police, the ANA general and the head of the intelligence services. These gents were invited to PRT House and presented with a document titled Security Agreement for the Road to Chora, which the Dutch requested they sign. Afghans don't set much store in written contracts, unless enforceable by the gun. The local leaders said they would take the document on notice.

On the subject of TLSR, Brigadier van Uhm and Michel made lengthy speeches expounding on security progress in the province, suggesting the time had come to recognise this with an official transfer of responsibility for security. I don't know how 'TLSR' translated in Pashtun, but the locals were wary.

Juma Gul, the police chief, never one to let a chance go by, said, 'Just leave all your weapons with us and we'll be fine.'

Governor Hamdam, sensing the Dutch were leaning towards the exit, was less cavalier.

'Throughout history, foreign forces always make the same mistake,' he said. 'You must not leave us halfway!'

History has a useful way of explaining why things are as they are, and I was reading a lot of it as the winter closed in on Uruzgan in 2009. I need a certain amount of my own company to stay sane, but my only privacy on base was two square metres of bed space. I had draped a blanket from the frame of the top bunk and installed a little reading light. I would spend the last hour of every day reading about the country beyond my shipping container. This was in part professional curiosity – I needed to understand the Afghans. One can never really know what it's like to be someone else; empathy is possible, but only as an act of the imagination.

Reading feeds the imagination and so is a gateway to empathy; to understanding other people's worlds you would otherwise have no access to.

It occurred to me that I had no idea about the reality for women in Afghanistan. I had been there four months and had not spoken once to an Afghan woman. In the conservative Pashtun-dominated south of Afghanistan, they simply were not part of public life. I had a conversation with Susanne Schmeidl from the TLO about it. She related a conversation she'd had with some woman in a village in Uruzgan who had said, 'If we educate the girls, maybe the next generation can find a way, but all is lost for this generation of women.' A series of experiences in November and December that year bore this out.

One evening, I was down at the US Special Forces compound, FOB Ripley, having dinner with Russ. It was like a Mexican village down there: adobe mud buildings, wide dusty streets, and their dining facility had great Mexican food. We were talking when out of the corner of my eye I saw a sprightly colourful figure moving about. It was a young Afghan woman in a maroon headscarf helping herself to some food. I was surprised at her presence on the FOB, and even more surprised when she turned and I saw her piercing blue eyes and, to my shock, a red bloody hole in her face where her nose should have been.

Russ, following my gaze, explained: 'Oh, that's Bibi Aisha. Interesting story. Apparently she was fourteen when her mom died and she was forced to marry some Taliban dude. He beat her regularly until she ran away. But the police caught her and her father gave her back to her husband. To punish her for running away, the husband and his brothers cut off her nose and ears and dumped her in the mountains. Our guys found her up north of Chora.'

Then, in late November, I met with the emerging warlord Matiullah Khan. MK was dressed in traditional shalwar kameez and turban rather than the Afghan National Police (ANP) uniform. He had the casual authority of a man accustomed to wielding both love and fear, depending on which was needed to get what he wanted.

We spoke about possible replacements for Governor Hamdam. I asked about the former Communist governor Aminullah Khaliqi, touted to be in the running.

'No, that wouldn't work,' said MK. 'When the Communists fell, people hated him so much they slaughtered all his children. The deputy governor, Khoday, is experienced and would be good for the job.'

He neglected to mention that Khoday was his uncle.

'Something needs to be done about corruption,' he continued. 'The education department is full of thieves. I send the children of my elder wife to school in Kabul.'

Pashtun men are allowed four wives, and are more inclined to take a chance on polygamy if and when they become wealthy. When an Afghan man takes a second wife, this is an indignity for the first wife, which she has no choice but to accept. Leaving the marriage is illegal for women and, in any case, would leave her economically marooned (the streets of Kabul are full of beggars in burqas, sitting in the dust or the snow with upturned palms). Polygamy has historically added fuel to the fire of the contest that is life in Afghanistan, with sons of the various wives of wealthy landowners fighting intergenerational feuds over inheritances.

'You have two wives?' I asked.

'Yes, it's good. By making them compete you can get them to treat you better.'

It occurred to me he probably took a similar approach to his tribal rivals, his minions, and us.

❖

At around the same time as MK was extolling the benefits of having two wives, the Dutch government sent out a cross-eyed comedian and a singer named Denise, complete with backing band. The comedian opened the night and had 500 Dutch rolling in the aisles of the Apache aircraft hangar. Then I got up and sang the 'Dixi song' with the No Synch Band (footage of this performance is on YouTube) before Denise took to the stage in a tight pair of shorts, a bikini top and kick-arse high-heeled boots. She knew what the audience wanted and did not hold back, singing provocative songs well, grinding her hips and purring.

From the side of the stage, I turned to the cross-eyed comedian.

'Audacious!' I said.

'No,' he corrected me. 'Authentic!'

He was right. She was natural, comfortable in her skin, which was why it worked.

A handful of young Afghan interpreters were up front watching, their eyes popping out of their heads. It was beyond anything they had ever seen, something their sisters would never contemplate for fear of being branded a 'whore' and stoned to death.

❖

The Dutch leadership in Uruzgan, meanwhile, were in dialogue with their political masters to continue the mission. My notes from the DCU on the morning of 30 November cover Dutch preparations for a visit by their Minister for Development.

'He is really making up his mind as to what should happen next year – perhaps looking for opportunities to continue development work, even if there is no military,' said Brigadier van Uhm.

Michel expanded on this. 'He will be looking closely at a number of development projects. He wants to see results, particularly on gender.'

The Dutch had worked hard on gender, but the dust of Uruzgan was not fertile soil. The provincial government did have a women's ministry, but its director was rumoured to be a nefarious fellow who, inter alia, ran the brothel in TK. And conditions for women in Uruzgan were very difficult, even by Afghan standards. The female literacy rate was close to zero (the male literacy rate was only 10 per cent). Nine out of ten women gave birth at home without a midwife. The mortality rate of children under five approached 40 per cent. According to surveys, more than half the girls in the province were married by the age of eighteen, with most marriages arranged – and in some cases forced.

Michel spoke of an initiative they had attempted in Chora earlier that week. The Dutch mission team up there had very publicly invited women from the district to rally at 2 pm on 29 November and march to the top of a hill in the village of Ali Sherzai. This 'Chora women's march', they hoped, would be a demonstration of solidarity for the women of the district. A group of Dutch soldiers and officials gathered at the appointed hour to escort the women, but none showed up. Perhaps they had been intimidated or simply knew they would pay a price for participating. Perhaps, isolated in their own homes, the women had no opportunity to encourage one another to get involved.

There were other Dutch efforts. They were supporting AusAID Kate in her negotiations with the education minister to secure a piece of land for the Malalai Girls' School, to be built by Australian engineers. The minister proposed a plot of land several hundred metres away from the town, up in the *dasht* (desert). Kate knew the teachers would not want to travel that far for fear of IEDs, and somehow managed to talk the minister into allocating the school a site in town originally designated for a counter-narcotics ministry.

There had been other noble failures on the issue of gender. The Dutch had built a prison facility in Deh Rahwud District with a special cell for women, as was standard in Western detention centres. Of course, women don't get out much in Uruzgan, so leading a life of crime is not easy. The cell was occupied just once, by a woman who had killed her abusive Taliban husband.

Gender is a major theme for Western development agencies seeking to redress the gross disadvantages experienced by women in the developing world. A sub-theme called Women, Peace and Security stems from two propositions: the first, that societies in which women are empowered tend to be more peaceful; and the second, that in societies racked by conflict, women suffer more. The accuracy of both these propositions is borne out by Afghan history.

For the last 3000 years, Afghanistan has been ruled by various ethnic groups: the Greco-Bactrians, Mauryas, Kushans, Kabul Shahi, Saffarids, Samanids, Ghaznavids, Ghurids, Timurids, Mughals, Hotakis and Durranis, all of which rose and, in due course, fell by the sword. In conflict studies parlance: the *political transitions* have been violent.

Interestingly, between 1933 and 1973, the country enjoyed a period of stability and modernisation under King Mohammad Zahir Shah. Photographs from 1960s and 70s Kabul show women walking the streets in miniskirts, working in offices and as fashionably dressed hostesses on the national airline.

I went there myself in the 1970s, though I don't remember it because I was just a little boy. We drove across the Khyber Pass from Pakistan to Kabul, where we stayed in a room on the fifth floor in the famous Serena Hotel. One morning, I was playing with my ball on the balcony, when the ball slipped through the grille and down into the courtyard, where twenty men were on their knees praying to Mecca. I called out, 'Hey, Mr Exercise Man, can you please chuck my ball up?' This was not the highlight of my diplomatic career, but the men below looked kindly on me and I survived the incident – those were gentler times in Afghanistan.

In July 1973, when the king went to Italy for medical treatment, his brother-in-law, Mohammad Daoud Khan, seized power in a non-violent coup, abolishing the monarchy, declaring Afghanistan a republic and proclaiming himself its first president. Daoud's agenda was progressive, but the political accord began to unravel. Daoud continued with his predecessors' social reforms, which did not sit well with many Afghans, particularly in the conservative Pashtun south. Meanwhile, his economic reforms were unsuccessful, encouraging the rise of a communist party on the other side of politics.

On 28 April 1978, Daoud and twenty-seven of his family members were murdered in the presidential palace during a coup by the Soviet-sponsored Communist People's Democratic Party of Afghanistan. They released a statement that President Daoud had 'resigned for health reasons' – the Communists were renowned for their understated sense of humour.

In 1979, the Soviet Union invaded Afghanistan and remained there for the next ten years, supporting a puppet government led by Mohammad Najibullah Amidzai. The Russians generally managed to control the cities, including Kabul, but in the countryside there was endless fighting between Russian soldiers and homegrown Mujahedin who were sponsored by the CIA and the Pakistan intelligence services.

There were paradoxes in the Russian approach. On the one hand, they were brutal, stupid and ham-fisted – using tanks, for example, to lay waste to the countryside around rural roads to deny Mujahedin snipers cover and concealment. Yet many Afghans

I worked with had fond memories of the Russians. The Russians believed in education and government institutions. Most of the senior Afghan military officers I met had trained with the Russians (and didn't mind a drink if they could get away with it). The Russians also believed in the importance of art and culture. And, to the point, they proactively sought to advance the station of women in the country: Afghan women were encouraged to seek an education and go to university, and it was safe for them to walk the city streets. The Russian approach to the advancement of women, however, inflamed resentment among men in the conservative countryside.

The Afghanistan mission became a bleeding sore for the Soviet Union, contributing to its ultimate demise: 30,000 Russian soldiers perished in Afghanistan. In the late 1980s, under Gorbachev, the Russians prepared to withdraw, and in February 1989, the last Russian soldier left Afghanistan. US political leaders celebrated the withdrawal as a victory. But the Russian departure let slip the dogs of a new war, now referred to by Afghans as 'the civil war'.

For the next three years, with Russian financial backing, the Communist government in Afghanistan managed to hold on to power. But four months after the Soviet Union dissolved in December 1991, they lost control of Kabul. Chaos ensued, a power vacuum in which warlords, representing various tribes, slugged it out for control of the country. Kabul, which had hitherto been a peaceful ethnic patchwork, fractured along tribal lines. There were militias led by various ex-Mujahedin commanders: Hekmatyer, Massoud, Rabbani, Fahim, Dostum, Sayyaf. Packs of armed men roamed the streets attacking rival tribal enclaves.

Rape and murder of women was a systematic part of these attacks. Afghan men stake their manhood on being able to protect their women, so these assaults were used to demoralise the men of the opposing tribe. Women could no longer walk the streets.

Meanwhile, militias on the mountainous peripheries of Kabul fired rockets and artillery into opposition enclaves in the city day and night, reducing it to ruins. Afghans take pride in refusing to cower in the face of death, so apparently would never run for cover when they heard the scream and whistle of incoming rockets.

Accounts vary of the Taliban's rise to power. It's a complex story in a land of many stories. One version was related to me by Fawad, a former Afghan air force pilot, trained by the Russians, now living the quiet life in the suburbs of Canberra.

'There was a mullah in a small village near Kandahar city,' he told me. 'The people of the village were tired of the local warlord. He had set up a checkpoint on the main road and was demanding money from anyone who wanted to pass through. The warlord liked little children, but not in a good way, and one day, his checkpoint commander kidnapped two young girls from a car and took them to the warlord's house. The people in the village were angry. So was the mullah. He led his students and some villagers to the warlord's home. They climbed over the walls, killed the warlord, set the girls free and destroyed the checkpoint. Throughout the south, people began to talk about this and rally around the mullah. And this is how the Taliban started.'

Whether or not this story is accurate, it is illustrative of what happened: Taliban leaders emerged from the ranks of religious judges and teachers, as well as former Mujahedin commanders, many trained by Pakistani intelligence services. Word spread to Pakistan and soon 15,000 students arrived from the madrassas (religious schools) to join the fight. 'Taliban' is Pashtun for 'student'.

The Taliban took Kandahar city in the summer of 1994; by year's end they controlled twelve of the thirty-four provinces across southern Afghanistan. Local militia leaders often surrendered without a fight. People were hungry for law and order and were attracted to the Taliban's adherence to Pashtun and Islamic values.

Meanwhile, in the north, various militias competing for Kabul were defeated by forces aligned with the defence minister of the 'Islamic State' (no relation), Ahmad Shah Massoud – known to locals as the Lion of Panjshir, and in the Western press as 'the Afghan who won the Cold War'. He invited the Taliban to negotiate and join a political process to consolidate the country under a democratically elected government. He travelled unarmed to the village of Maidan Shar to talk with Taliban leaders. The men he spoke with declined to join the political process. When Massoud returned unharmed to Kabul, the Taliban commander who had received him was killed by other senior Taliban for failing to murder Massoud while he had the chance.

The Taliban moved north. In early 1995, they began shelling military targets and residential areas in Kabul. In the year that followed, they suffered defeats at the hands of Massoud's soldiers and appeared to be a spent force. Then Pakistan ramped up its military support; this, combined with financial backing from Saudi Arabia, shifted the momentum back in the Taliban's favour. In September 1996, as Taliban forces prepared for a major offensive, Massoud ordered his men to retreat from Kabul and regather in the Hindu Kush mountains to the north to fight another day.

On 27 September 1996, the Taliban swept into Kabul and declared the Islamic Emirate of Afghanistan. Many of the local population welcomed them, promising as they did some level of order, albeit based on a more austere interpretation of the Islamic faith than most Afghans were comfortable with.

The treatment of women in the years to come has been well documented. The Taliban's approach to women can be seen as an extension of Pashtun/Islamic conservatism, or as a codification of the protected species women had become during the violent years of the civil war. Either way, women suffered enormously under the Taliban. Demand for Prozac on the black market was huge, with women absolutely disempowered, and literally living in darkness.

The Taliban created a Ministry for the Propagation of Virtue and the Prevention of Vice. Their stated aim was to create a 'secure environment where the chasteness and dignity of women may once again be sacrosanct'. They published a set of rules, which included:

> All ground and first-floor residential windows should be painted over or screened to prevent women being visible from the street.

> Women are forbidden to appear on the balconies of their apartments or houses.

> Women should not wear high-heeled shoes as no man should hear a woman's footsteps lest it excite him.

Afghan women were forbidden from walking the streets without a male relative. Those going out in public were forced to wear a burqa, because, as one Taliban spokesman put it, 'The face of a woman is a source of corruption for men not related to them.'

Women seeking education attended clandestine schools in the basements of homes, where they and their teachers risked execution if caught. Employment for women was restricted to medicine, because male medical personnel were not allowed to treat women and girls. But there were very few female doctors, so many died in childbirth and from easily treated conditions.

The photographing or filming of women was banned, as was displaying pictures of females in newspapers, books, shops and in homes. Women were banned from appearing on radio, TV or at public gatherings.

These rules were enforced with violent punishments. Women who broke them were deemed 'adulterers' and lashed in public, or executed with Kalashnikovs in the goal square at half-time during public football matches.

Reading all this in the comfort of my little bedspace as winter came to Uruzgan certainly didn't help me sleep. On 1 December, I flew up to Kabul to touch base with the embassy, ahead of the ambassador's departure from his post. On the way from the airport, as the CPP guys negotiated Kabul's potholes and check-points, I looked with new eyes through the inch-thick, bulletproof windows of the up-armoured SUV at the high compound walls behind which people lived. I thought about the lives of the women inside, both imprisoned and protected through years of slaughter and chaos by these rammed earth walls.

A Thousand Splendid Suns

The soldier down by the road had manned his checkpoint all day
Out in the hot summer sun, old uniform and AK
I too had worked a long day, behind this high compound wall
Felt the evening breeze, and took some time to recall

Seems like a long time ago, back when this city was green
We walked the streets of Kabul, were not afraid to be seen

Now hid behind these walls a thousand splendid suns
A mind and hopeful heart behind each veil

The Russians came from the north, with their tanks and
    their planes
Kabul took no time to fall, for years the Communists reigned
But the countryside held, and killed enough of their men
Until they finally left, then trouble started again

The Mudj turned in on themselves, whoever guessed that
    they would
Dostum, Sayyaf and Fahim, Hekmatyar and Massoud
The rockets rained from the south, so many long nights of fear
before the Talibs swept in, Kalashnikovs and long beards

And hid behind these walls a thousand splendid suns
A mind and hopeful heart behind each veil

Why did this struggle begin? When will this war ever end?
A time of triumph of sin, a time of dangerous men
The soldier down by the road, asked his friend for a light
Smoked a quick cigarette then wandered home for the night

Hid behind these walls a thousand splendid suns
A mind and hopeful heart behind each veil

I set the song on a summer afternoon, I suppose because it better suits the languorous melody. I finished writing it in May 2011, then asked Liz Frencham to sing the vocal. Before heading south to record it in her backyard studio in Trentham, Victoria, I sent her a copy of A Thousand Splendid Suns, a novel by Afghan American author Khalid Hosseini. It's a heartbreaking story about two women living in a household in Kabul through the chaos of the 1990s. She had read it ahead of the session. Her initial vocal take was very emotional, with a tinge of anger. I asked her to sing it again – 'Once more, with less feeling.' It seems to me that people telling stories of their own suffering earn dignity by relating the facts dispassionately.

A THOUSAND SPLENDID SUNS

CHAPTER 5

DUST OF URUZGAN

In war, you win or lose, live or die – and
the difference is just an eyelash.
GENERAL DOUGLAS MACARTHUR

. . . nothing can prepare you for the dust of Uruzgan
FRED SMITH, 'DUST OF URUZGAN'

ON THE PAGE ACROSS FROM MY NOTES FROM 30 NOVEMBER'S BATTLE
update brief are the first scribblings for a new song. At the top of
that page is written 'Dust of Uruzgan'; it seems I knew the title
of the song before I knew anything else about it.

From the day I arrived in Tarin Kowt, I had a feeling I needed
to write a song called 'Dust of Uruzgan'. The dust was persistent
and annoying. It made everything difficult. Trucks broke down,
laptops seized up, helicopters couldn't land, and it made your
shins itchy. An abiding memory of Afghanistan is going to bed
at night with itchy shins.

The dust also struck me as a metaphor for the opaqueness
of the province. There was so much more going on than met

the eye – networks of connections, agendas and conspiracies. Murderers did their business indirectly through IEDs or proxies, so when someone got killed, you couldn't prove who was behind it. It was a competitive, feudal, subsistence agricultural society with a heavy overlay of Islam; I had never been anywhere that felt so foreign.

So I had a title and a central metaphor – 'the Dust of Uruzgan'.

Looking at my diary pages from the few days that followed, I had a go at writing more verses, but didn't push on. Songs come when they're ready, I knew that. And I also knew I didn't yet know what I needed to know in order to write it. On one of those pages of scribbles I wrote the name Ben Ranaudo, so I had an early intuition the song related to his story. I knew the what, the where and the when, but I did not know the how or, more importantly, the *who* – who was the storyteller?

Every story needs a storyteller, a pair of eyes through which to see events. I write a lot of songs in the first person, but the first person is not always me. This device buys freedom to explore worlds beyond my own. And it can work artistically: 'I Was Only Nineteen', 'The Band Played Waltzing Matilda' – would these stories be as compelling if you weren't watching events unfold through the eyes of the man bearing the brunt?

But the device can occasionally get me into trouble. People confuse the 'I' in many of my songs with Fred Smith and admonish me for expressing unwholesome sentiments.

It's presumptuous, too, to presume to know someone else's world. You can get away with it if you get it right, but in the case of 'Dust' and the story of Ben Ranaudo's death, I didn't know enough facts to get it right. I had learned a bit about the environment in which Ben was working, up around Combat Outpost Mashal, from a conversation I'd had with an interpreter assigned to work with me at one of the Provincial Security Council meetings.

I'd met him out by the Dixis one Saturday morning in November. He was a serious young man with a good haircut and a troubled look on his face. I asked his name.

'Noari, N-o-a-r-i,' he said spelling it out, evidently sick of having his name mispronounced.

He told me he'd been working at Combat Outpost Mashal.

'What's it like up there?' I asked.

'Oh, the fucking IEDs every day, and fucking RPGs all the time.'

The way interpreters spoke English tended to reflect who they were working with – he'd clearly been working with Australians.

'How many guys up there?'

'Only ten.'

'You go on patrol every day?'

'Every day, six to seven hours, sometimes at night. Every day IEDs and mortars. But thank you God, no one killed.'

'Where is Mashal?' I asked, though I had a rough idea.

'Up in the Baluchi.'

❖

I knew a bit about the Baluchi Valley from the Dutch and their Road to Chora anguish. Tarin Kowt is located at the meeting place of two rivers. One of those, the Tiri Rud, flowed in from the east, from Khas Uruzgan into the Mirabad Valley and then to Tarin Kowt. The other, the Dorafshan, flowed north–south from Chora through the narrow path of the Baluchi Valley, down into the wide alluvial plains of Dorafshan, then into the Tarin Kowt bowl.

Eastern Dorafshan was apparently impenetrable in 2006, but it was mostly under control by 2009. Clearance operations by Dutch and Australian forces had paved the way for patrol bases and checkpoints up to the mouth of the Baluchi Valley. These gains were consolidated by good relations between the Dutch and local tribal leaders – particularly with MDK from the Barakzai and

Mohammad Nabi Khan Tokhi (MNKT) from the Ghilzai. Their militias helped keep things in check. After the original contract for the Road to Chora collapsed, the Dutch began working directly with these tribal leaders, and with the security they provided, had managed to to pave the Road most of the way to the mouth of the Baluchi Valley.

But the Baluchi Valley itself was Taliban country. Traditional leaders in the area had either been killed or had fled, and insurgent leaders had filled the vacuum.

This was the general pattern. When local leaders and communities were strong, they could keep the Taliban out. When they were weak, the Taliban found ways to control a village by doing what they did best – intimidation. In a highly decentralised country where everyone just wanted to survive, this was a pretty good business model. I got a sense of the way they operated at BUBs I attended in November and December. Up on the screen one evening, the 2 Shop showed samples of the 'night letters' insurgents had left under doors, threatening to kill locals if they cooperated with the government or coalition forces. Another evening they showed a photograph of a national hanged from a tree with greenbacks stuffed in his mouth. He had been seen by insurgents walking out the gate of a Dutch team site.

As for the broader Uruzgan picture, I kept busy learning from the Dutch. At the heart of the Dutch PRT operation were their two cultural advisers, Willem and Hamidi.

Willem was a Dutchman, an Afghan expert who, as a young tearaway in the 1980s, had travelled to Afghanistan and spent time kicking around with the Mujahedin. He wore spectacles and had a mop of silver hair cut Beatles-style, circa 1964. He got around the base in sandals and socks; the Dutch soldiers referred to him affectionately as *'geitenwollen sokkendrager'* – 'wearer of the goat-wool socks'.

Hamidi had escaped Afghanistan as a teenager during the Taliban years and made his way to the Netherlands. A good-looking man with a clean-shaven face and faded blue jeans, he was resourceful, softly spoken, strategic and measured in his views. He had a little daughter in Kabul whom he loved to the end of the earth.

Willem and Hamidi shared an office with AusAID Kate, and had worked from that office for three years while soldiers and diplomats came and went on six-month rotations. Their long-cycle knowledge was a rare and valuable commodity on base. I learned a lot from these guys. I have seven pages of notes just from one afternoon spent sitting with them.

'When I was in Afghanistan in 1984,' Willem told me, 'the population was fifteen million. Now it is thirty-two million. So pressure on land and water is very tight and feeding people is a struggle. People are very focused on daily survival. They will always be asking themselves, "Who do I cooperate with to survive, the government or the Taliban?"'

He said land ownership had forever been contested, but was further unsettled by the coming and going of regimes over the last three decades, each with their own legal systems. Localised competition for land and water was a bigger influence on Uruzgan dynamics than the struggle with the Taliban.

He explained that no one wanted the Taliban back, but nationals needed to feel they would be protected by the government. 'Part of this job,' Willem said, 'is making the provincial government more trustworthy. But this is difficult: many government officials are poorly trained and corrupt.'

Hamidi said there were government officers who could be both corrupt and constructive. If an official's first priority was to do his job and his second was to make money, you could still get things done.

Willem said the current Director of Education, a charismatic but nefarious Popalzai figure rumoured to be illiterate, was a big problem. Education projects rarely went ahead; teachers were often not paid.

'He's a disaster for the children of Uruzgan – the third-most powerful Popalzai, and he undermines everything.' The Dutch had tried to get him sacked but he had 'protection' in Kabul.

And on they went. I could have listened for hours, and did.

When writing a song through another man's eyes, getting the language right matters. The ADF speak a language of their own: a staccato creole combining acronyms and expletives with a smattering of the Queen's English. By December 2009, I had learned the language of Australian soldiers by absorption – at night back at Chalet 6, working in the headquarters, and attending the daily battle update brief.

At the BUBs, I would often present points on what the governor was up to or discuss the latest twist in tribal politics in the province, but most of the time I was listening and taking notes. Whenever a new acronym popped up, I'd write it down and ask the padre, Al Lavaki, about it afterwards. (The atmosphere in the BUB could be a little combative; the padre's job, however, was forgiveness.)

I was pretty solid on the basics: LNs were local nationals, a respectful way of referring to the citizens of the land. TTPs were the standard tactics, trainings and procedures that had been drilled into diggers before deploying: patrol formations, watching your arc of fire, noticing symptoms of an imminent attack, such as women, children and the elderly leaving an area.

As for IEDs, by 2009, the Taliban was becoming increasingly creative with their use, and the acronyms flowed. There were PPIEDs (pressure-plate initiated IEDs), VBIEDs (vehicle-borne

IEDs) and DBIEDs (donkey-borne IEDs). The Taliban were now using small, commercially manufactured AP (antipersonnel) mines, as well as daisy-chain arrangements where one bomb would be connected to another by detonation cord.

By December, winter had set in and daily temperatures in Tarin Kowt hovered between 4 and 8 degrees Celsius. It was colder up in the valleys. Seven Aussie soldiers had been sent home with frostbite. Weather and moonlight played a big role in the way we operated, so each BUB began with the 2 Shop giving a basic readout on conditions, including a presentation of the 'weather effects matrix'.

At the BUB on the evening of 17 December, for some reason they presented two separate weather effects matrixes. An amusing exchange followed.

'Why do we have conflicting weather effects matrixes?' asked Commanding Officer Lieutenant Colonel Peter Connolly.

'One's Dutch, one's American, sir.'

'Which one's better?'

'I'll tell you tomorrow, sir.'

When it was Pete's time to wrap up, his tone got serious, and he announced that the inquiry report into the death of Ben Ranaudo had been released. I could see this was a matter of intense interest to those gathered. The task force had only been deployed a month when Ben was killed. His death had been an early and serious kick in the guts for the battle group. And, of course, the report looked very closely at who made what decision when.

My notes read: *Report released to media by VCDF [vice chief of Defence Force] . . . shown first to Ben's family: Jennifer, Terry, father Angelo, Haylee (GF) . . . KIA as a result of insurgent activity . . . IED exploded while manning a cordon . . . unclassified version of report on Defence website.*

After dinner, I finished off a cable and was about to go to bed when curiosity got the better of me and I went looking for the report on the website. I found the public version, heavily redacted, omitted chunks of text appearing as white blanks between words, rather than blacked-out in the old World War II style.

The report began:

> On receipt of intelligence regarding [blank] CO MRTF directed OC CT to prepare a cordon and search operation . . .

And then:

> The incident took place on 18 July 09 at approximately 0647h local time on the 18 July 2009, while conducting a cordon and search as part of Operation [blank] in the Baluchi Valley, an improvised explosive device (IED) initiated by an antipersonnel mine was struck at [blank]. It resulted in two Australian military and three local national civilian casualties. Private Ranaudo was evacuated via aero medical evacuation to Kamp Holland near Tarin Kowt where he was pronounced dead by a medical officer.

Ben's name featured often in the report, but there was a second Australian casualty whose name was blanked out.

> At 0647h an explosion occurred. Some members [Australian soldiers] in the vicinity indicated they initially thought it was a suicide bomber. Among several nearby, [blank – a soldier] and [blank – a second soldier] went to Private Ranaudo's assistance. They both reported that it was clear to them from his head injuries that Private Ranaudo was killed outright and after confirming there were no signs of life they moved

to assist Private [blank]. The mine which injured him was also [blank] the IED charge which [blank] caused the death of Private Ranaudo. The location of the two victims was within metres of the craters.

Who was this second soldier – Private blank? It wasn't too hard to find out. I went online and entered 'Ranaudo' into the search engine. I found reference to a Paul Warren, injured on the same day, in an online article from the *Toowoomba Chronicle* and in a press release dated 24 July that Defence had put out on behalf of Paul's mother.

I continued reading the report, which concluded:

> The Quick Assessment reported that approximately 30 civilians had moved through the general vicinity of the incident and that the atmospherics were normal (that is, they showed no concerns).

According to the report, all other elements had worked as they should: command and control; tactics, training and procedures; individual training; protective equipment; human factors; medical treatment; casualty evacuation; casualty notification (i.e. telling Ben's parents); and repatriation. In the report's assessment, 'this attack reflects the tactical sophistication of the insurgents in their ability to adapt and develop new methods of targeting'. It concluded: 'The evidence does not indicate any substantial shortcomings by ADF personnel in the context of Private Ranaudo's death.'

Not all inquiry reports are created equal. But from what I knew of the facts, the Ranaudo report seemed pretty fair in its assessment that no one was at fault. Nonetheless, my experience in Afghanistan was that whenever a soldier was killed, a couple of dozen people up and down the food chain started thinking, 'If only

I had done this or that, he'd still be alive.' The report didn't imply that Paul did anything wrong, but I imagined that in his current state of mind he might have felt responsible for what happened.

❖

I went to bed that night with all of this shifting around in my head. A guitar riff for this 'Dust of Uruzgan' song had come to me a month earlier, based around a D suspended 2nd chord. Neither a major nor a minor chord, it conveyed ambiguity and danger, unresolved tension. So I had a metre and tempo looping through my mind, and, lying there in my bunk, I realised I now had a narrator for the song, a voice – Paul Warren. Here was a soldier whose story needed telling. As the verses started to come to me, I lifted the blanket over my head and whispered them into my little Zoom digital recording device so as not to wake the other blokes. A dozen or so verses came before I went to sleep, probably at around 0230.

The next morning, I was due to fly out on leave. In the back of a Herc careening towards Dubai, more verses came and I scrawled them into my little green military notepad.

Arriving at Al Minhad Air Base in Dubai, I jettisoned my body armour in some accountable direction, and got the first car I could back to civvy street, the urban Disneyland that is Dubai. I checked myself into the Méridien, washed away the dust, had a meal in a real restaurant and slept.

I woke the next morning in clean sheets and a queen-size bed with an entire hotel room – and the day – to myself. After months of sharing a dusty shipping container with seven diggers, this felt like a wicked indulgence. I spread my notes and scribbles for the song all over the room, put the Indian cricket on TV, plugged the headphones into my Zoom recorder and started punching verses for this new song into my laptop.

I ended up with twenty-one verses. This was a problem. Economy is the golden rule in songwriting and twenty-one verses were way too many. I tried to wield the blade, but only two or three of the verses seemed superfluous. The only way to make a song that long work is to tell a story. I had heard it done well before, but not often.

One example was Kev Carmody's 'Droving Woman'. I knew all the lyrics by heart, and understood its movements. Kev's ballad spins its yarn through the lips of a woman at the funeral of her drover husband, killed while breaking a horse on a hot summer morning in inland Queensland. It's a little-known Australian masterpiece. Nine minutes long, the song holds a listener's attention because everything about it works to engage the imagination: a human voice, vivid detail, conversational tone, serious narrative architecture and music that helped the cause.

Sitting there with twenty-one verses spread out before me, I could have thrown my hands up in despair and joined the pink Poms beside the pool. But, having listened to Kev's song a hundred times, I had the instincts and the toolkit to make 'Dust' work. I can now see the similarities between 'Droving Woman' and 'Dust of Uruzgan': both songs begin, and indeed are set, in a conversation; and you know from the start that something really bad has happened. They relate a journey through a rugged and beautiful landscape, describing the hardships and pleasures of the work, before narrowing to the particular morning when the fatal chain of events play out. All these narrative movements in the song are separated by instrumental breaks to give the listener time to take a breath and absorb.

So I organised the arc of the narrative in that hotel room in Dubai, shifting verses around on a Word document until it all seemed to flow. By the time I got back to Sydney for leave, I had it pretty much sorted. I knocked out a demo into my digital recorder and played it to my dad.

'This is a bit more serious than anything you've done before,' he said. 'This is a real person's story – and not a happy one.'

We agreed that before I could do anything public with the song, I needed to get an okay from its subject.

This filled me with mild anxiety. I had heard Paul was struggling, and I was loath to disturb a man who was already disturbed. But the song felt important; I knew I had to do it. I emailed my mate Matt Moran, an army reservist and Channel Ten journalist, who was doing a stint in Tarin Kowt as a public affairs officer. He suggested I try to contact Paul through the 1 RAR rear details officer, Major Robert Wallace, who had remained behind in Townsville to look after soldiers' families.

I emailed the MP3 demo to Robert Wallace with an explanatory note. A couple of days later, Robert forwarded me Paul's response, a polite one sentence email that read: 'Thanks for passing that on, sir, I really like it and find it flattering that people take an interest.'

I wanted to ask a few more questions in order to get the facts right. But there was an air of finality about Paul's response. I didn't want to push him, and in any case, the song seemed to be working.

A few days later I rolled up to the Woodford Folk Festival. One of the venues I was scheduled to play was called the Mystery Bus. It was a quirky idea: festival-goers would show up to this lucky dip venue and take their chances on a ten-minute set from whichever performer was scheduled. I couldn't take my band in there because the stage was the front seat of a bus – they wouldn't fit. I decided to chance my arm with this new song: 'Dust of Uruzgan'. I played it imperfectly, stumbling on a few of the lyrics as one tends to do in the first public performance of a song, especially one that now had eighteen verses. Yet as I struck the last chord, there was a brief silence, almost a gasp, before the assorted punters who'd showed up on spec for an afternoon's light entertainment started applauding.

❖

I set about recording 'Dust of Uruzgan' with some urgency. I was due to go back to TK soon and wanted to take a copy of the song with me. The process began in Peter Kennard's studio in the Blue Mountains, laying down the guitar tracks: a twelve-string, a six-string and an electric on the solo riff. Then I brought some heavyweight Sydney session men into Megaphon Studios: Hamish Stewart on drums and Leon Gaer on bass. I was in a hurry, had worked with these guys before, and knew they wouldn't miss.

That weekend, I played a rough mix to my Western Australian songwriter mate, Bernard Carney, at the Illawarra Folk Festival. Bernard suggested I add lap steel guitar. Happily, there was a good lap steel player at the festival, Damon Davies. He took an MP3 back to his home studio on the New South Wales South Coast and added something tastefully nasty. I had the guys at Megaphon mix it along with two other songs I'd knocked down with Hamish and Leon: 'Christmas in Kandahar' and 'Niet Swaffelen op de Dixi'. I burned the three songs onto a disc, printed fifty copies, chucked them in my suitcase and returned to Uruzgan at the end of January.

I came back in via Kandahar airfield. It had been a big month: two festivals, several gigs with the Spooky Men's Chorale, my fortieth birthday party and, at the end of it all, Maryanne announced she was pregnant again!

In the terminal I was lucky enough to run into my Dutch mates: Michel, Marc van Uhm, Eric and Sebastian. They had finished their six-month posting and were on the way home. I bid them a hasty and hearty farewell and got myself on the next bird.

Back in TK, MRTF 2 were also in the early stages of a RIP (relief in place) with the new MTF 1. The 'R' for 'reconstruction' had been dropped from MRTF to reflect that the focus was now squarely on the mentoring effort. MTF 1 were mostly drawn from 6 RAR in Brisbane, and their guys mingled with the MRTF 2 crew copping handovers and learning what they could. With the overlap from both task forces, the base was pretty full. There were soldiers who had recently returned from the combat outposts lurking around on the base in Tarin Kowt, handing over weapons and body armour, doing psych tests and taking warm showers. They looked gaunt, sunburned and utterly exhausted. Their uniforms were faded and torn.

Every now and then a FACE – Forces Entertainment Unit – tour would come through. On my first Saturday back, they brought over Jenny Morris with a backing band of Sydney young guns. During the afternoon, they had set up a big truck with lights and a PA system on the volleyball court/parade ground, and by sunset they were ready to go.

FACE tours were generally a pretty overwhelming experience for the musicians: a week of briefing and jargon then thirty hours of flying in to a war zone. The Taliban didn't make things easy for Jenny Morris. The scheduled performance seemed to have ignited the indignation of the Taliban, who, philistines that they are, tended to view Jenny's music as a bit dated. At 1800, two hours before the concert was due to start, old mate in the hills fired a couple of rockets on the base. We all scurried indoors and remained there under orders for the next hour. By the time Jenny and the band finally emerged, they seemed a little giddy.

My mate Major Julian Thirkill, who was facilitating all this from the TK end, had arranged for me to go on and play a couple of songs between Jenny's sets. I got up there on the back of the truck and plugged in my guitar. There were about 150 Australian soldiers on the parade ground out there in the darkness, and maybe fifty Dutch sitting on top of the adjacent chalets. I guess the Aussie soldiers on the base didn't know who I was – just that civvy guy who got around with the beard and the hat. I could see them bracing themselves in anticipation.

A made a little introductory gag suggesting a few things returning soldiers could do to ease the transition back home: fill the backyard with rocks, install a portaloo and get the neighbour to throw firecrackers over the fence every now and then. Then I took a deep breath and punched out 'Dust of Uruzgan' through the big PA system. I looked out in the direction of the Dorafshan Valley when I was singing about it, and down at the dust on the parade ground when I was singing about that.

The impact was immediate. I was talking about their reality, about people they knew, and terrain they had studied and patrolled day in, day out.

Afterwards, we went back to Poppy's for tea and biscuits while Jenny signed CDs. I spoke to a handful of soldiers just back from the COPs.

'Mate,' one of them told me, 'that song – it was like you'd read my diary.'

A patrol commander named Nigel told me about a recent near miss.

'There were eight of us out on patrol with a group of about forty ANA boys. The 2 Shop called over the Icom radio to say they had picked up chatter indicating we were walking in the direction of a remote-controlled IED ambush. I stopped the patrol while we looked at a map to see if there was a way we could turn the situation around and catch the bastards. Then they called again to say the insurgents were frustrated because they couldn't initiate the IED. Maybe it had malfunctioned, maybe our jammers were working. Either way, I looked down to my right and saw what they were talking about – a dirty big IED sitting right there beside me! Mate, we were lucky.'

I spoke to another soldier who'd been saved when an enemy round lodged in the radio strapped to his hip.

It occurred to me that a lot of what happened out there came down to luck. Young men are driven to prove themselves in a physical contest. These guys trained hard and bonded intensely before deployment. By the time they saw action, they were highly motivated to perform. Their deepest desire was to prove themselves in the heat of battle. Their greatest fear was of letting their mates down. From what people were telling me about Paul Warren, he felt that he had.

What I wanted to say to Paul with this song was simple. 'Mate, anyone can have a bad day at the office, you were just unlucky.'

Dust of Uruzgan

In the ring they called me Warlord, my mother called me Paul
You can call me Private Warren when you're filing your report
As to how I came to be here, this is what I understand
In this hospital in Germany from the dust of Uruzgan

I had just turned twenty-eight, just bought a new car
When I joined the first battalion of the Big 1 RAR
We were next up for deployment into south Afghanistan
To combat the insurgence in the dust of Uruzgan

It took seven months of training just to get into the joint
There were push-ups and procedures, there was death
    by PowerPoint
Then the RSO&I course in Ali Al Salem
But nothing can prepare you for the dust of Uruzgan

Me and Benny sat together flying into Kandahar
Sucked back on our 'near beers' in the Camp Baker bar

Then up at 0530 we were on the Herc and out
In twenty flying minutes we were into Tarin Kowt

We shook hands as the boys RIPped out from MRTF 1
And pretty soon were out patrolling in the Afghan summer sun
Walking through the green zone with a Steyr in my hand
Body armour chafing through the dust of Uruzgan

We started up near Chora working fourteen hours a day
Mentoring a Kandak from the Afghan fourth brigade
Down through the Baluchi into eastern Dorafshan
Working under open skies in the dust of Uruzgan

It's a long way from Townsville, not like any place you've seen
Suddenly you're walking through from the fourteenth century
Women under burqas, tribal warlords rule a land
Full of goats and muck and jingle trucks is the dust of Uruzgan

And the education minister can neither read nor write
And the Minister for Women runs the knock shop there at night
They've been fighting there forever over water, food and land
Murdering each other in the dust of Uruzgan

There's nothing about the province that's remotely fair or just
But worse than the corruption is the endless fucking dust
Fine as talcum powder on the ground and in the air
And it gets into your eyes and it gets into your hair

And it gets into your weapon and it gets into your boots
And when bureaucrats all show up there it gets into their suits
Gets in the machinery and foils every plan
There's something quite symbolic 'bout the dust of Uruzgan

Still the people can be gracious and they're funny and
    they're smart
And when the children look into your eyes they walk into
    your heart
They face each day with courage and each year without a plan
Beyond scratching for survival in the dust of Uruzgan

But the Taliban are ruthless, keep the people terrorised
With roadside bombs and hangings and leaving letters in the night
And they have no useful vision for the children of this land
But to keep them praying on their knees in the dust of Uruzgan

It was a quiet Saturday morning when the 2 Shop made a call
On a compound of interest to the east of COP Mashal
We had some information they were building IEDs
So we cordoned and we searched it in accord with SOPs

I was on the west flank picket, propped there with Ben
There to keep a watchful eye out while the other blokes went in
We looked for signs of danger from the TTPs we'd learned
But the nationals were moving back and forth without concern

We'd been static there for hours when I took a quick step back
Kicked a small AP mine and everything went black
Woke up on a gurney flat out on my back
Had to ask them seven times just to get the facts

That I lived to tell this story through a simple twist of fate
The main charge lay ten feet away from the pressure plate
You see the mine was linked by det cord to a big charge laid
    by hand
Hidden under Benny by the dust of Uruzgan . . .

I was a Queensland champ Thai boxer now I look south of
    my knee
And all I see are bedsheets where my right foot used to be
Benny's dead and buried underneath Australian sand
But his spirit's out their wandering through the dust, the dust
    of Uruzgan

Now I'm going back to Townsville, it's the city of my birth
Some go back to Ballarat and some go back to Perth
I'll be living with my mother who's still trying to understand
Why we're spending blood and treasure in the dust of Uruzgan

CHAPTER 6

LIVE LIKE AN AFGHAN

The Afghans are an extremely hardy, bold, independent
race, intelligent with a ready fund of conversation and
pleasantry which renders them agreeable companions
. . . Afghan gentlemen are extremely sensitive to
courtesy, having excellent manners themselves.

BRIGADIER COLIN MCKENZIE, KABUL, 1842

I love the Afghans, they're great people –
except the ones that are trying to kill you!

BOB MULLEN, US AGRICULTURE OFFICER IN URUZGAN, 2013

. . . Manners matter when you fight like an Afghan,
fight like an Afghan lives

FRED SMITH, 'LIVE LIKE AN AFGHAN'

MOST BOOKS HAVE A FINITE AND STABLE DRAMATIS PERSONAE –
a handful of characters the reader can get to know and follow
through the story. I can't oblige herein. Western colleagues came
and went from Afghanistan on six-to-twelve-month postings, and

many of the Afghans I have described did not survive through to 2013.

Early on the morning of 14 February 2010, I headed out the back of the PRT chalet towards the Dixis and found the civil military officer, my good mate Major Andrew Elgey, feeding reams of redundant paperwork into the fire bin in preparation for leaving. He showed me a copy of the death certificate for a sixty-year-old national who had thrown himself under the wheels of a Bushmaster, perhaps planning to survive and claim compensation – or perhaps just to earn compensation for his family.

The BUB that night was overflowing with staff from both MRTF 2 and the incoming MTF 1. At the Transfer of Authority ceremony the following morning, Elgey was awarded a medal and S2 a promotion. I felt a little bubble of pride to see my friends recognised.

The following afternoon I went to see them off: S2 gave me a real hug, Julian Thirkill a 'MCBASS hug' through the inch-thick plates of his body armour. Then they hopped up into the truck, and it took off for the flight line, leaving me with a face full of diesel fumes.

Other transitions followed. Among the Dutch, Eric was replaced by Huip, and Michel was replaced by Yennes. Meanwhile, back in The Hague, a political crisis was brewing with cabinet meeting after cabinet meeting on the future of the Dutch mission breaking down in acrimony. Finally, on 21 February, they decided they couldn't decide, the ruling coalition was dissolved and an election was called. Wrangling over the future of the Uruzgan mission had brought down the Dutch government! The upshot was that the original mandate would simply expire on 1 August, and that would be it for the Dutch military mission in Uruzgan.

All these comings and goings could be fatiguing. In a war zone, you bond intensely with colleagues, then before you know it, they are gone. Those of us who did longer stints often complained of 'people fatigue' – an instinctive wariness of investing in getting to know people, combined with a persistent low-level grief as friends disappear. Still, you try to help the newbies learn the ropes and make the best of it.

The comings and goings also made it difficult to build long-term relationships with Afghans, but I suppose they were used to that. Foreigners have come and gone forever. Located at the crossroads of Central Asia, on the trade and migration routes between China, India, Persia and the Mediterranean, the country has been notoriously prone to invasion.

In the third century BC, after a smooth run through the Balkans and Persia, Alexander the Great took three years to conquer what is now Afghanistan. The southern city of Kandahar is named after him, a derivation: Alexander – Sekander – Kandahar.

Genghis Khan swept through in the early thirteenth century, killing millions, destroying cities and ruining farmlands with salt. He is reported to have said, 'It is not sufficient that I succeed – all others must fail.' This mindset seems to have informed the foreign policies of a number of countries in the region, and the outlook of most Afghan warlords.

The story of the first British invasion of Afghanistan is inter-esting to me; I'll relate it from the point of view of two 'political officers', since that was essentially my role some 170 years later. In the 1830s, Lord Auckland – the governor-general of India – and others in the British East India Company became anxious about Russian influence in 'Kabool', fearing the Russians would use Afghanistan as a staging post to attack India.

In 1836, they dispatched the renowned explorer, author and linguist Alexander Burnes on a political mission to meet the Barakzai king, Dost Mohammad Khan. Burnes and Dost got on famously. Burnes was charismatic and a lot of fun, and

Dost Mohammad was keen to forge an alliance with the British, particularly as he needed help recapturing Peshawar from the Sikhs. Burnes sent dispatches advising Lord Auckland to support Dost Mohammad on the throne in Kabul, assessing that Dost had both the firepower and support base to govern this fractious land.

Auckland ignored the man on the ground, instead heeding the advice of a second political officer, Claude Martin Wade, a diplomatic agent based in Ludhiana in north-west India near what is now the Pakistan border. There, a former Popalzai king, Shah Shuja, under the protection of Wade, was licking his wounds and reorganising, having been removed from the throne by the Barakzai in 1809. Shuja persuaded Wade that he was the rightful King of Afghanistan, and with a little help from the Brits and the Sikhs, could summon a fighting force to make it so.

Later, it came to light that some of Burnes's reporting from Kabul in 1839 might have been doctored in Ludhiana to convey negative opinions of Dost Mohammad. In any case, on the advice of Wade's patron, Sir William Hay Macnaghten, Lord Auckland decided that it was time to pre-empt Russian moves by invading, and Shah Shuja would be their man. Twenty-one thousand British and Indian troops set out from Punjab in December 1838. After dragging their cannons over the Bolan Pass, they made it to Kandahar in April 1839. The local leaders surrendered without firing a shot.

The British then set their sights on Dost Mohammad's heavily armed fortress in Ghazni. At three o'clock on the morning of 23 July 1839, Indian engineers from the Bengal and Bombay Sappers Regiment managed to steal their way up to the northern city gate and blow it up. The British forces stormed in. By dawn they'd lost 200 men but taken the city. Dost Mohammad sent a force led by one of his sons, but when they were routed, the momentum was with the British. Dost, like most Afghans, concluded the British could not be defeated and fled with his followers to Bokhara.

From Ghazni, the British marched on Kabul and took the city with little opposition in August 1839. They restored Shah Shuja to the throne after thirty years' exile, and, for a while, things were looking good. They reduced their fighting force to 8000. Wives, children and servants of those who remained were sent from India; there were polo matches, picnics and theatre shows. They paid off the Ghilzai tribesmen in the mountainous passes to the east of Kabul to guarantee the British convoys safe passage from India.

The Afghans, however, came to resent the British presence. British soldiers were consorting with the local women, an unforgivable affront to Afghan men. And they made political mistakes, such as reducing the payments to the Ghilzai tribesmen. But the fundamental political mistake was backing Shah Shuja. He did not have the personality or support base to hold power in this fractious land. Being seen as a British puppet added to his 'image problem'.

Meanwhile, not wishing to miss out on the fun, Burnes had joined the British mission and become a respected political agent in Kabul. He was knighted. But he was known to be particularly enthusiastic about the local women; this, combined with what looked to be his betrayal of Dost Mohammad, made him a lightning rod for resentment among Afghans.

On the afternoon of 1 November 1841, Burnes's servants told him there was trouble brewing and suggested he leave Kabul. Burnes decided to stay. Early the following morning an angry mob gathered outside his house and set fire to the gate. Burnes and a few colleagues went up on the roof and began firing at the mob. A representative from the crowd promised him that if he stopped shooting, he would be given safe passage to a nearby fort held by Shuja's men. Burnes led his household out the front door. The mob descended and cut him to pieces with long knives. His brother, fifteen Sepoys and several Hindu servants suffered the same fate.

Shuja tried but failed to urge the British to exact retribution for Burnes's death, and the disaffected in Kabul grew bolder. Meanwhile, tribes in the countryside were rallying around Dost Mohammad's son, Abdul Khan. Macnaghten knew the British mission was in trouble and set up a meeting with Abdul Khan to negotiate a way out. When Macnaghten showed up, he was slaughtered, his body dragged through the streets and put on display in the bazaar.

The British cantonment in Kabul went into siege mode, but they were running out of supplies and the cantonment itself was hard to defend. In January 1842, the remaining 4500 soldiers and 12,000 camp followers struck out for India. Abdul Khan had guaranteed safe passage out of Kabul, but could not vouch for the Ghilzai riflemen, who picked off those who did not perish from exposure in the waist-deep snow of the mountain passes. Just one member of the party that had left the Kabul Containment, Dr William Brydon, made it to the British garrison in Jalalabad.

One could learn at least three things from this story – 'Auckland's Folly', as it became known – about the way we foreigners tend to work in Afghanistan. First, we tend to take sides; to pick our man and back him. Sitting on the fence doesn't seem to be an option. Then, having picked our man, we tend to believe him, and see the country through his eyes. His version of Afghanistan becomes ours. And, in the eternal contest that is Afghanistan, local leaders see us as a source of power and resources in their competition with one another. We go in there for our own purposes, but can pretty quickly find ourselves being used for theirs.

And there's a fourth, more specific, lesson: the Barakzai and Popalzai have been at it for a while! Afghan kings for the last 400 years have come from these two Pashtun sub-tribes, and the contest has been fierce. Karzai's ascension to the presidency in 2002 began a relatively brief period of Popalzai dominance, although democracy was beginning to open up the field to a broader range of tribal influences.

This contest continued to play out at the national level, with high-level powerbrokers marshalling their clients in pursuit of wealth and influence. But it also played out locally. Deciding what we needed to do about this contest in Uruzgan became my focus in March 2010. With the Dutch going, it seemed probable that Australia would be expected to take over the PRT, in which case these problems would become ours whether we liked it or not. We needed a political strategy.

Susanne Schmeidl from The Liaison Office was visiting Tarin Kowt and offered some basic principles.

'We can't play God, but we can understand our role in the ecosystem. Our role is as a source of power and resources, and we can either decide how to allocate those in support of our goals, or have it decided for us. In any case, we need to be aware of this so as not to be manipulated.'

Jason Katz, a passionate and intrepid aid worker in his thirties, had been running USAID's program in Uruzgan for eighteen months. He put it in simple terms: 'I guess you've got two choices. You could keep the balance, or you could let MK rule.'

The let-MK-rule option had some logic to it. MK was showing signs of transitioning from thug to businessman to statesman. In February he had begun running weekly shuras (meetings), at which community elders would discuss local issues and resolve disputes. These were mostly attended by MK's friends and fellow tribesmen, but Barakzai and Ghilzai were starting to show up too. The forum was thought to be constructive.

Russ went out to observe one of these shuras and came back impressed. 'This is governance Afghan-style! People go to MK for favours, not the governor.'

He had a point. In a country where the formal government was weak, often corrupt, sometimes partisan and occasionally predatory, what constituted legitimate 'governance' was in the eye of the beholder.

Even the TLO felt that, unlike JMK, MK was a powerbroker we could work with. He was local and in for the long haul, so even when he did extort money, at least it stayed in Uruzgan.

❖

In early March, I went up to the embassy in Kabul to talk about the political strategy. On my first afternoon, we met with the Dutch ambassador. He suspected MK's new weekly shura was another Popalzai power play. I said my impression was that the shuras were constructive and that MK was maturing as a leader.

That evening a few members of the Australian business community in Kabul came to dinner. I spoke to Barry Stevens, a former 6 RAR soldier working as a contractor to build a road between Chora and Gizab, a project MK was muscling in on. He was vitriolic.

'MK! That bastard killed six of my workers!'

The following afternoon we met with Jelani Popal, the director of the Independent Directorate of Local Governance. He was responsible, to the extent anyone other than Karzai could be, for staffing decisions in the provincial governments. He said Governor Hamdam's days were numbered. There had been too many complaints about his corruption, including from MK. As for MK, Popal (as his name implied, a Popalzai) felt MK could be constructive. 'But he needs to be constrained too.'

On return to TK, Huip, Russ and I had a series of meetings with elders from around the province to help us think this through and to explain the Dutch departure to them. Many were anxious about what would happen once they left.

Haji Zahir Barakzai was an ancient tribal leader from the Dorafshan, a slight old fellow with a grey beard and round spectacles that reflected the light that came through the window of PRT House. When Huip told him of the imminent Dutch departure, he replied: 'Yes, I know. We thank you for supporting our tribe against Al Qaeda, but this is a bad sign, the first country to leave. The insurgents are making propaganda about this!' He gave us a harrowing account of the death of his son and four of his grandchildren by IEDs. 'JMK ordered the police to leave our area, and took away the checkpoints. The insurgents just came in and set up IEDs everywhere.'

Mauladad was a genial old leader of the Kuchi tribe, with a warm smile and no front teeth. He said he didn't trust MK's shuras.

'His shura is not for us. But people are afraid that if they don't attend, MK will tell coalition forces they are insurgents and they will be targeted.'

More generally, he advised us to 'Talk to people, organise shuras, have good relations with tribal leaders, bring development, and protect people against other groups like the Taliban and the old government of JMK. If you support all tribes, we will support you.'

This seemed sound. We needed to support all the tribes, but we also needed to work with MK while doing what we could to make him accountable. The ambassador agreed, but the matter was still being discussed with the Australian military leaders on the ground in Uruzgan.

The political strategy needed to be settled, and soon. Many people in the province were concerned that when the Dutch left the Americans would slide in behind the Popalzai warlords, and the Taliban propaganda machine was fanning the flames of this anxiety.

MDK told us as much when we met on 17 March. 'It's time to get our tribes together and talk about this, so I will hold a shura next month at my compound on the day after Afghan New Year. Can you come and speak?' he said.

'I'll see if I can get there,' I said, knowing the symbolic import-ance of attending, but also that I would need to line up security and transport, and make sure of my ground with the ADF.

I met with the new Mentoring Task Force CO, Lieutenant Colonel Jason Blain – a down-to-earth bloke from North Queensland sugarcane country. I had got to know him during games of corridor cricket that began to break out in the evenings following the arrival of 6 RAR.

I explained the powerbroker management theories under-pinning my thoughts on a 'political strategy', and the whys and wherefores of a proactive and deliberate approach to supporting the non-Popalzai tribes.

He saw it in simpler terms.

'My guys are out there in Barakzai, Ghilzai, Noorzai country. If we don't have a good relationship with those tribes, more of my soldiers will die.'

I told him about MDK's shura, and suggested it was a timely opportunity to counter the Taliban's fear-mongering. He agreed and gave me a green light to speak at the shura.

February and early March 2010 were busy. I was feeding into deliberations in Canberra on what the Australian civilian contri-bution would look like once the Dutch left, while trying to shape our political strategy for managing the nasty and competitive dynamics of Afghan culture. But at the same time, I was beginning to immerse myself in some of the gentler sides of the Afghan world.

People I have met who travelled to Afghanistan in the 1970s had told me they found the people kind, hospitable and trustworthy. Thirty years of bitter war has damaged that. As people's mindsets shifted into survival mode, trust became a rare commodity. And yet the Afghans remain very likeable.

Hospitality is valued in Afghan culture. Guests are lavished with food and tea until they can take no more. Courtesy likewise. When Afghan friends meet there is always a hug and kisses on both cheeks followed by a long list of inquiries about the welfare of family members. When a young man meets an elder, he will bow his head slightly and place his left hand on his heart while shaking hands with the right.

I observed this practice with the interpreters. And it was through the interpreters that I got my clearest insights into Afghan culture. There were around 100 of them on MNBTK, and perhaps fifty out at the FOBs in the valleys. Most of those were classified Category 1, Afghan citizens, typically young men from the northern provinces who had come down hoping to make enough money to pay a wedding dowry or support their younger siblings through school. Many of them ended up staying for five or six years, because a job is a job – and the conditions were good, when they weren't being shot at.

The 'terps' would often play ping-pong or chess late into the night under the lights at Poppy's. Every evening there were five-a-side soccer games on the concrete basketball court up near the gym. They would compete fiercely, diving around as if their lives, or more importantly their honour, depended on it. Decisions of the non-existent umpire were contested furiously before the match ended in hugs and handshakes.

Many had learned English in refugee camps in Pakistan during the Taliban years. They took on English names, to prevent us butchering their real ones, but also to conceal their identities. Most kept their employment with us a secret even from their families, so no one in their home towns knew they were working for international forces; the Taliban sometimes targeted their families. This created all sorts of awkwardness in their lives. As one of them said to me, 'In Afghanistan, we say one lie is the mother of a hundred.'

They would often share with me sayings like this, Afghan jokes and folk stories, each offering a little insight into their culture and world view. The story of Amin, for example:

> A young guy called Amin moves from his home in Jalalabad to Kabul and gets a job working as a waiter in a teahouse. One morning, Death comes in for a cup of tea with his friend.
>
> 'Busy day ahead?' asks Death's friend.
>
> 'Not too much on,' says Death, 'just a young man named Amin whose time has come.'
>
> Overhearing this conversation, Amin hangs up his apron, runs out the back door of the restaurant and catches the next bus to Jalalabad.
>
> Ten minutes later, Death stands up and says to his friend, 'Nice to see you again, but I'd better get going, I have a job today in Jalalabad.'

The terps on MNBTK shared a cluster of bunkrooms on the edge of our accommodation lines. I remember the first time I went there. I was looking to clarify my notes from a Provincial Security Council meeting. I liked to show them my meeting reports to improve their writing and reading and to let them know their work mattered. I ventured out to their quarters and asked a few of the boys where I might find Ian. They took me to his room.

We sat on a bed, which was the only horizontal furniture, and he corrected a few things in my report. He introduced me to his room mates. One said, 'I am Farid, but I want to be called Tony.'

Another introduced himself as Barry and asked if I was married.

I said I was.

'I have a girlfriend in Istanbul,' he said. 'I was studying civil engineering there but needed to come and make some money. I have been working up in Chora. A lot of foot patrols. Sometimes it is dangerous – IEDs, grenades.'

I was about to leave when another interpreter showed up at the door, dressed in uniform, carrying his body armour. He said something to the others and they all got up, and gave him a hug and kiss on both cheeks before he turned and left.

'He is about to go up to COP Mashal,' Ian explained. 'It's dangerous up there, so we wish him good luck.'

What struck me was the gentleness, almost tenderness, with which they related to each other. It stood in sharp contrast to the interaction in the shipping container I was sharing with seven Aussie diggers who seemed to communicate via a mutually understood set of jibes, grunts and farts.

In addition to the pool of Category 1 interpreters, there were twenty or so 'Cat 2s' on the base – Afghans who had fled the country in the Taliban years and gained citizenship as refugees in the US or Holland. The US Cat 2s were on civilian contracts, most of them pleased not to be working in a gas station in New Jersey. The Dutch Cat 2s had been recruited into the Netherlands army and wore uniforms with captain rank. One of these was Dr Mokamel.

An older fellow with a dapper moustache, he reminded me of the Peter Sellers version of a gentleman from the Subcontinent. He walked with his hands clasped behind his back, and taught Pashtun language classes in the PRT conference room on Tuesday nights. He was passionate about culture, particularly Afghan music and poetry. We struck up a friendship, and he led me on a series of adventures into the wilds of Afghan culture.

'Afghan New Year – Nowruz – it is in one month. We will make a band and have a party,' he said.

I hoped he was joking.

He wasn't. He came around the next day with a rehearsal schedule – every Saturday night for the four weeks leading up to Nowruz, which fell on the first day of spring.

That Saturday I fetched my guitar and made my way down to PRT House with Mokamel. He had pulled together a motley band of musicians. There were guys from Tarin Kowt town: Hormut played the harmonium, a traditional instrument that looked like an accordion set in timber; Rassoud played rubab, a multi-stringed, Central Asian lute, plucked with a heavy pick; and a blind old gent they called 'the Communist' (he'd worked in the provincial government in the 80s) played the djembe drum with a feverish passion.

From the base was Matin, on tabla. I recognised him – he drove the truck that sucked out the Dixis. And on the tanboor there was Wali, whose shifts with the ASG, the Afghan Security Guards, out on the walls were adjusted to accommodate rehearsals.

Mokamel introduced me and the rehearsal began. It was hard going. Afghan and Western musical traditions have little common ground. The chord changes that underpin Western pop are rare in Afghan music, and our scales are very different. Their rhythms are intricate but all based on the one beat; no waltzes on lazy back beats in Central Asia – every beat drives the music forward.

We spent the first half hour sifting through these differences, looking for common ground. We were making some headway when one of the young terps stuck his head in the door. One text message later and about thirty others were sitting around the rug, ready to party. The band and I just kicked into whatever we could find that was danceable.

The boys sat themselves on the cushions around the edge of the large rectangular rug and got up one at a time, each doing their own dance while the others clapped and cheered. Mokamel looked on, his facial expression changing from pride to disapproval according to the quality of the dancing. Some dancers were reticent, others knew what they were doing, like Rocky. A young guy down from the wilds of FOB Mirwais, he danced with the angular virility of a goat. There was intensity, wickedness, control and danger in his movements.

Others were softer and even feminine in their moves, shaking their hips and shoulders suggestively, batting their eyelids and pouting behind scarves they flicked back and forth. This drove the mob berserk with its hilarity and naughtiness.

In Afghanistan, men and women dance separately, and there is a homoerotic edge to the dancing that seems to sit comfortably in the culture, notwithstanding the strictures of the religion. It was all good clean fun on these Saturday nights. The terps were like young men from anywhere, in need of a bit of release once a week. In the absence of alcohol, this was how they cut loose.

This pattern continued for the next three Saturday nights; I'd be tired and longing to go and hide in my bunk. But instead, I'd drag my guitar down to PRT House and rehearse with the band before the terps descended and we turned into a dance band. We built a viable repertoire of songs, theirs and mine, including a duet in English and Pashtun of the Mary Hopkins song 'Those Were the Days', which was a hit in Afghanistan and dozens of other countries in the 1960s.

It was the only ballad in the repertoire; the rest was designed to provide the audience with opportunities for dancing, yelling and clapping. I even custom-built a song around the band (which had effectively grown to include the interpreters), a variation on the Chuck Berry classic 'Johnny B. Goode'. I called it 'Rassoud Be Good'.

> Down the Tiri Rud into Tarin Kowt,
> Deep beneath the valley of the deep devout
> in a little Qualla made of earth and wood
> there lived a country boy named Rassoud Be Good
> Rassoud never learned to read or write so well
> But he could play the rubab just like he ringin' a bell

Then the terps would sing the chorus:

> Za! Za Rassoud Za Za Za!

One of the terps told me 'Za' was Pashtun for 'go', but it turned out it meant more like 'go away!', not far from 'get stuffed'. This misunderstanding only seemed to add to the mirth. After the chorus the band would stop and Rassoud would play a solo, then I'd launch into the second verse.

> Wali's here working for the ASG,
> out there on the wire protecting you and me ...
> *then* Za, Za Wali, Za, Za, Za!

And on it went with a verse for every band member followed by the shouted Za! chorus and a solo on an Afghan instrument.

The beginning of the Afghan New Year celebrations, 20 March, was to be our first 'proper' gig at PRT House, starting at 1630. The band was starting to click to the point that I was really looking forward to our public debut. But on the morning before the gig, it all fell apart! I had seen bands unravel in Australia, but never this efficiently. The Dutch tended to blame everything that went wrong in Uruzgan on the Popalzai, and on this occasion they were right.

President Karzai decided to visit TK that morning, for the first time since late 2001, to attend a huge shura controlled by JMK. The Afghan security forces got serious about security and locked down traffic in Tarin Kowt town. As a consequence, 'the Communist' was left stranded on the other side of town; he couldn't make the gig. This somehow led to an argument between Mokamel and Hormut and Rassoud; they quit the band simultaneously.

At 1400, Mokamel rushed in to my office, sweating and embarrassed, to let me know the band we had so patiently nurtured had disintegrated.

'There is good news, though,' he said. 'We have another band!'

He drove me out to the ASG compound where the band of Dr Farouk from Kandahar was assembled in a wooden shed. I was introduced to the players. Farouk, the father figure and bandleader, played the rubab. There was a second rubab player and Farouk's two sons; one played a Western electronic keyboard, the other the tabla. Then there was a guy with lightning in his eyes and a cheeky little moustache like Oliver Hardy. His only instrument appeared to be a suitcase full of notebooks. He was the singer, and in his notebooks were song lyrics.

An old geezer ran the PA system; they had their own, which was a good sign. Things got even better when we started rehearsing. I'm no expert in Afghan music, but these guys could play. We rushed through 'Dust of Uruzgan'. They didn't latch on to the third chord change in the riff but I let it be – given the rarity of chord changes in Afghan music I figured two chords was as much as one could ask of them on short notice. We rehearsed 'Those Were the Days', then hightailed it out to the Slovak Gate for the gig.

Getting six Afghans with no security passes and a vanload of electronic equipment through the Slovak security gate was not straightforward. By the time we reached PRT House, the room was half full; we had to fight our way in to the stage area up against the back wall. An ornamental set of traditional Afghan clothes hung from a coathanger on the wall; Mokamel insisted I put them on. I was reluctant, thinking I'd look silly, but it was their New Year's Eve so I obliged. By the time we were ready to play, the room was full and chaotic. All the commanding officers from the various contingents were present, along with a large number of Dutch and a handful of Aussies. The heat was on: literally, it being the first day of spring.

The band broke into the theme song from *Titanic* (the film was an underground hit in Kabul in the Taliban years when movies were banned and television sets were strung up from lampposts). Then they rocked an Afghan song with electronic drums from the keyboard thumping loud, complemented by the more organic-sounding traditional instruments. We created some dancing space on the rug and I led by example. It felt good to dance barefoot on the carpet in the Afghan pantaloons – there was a lot of room to move in there.

I joined the band on 'Those Were the Days' as a duet with the moustachioed singer; it picked up nicely as the guys kicked in behind the choruses of the old Russian melody. Then I led into 'Dust of Uruzgan', which, to my surprise, worked fantastically. When we reached the crisis point after the seventeenth verse, I pulled the band down to almost nothing then screamed into the mike and the band exploded into the instrumental. The tempo went up through the roof and the rubab player picked the melody feverishly while the guys on the djembe and tabla hammered away. (There is a video of this performance on YouTube, filmed with a shaky hand.)

Mokamel announced a break and the ASG cooks laid on a feast of flatbread, meats and rice served from twenty-two-gallon aluminium pots. Then the band cranked up again. Initially only the Afghans were dancing, then they pulled me up, along with some Dutch girls. Pretty soon the whole room was a mosh pit of flailing limbs: soldiers in their uniforms and the Afghans in traditional clothes. A couple of the older interpreters turned out to be great singers; they chimed in too.

Things started to wrap up at 2100. I was shaping to leave when Nazir, the ASG commander, invited me to another New Year's Day bash the following evening. Mokamel – by this stage my manager, it seemed – immediately agreed.

As we drove back to the office, Mokamel was high on life and the success of the evening. Prone to moments of eloquence, he said, 'There is a Persian saying: Music – it is a ladder for the soul!'

It occurred to me that in this part of the world you need something for that purpose, since daily life seemed a series of vexations and antagonisms leading to an early death.

'I'm very tired but very happy,' he said. I felt the same way: *Fucking exhausted* is what I wrote in my diary.

The next day passed in a haze. I was getting dirty looks around the headquarters; half of those who had eaten the meal at the party had come down with diarrhoea and seemed to be holding me responsible as the main white face of the party. I had suffered the same affliction from an Afghan meal the week before – it was always a risk – but dodged the bullet this time round. It was just one of those weeks when the Role 2 ran out of Gastro-Stop. That happened every few months.

It was on my mind that I needed to make an important speech the following day at MDK's shura. Leaders were coming in from all around the province. I had requested transport and protection from the Dutch for the trip and assumed it was all squared away.

But at the BUB at 1800, Major Mark Griffiths, the new civil military officer responsible for liaising with the PRT, announced that the mission to MDK's shura had been cancelled as the Dutch were unable to spare force protection. This was news to me – and a big problem. MDK's credibility and the confidence of 90 per cent of the province about the direction of the ISAF mission hinged on us showing up at this shura.

Driving out to the ASG compound with Mokamel, I was thinking this through while wondering whether a little gig in the ASG meeting room was worth my trouble with so much else going on. I arrived to find that the ASG Commander, Nazir, had spared no effort; he had set up a twenty-foot stage on the grass and Dr Farouk's band had their full PA rigged up with lights and instruments. I was halfway through enjoying a pre-gig meal with the band when MDK and forty of his tribesmen showed up. Among them was a portly fellow named Habib Barakzai who wore the traditional Afghan shalwar kameez and Nike basketball boots. A former Barakzai tribesman, he had made it to the US as a refugee during the civil war. He spoke fluent English with a New Jersey accent.

I knew I had to break the news to MDK that we might not be able to make it to his shura, so I told Habib.

'This is serious,' he replied. 'Daoud told everyone you would be there. He has spent 400,000 Afghanis on the shura – you have to come!'

The problem was explained to MDK. He understood the theatre of power and that he couldn't be seen to be panicking at this most public occasion, but I could see him sweating under his turban.

I got on the Nokia, first to Lieutenant Colonel Jason Blain, then to TF66, then to Russ to see what could be done. There were no Bushmasters left in Bethlehem. So it came back to the Dutch. I called Jennes, the new Dutch CivRep, explained that the future of their 'tribal balance' approach was in the balance; what could he do to find me some Bushmasters and a couple of dozen heavily armed men? Hamidi, the Dutch Afghan cultural adviser, showed up and confirmed my view that this was serious. He began calling his contacts in the PRT.

Meanwhile, at the party, the ANA general and his coterie of colonels sat down in the front row to the right, while MDK and the senior Barakzai sat to the left. There was a guy getting around with a video camera; the vision was projected onto a screen at the side of the stage. I was waved to the front and sat with MDK and Habib. I noticed the camera panning in on me, then him. This was the theatre of power, Afghan style, and I was a symbol of prestige and influence.

The band cranked out a couple of tunes, then Mokamel gave the signal – time to play. I plugged in my guitar, asked the singer to move his suitcase over a little and sat on the front of the stage.

We knocked out a respectable version of 'Dust of Uruzgan', and then the band and crowd went nuts at our version of 'Minnie the Moocher'. A couple of the ANA soldiers danced very formally on the grass in front of us, barely adjusting their traditional Afghan stylings to Cab Calloway's classic stomp.

I went backstage and made more calls; things were still looking bad for the shura. I sat down on the couch next to MDK and Habib. The singer started a song from his notebook – a ballad about Rozi Khan! A photograph of the revered Barakzai warrior appeared on half the screen; the other half showed his son MDK, as he sat there stoically to my left. Habib started blubbering, 'He saved my family, you know,' while MDK began pulling $US100 bills out of his pouch – and had one of his boys take the bills to the stage and drape them on the mic stand. I sat there between them thinking, 'We killed this guy's dad and I can't even get the force protection to make it to his shura.'

Another song started. On Mokamel's suggestion I got up and danced, thrashing around like Peter Garrett in front of the stage. The Afghans started clapping and cheering.

When I sat down Hamidi tapped me on the shoulder and said quietly: 'It has all been arranged – the Dutch soldiers can do it.'

Habib looked like a man released from death row, and I noticed MDK had stopped sweating.

After the gig, Mokamel and I drove back to the PRT in high spirits. 'If you do not take the risk, you cannot drink the champagne – it is a Russian proverb,' said Mokamel.

I slept for four hours, waking at 0630 knowing I still needed to finish organising my thoughts to speak at the shura. I found Mark Griffiths in the DFAC eating breakfast; as we spoke, it occurred to me it would be good to get Russ on board for an American presence.

'Possible?' I asked.

'Nope,' Mark said. 'With all the shooters there's only four spots and they're taken: you, me, Hamidi and the interpreter.'

'We've got Hamidi; we don't need to bother the terp!'

I called Russ, who, though half asleep, saw the logic in coming and dragged himself out of bed and into some body armour.

The convoy forged through the streets of Tarin Kowt and out over Irish Crossing. Through the front window I could see children playing in the river. MDK's compound was on the left of the main drag, some four kilometres north of TK up the paved road. At the entrance was a pillbox with a mounted fifty-calibre machine gun. We drove through a cluster of *qallas*, the homes behind the high mud-brick walls that are the staple housing construction in rural Afghanistan. We pulled up in a gravel car park, alighting from the rear hatch of the Bushmaster to find ourselves in rural Barakzailand – a walled village the size of a small suburb. With its narrow cobbled streets, it felt like a Tuscan town. We entered a large courtyard covered with shade cloth; it was full, with some 300 elders there. I noticed a pair of Blundstone boots among the collection of 600 removed shoes arranged at the entrance; they belonged to a Dutch journalist who I saw sitting there with his camera among the sea of turbans. With his presence, the stakes went up another notch.

We were seated in the prime positions and shook hands with the elders while MDK breezed around in host-with-the-most mode. A sole Dutch marine stood there, eyes scanning the group, but we sensed we were among friends. Speeches began, mostly addressed to us, from half a dozen elders, including the venerable Haji Zahir Barakzai. Hamidi interpreted, whispering his translations over our shoulders. I heard the usual themes: the need for inclusive government; respect for local culture; and tribal realities. MDK made a short speech then Hamidi tapped me on the shoulder.

After years on stages I can read an Australian crowd and calibrate my voice and tempo to the size and mood of the room instinctively, like a surfer feels a wave. But speaking in Afghanistan, I never knew how my words were being translated, let alone received. I could only organise my thoughts, back myself to deliver them, trust the interpreter, and leave the rest to fate. The vast gathering of wizened faces peered at me through sceptical eyes; they'd seen so many foreigners come and go. I made one point at a time to allow Hamidi to translate. I spoke for perhaps ten minutes, letting them know we understood the tribal dynamics of the province, and would work to support all tribes. Then I sat down.

Haji Zahir got up and thanked us. Then the mandatory feast of mutton and rice was served. After all the pressure, I ate too much and spread rice all over my trousers. Afghans are adept at eating with their hands; I'm not.

An old fella approached me.

'Thank you,' he said. 'Your speech gave me hope.'

I was pleased to hear this, though wary that I'd written a cheque my successors might not be inclined to cash.

We drove out of the compound in the back of the Bushmaster, children running alongside waving at us. Hamidi, usually measured in all things, said my speech was 'perfect'. We arrived back at MNBTK feeling as triumphant as you can when working in a place like Uruzgan. But I knew I needed to get the tribal and political engagement strategy solid if my words were to have any real value.

The next week, the ambassador Paul Foley came down for a visit. We discussed the Uruzgan political strategy which Hugh's replacement down in Kandahar, James Fisher, had fleshed out and documented. We agreed that tribal balance – not to favour one tribe against the other – was the key element. We would engage with Matiullah Khan but encourage him to work with other tribes, and let him know we were watching him for any abuses of power. The other element of the political strategy was to try to connect the province with the capital; to encourage the provincial government to reach out to the central government for support and resources rather than warlords. Paul and I gave the political strategy document a few touch-ups and sent it back down to James to submit to Regional Command South for confirmation.

Meanwhile, Maryanne had had another miscarriage and bought us a house. And I came down with a second dose of the shits from the mutton I had eaten at MDK's shura. I was exhausted from the work and depleted by the diarrhoea. It was time for a break.

On a sunny morning in late March, I boarded a little USAID Beechcraft bound for Kabul. Peering out the window at the snow beginning to melt on the peaks of the Hindu Kush, I looked down at the tiny villages nestled deep in the mountain valleys. I wondered at the lives they lived down there, but knew that I could never really know what it's like to live like an Afghan.

Live like an Afghan

When I live, I want to live like an Afghan, live like an Afghan lives
Walk tall as the rockets are falling around me, laugh as they
    barely miss
If you meet me in the streets of Kandahar greet me with a
    bearded kiss
We shall live, yes we shall live like the Afghans, live like the
    Afghans live

When I love I want to love like an Afghan, love like the Afghans do
Everyone needs someone to love and today I'm in love with you
Meet the boys on a Thursday evening but a man needs a wife
    or two
And we shall love, yes we shall love like the Afghans, love like the
    Afghans do

When I dance I want to dance like an Afghan, dance like the
    Afghans dance
You never know what's going to happen tomorrow, this could be
    our last chance
So shake your hips and swing your hands to heaven, let your feet
    pound the dusty floor
Wake in the morning to tea and some flatbread and get stuck
    back in to the war

When I fight I want to fight like an Afghan, fight like the
    Afghans fight
Kiss your cheek if we should meet in the market out in the
    broad daylight
But cut your throat under the cover of darkness with a courteous
    flick of the wrist
Manners matter when you fight like an Afghan, fight like an
    Afghan lives

When I die I want to die like an Afghan, die like an Afghan dies
Hope there'll be someone present who loves me to brush away all
    the flies
In the end you might go with a whimper or a bang like our
    dear Massoud
Either way I want to die like an Afghan, die like an Afghan would
'Cause in the end you know these things happen and you'll want
    to get on with it
When I die I want to die like an Afghan, die like an Afghan lives

CHAPTER 7

SAPPER'S LULLABY

These young engineers, whose job is to clear
the roads that we may pass
They're always out front, and when they bear the brunt,
man it happens fast

FRED SMITH, 'SAPPER'S LULLABY'

I WAS A NORMAL ENOUGH TEN-YEAR-OLD WHEN MY FAMILY ARRIVED in Manila on a posting, although not entirely happy to be there. Having returned from Israel two years beforehand, I had just got used to being an Aussie kid and had become passionate about the Collingwood Football Club. I was slow to let go of that in the Neapolitan company of my new colleagues at the International School, who neither knew nor cared for Australian Rules football.

Still, I made the most of it, playing tennis, learning Spanish guitar and riding my bike around the streets of our walled suburb, like I did in Australia. I was doing just that one afternoon after a monsoonal downpour when a security guard from one of the households started chasing a pet monkey up a tree with a metal pole. The tree branch touched the power lines and I heard a loud *pop!* I turned to see the man lying on the road, dead, smoke pouring from a hole in his stomach, his eyes fixed in shock. Soon after that, news came through that my uncle had died in a horseriding accident on his farm in Western Australia.

Death and impermanence seemed everywhere, and I went into a junior league existential meltdown. I couldn't sleep at night; I became fixated on the notion that I and everyone I knew would one day die.

I recovered, on the existential front, by getting baptised at the local church, which seemed to promise at least some sort of post-mortem after-party. And I solved the sleeping problem by taking a little blue teddy bear to bed. The bear's name was Fred.

The following year, I went off to boarding school in Australia. In my first term, I developed a strange habit: I would hold on to things that meant something to me – wrappers of chocolates people had given me, or stickers my mum sent in the mail – and I would blu-tack them to the wall of my little cubicle. I had a simple camera and would take photographs of anything significant that happened in the boarding house. I soon became the 'house photographer'. For example, when occasionally a day boy, loitering around the entrance to the boarding house, was seized and prostrated at the bottom of a significant 'pile on' that reached almost to the ceiling, I would be called in to photograph this remarkable feat of pubescent corporeal engineering for posterity.

Christianity soon went by the wayside for me. But I have kept Fred, and retained the impulse to document in the face of our chronic impermanence.

❖

Speaking of impermanence, by the time I arrived back in Uruzgan in early May 2010, much had changed. I had been moved into a single container in Chalet 13 with a couple of new AusAID officers, a fellow named Andrew and my old mate Tony whom I'd worked with in Port Moresby in 1999.

I called Dad soon after arriving. He had just come out of a cabinet meeting where it had been decided henceforth to spell Uruzgan with a U rather than an O. The Afghans didn't seem to mind either way – they pronounced that first vowel somewhere between an O and a U depending on the wind direction.

More significantly, ministers had agreed that, come summer, the Dutch task force would be replaced with a new Combined Team Uruzgan (CTU) staffed by US and Australian soldiers, and led by a US colonel. Australia would send a senior diplomat to lead a combined US/Australian PRT, the US military element of which would be led by a navy commander. News of this prompted the Dutch CivRep to ask, 'Do they know it's a landlocked country?'

I applied for a six-month extension of my posting. I was engrossed in the work and intrigued by the prospect of working in an Australian-led PRT. And besides, I was becoming reasonably famous on base. One morning I had cause to call The Geeks, the young privates who provided IT support. When the lad at the helpdesk picked up the phone I could hear the harmonica solo to 'Dust of Uruzgan' playing in the background.

'You're listening to that "Dust of Uruzgan" song?' I asked.

'Yeah,' he said. 'I found the dude's website and figured out how to rip it off without paying!'

'Good work digger, crack on,' I said, pleased to know that a new generation of ADF technicians were honing their skills on my intellectual property.

Out beyond the wire, Governor Hamdam had been sacked and Deputy Governor Khoday Rahim was acting in the position. The Dutch had Khoday pegged as 'a toothless tiger related to JMK'. It was true that he had no real power base and that he was a Popalzai, blood relative of JMK and MK. On the other hand, he was a likeable old fellow in his early seventies who spoke with a high crack in his voice – a habit he had probably developed to keep children awake during through those long afternoons in his previous career as a teacher out in the districts of Uruzgan Province.

Meanwhile, the war, like the weather, was hotting up. *Nesht* – Pashtun for the harvest – ran from late April to mid-May and absorbed most of the fighting-age males, FAMs as we called them, in honest labour. But we knew that the end of *nesht* would mark the beginning of the fighting season, and that with the Dutch pulling out and the Taliban under pressure in Helmand and Kandahar, things would get nasty.

First blood went to the Taliban on 22 May, when a French captain and a Dutch soldier were killed in the Tangi Valley by an IED strike. Down range, IEDs were our greatest fear. Coalition forces were better armed and trained than the Taliban and tended to win whenever the situation turned into a 'two-way firing range'. So the Taliban engaged in 'asymmetric warfare' against us, and IEDs were their weapon of choice. Tactically, IEDs restricted our mobility. Strategically, the idea was to kill a lot of our soldiers so as to weaken the resolve of leaders in Western capitals. The Taliban had a saying, 'A small bomb in Kabul is worth two big ones in the country,' the logic of which derived from the fact that Western journalists were concentrated in the capital. So while our soldiers were the immediate prey, our media was the real target.

IEDs were mostly primitive devices, made of fertiliser packed into a container of some sort and wired up with basic consumer electronics. But they killed a lot of people, and were on the rise. There had been 200 IED attacks in Afghanistan in 2007, and 8000 in 2009. About 60 per cent of the coalition soldiers who died in 2009 and 2010 were killed by IEDs. But it wasn't just us they killed. According to UN figures, the Taliban were responsible for 75 per cent of the 2777 Afghan civilians killed in the war in

2010, most by IEDs. At one of the BUBs, the 2 Shop offered their assessment that in March alone thirty insurgents had been killed when the bombs they were building or planting had blown up in their faces. We called these 'own goals', and the announcement of another own goal in the districts was always greeted with a cheer at the BUB.

The statistics tell only part of the story. It was the injuries from IEDs that shocked me most. When energy, heat and shrapnel meet with soft flesh, the results are horrific – shock, blood loss, brain injuries, burns, lost limbs and psychological trauma are all likely outcomes. Paul Warren had eighteen operations after his injury.

As the war continued, coalition forces invested more in counter-IED technology. The US Army fitted extension arms that would drag a chain out ten feet in front of the vehicle to set off IEDs. The Taliban responded by placing pressure plates ten feet in front of the kill zone – an ongoing game of cat and mouse. But the best way to deal with the IEDs was to find them, and the best way to find them was with a sapper and his dog.

Sappers, or combat engineers, earned their name on the battlefields of seventeenth-century France for their ability to dig covered trenches (*sappes*) approaching the walls of a fort or castle that you might be laying siege to on a Saturday morning. Being a sapper was dirty and dangerous work then, as it is now. In Afghanistan and Iraq, construction roles aside, the main job of the sapper was to travel at the front of a patrol or convoy looking for signs of IEDs. If they saw something suspicious they would approach it on hands and knees, brush away the dust and deal with it. This meant convoys sometimes moved at walking pace, sappers out front with their dogs and metal detectors, edging forward in full body armour in the heat of the day, knowing a slip in concentration could mean death or permanent injury for them or the men behind them. Intense stuff, and I had a lot of respect for the work they did; without it neither the infantry nor diplomats could have operated in the province.

The ADF had three combat engineer regiments (CER) that would supply detachments to the infantry regiments, who provided the bulk of the Australian battlegroups sent to Afghanistan. In the summer of 2010, it was mostly sappers from 2CER working in support of 6 RAR, their co-tenants from Enoggera Barracks.

If the IEDs were on our minds when we left the base, IDF was the acronym of concern while on base. It stood for indirect fire and basically meant rockets. There had been a spate of them before I arrived in early 2009. One evening Jason Katz had applied first aid in a failed attempt to save the life of a Dutch interpreter whose throat had been torn out by shrapnel from a rocket, blown through the thin walls of a toilet block in which he was taking a shower. Jason was worried about rockets and often slept in his office Drehtainer rather than his tile-roofed accommodation down at FOB Ripley.

The rockets were mostly old Chinese 107mm self-propelled things that had been lying around since the Mujahedin years. The Taliban had no rocket launchers, so 'Rocket Man', as we referred to him generically, would prop the thing up on a rock about three kilometres away, point it in the general direction of the base and set it off with a timer. Mostly the rockets missed by a mile. Sometimes they landed near MK's place; then Rocket Man knew he was in trouble.

So accurate they were not, but on the night of 6 May, Rocket Man got lucky, as I recorded in my diary:

Last night at 1.30 am, I heard Tony get up and leave the Drehtainer for his nightly piss. I was drifting back to sleep when suddenly: BOOM! The walls shook, then the sound of scattering shrapnel and dislodged dirt falling off ceilings. Then a ten-second pause and the IDF siren sounded (thanks for letting us know!). I went out into the corridor. Other blokes had done the same and were chatting in excited bravado - 'Fuck me, you lighting your farts again, Johnno?' etc. - when BOOM! Another rocket landed just outside the chalet. We felt the blast wave, smelled the cordite and scurried back into our Drehtainers like rabbits into a hole. I felt the anger of the guy who fired the rocket. I felt hugely vulnerable against their force, real fear like I've never felt before. I lay in bed needing to piss. Eventually I got up and scurried out to the latrines abutting the east side of the building, knowing that most rockets come in on a flat trajectory from the west. I couldn't get back to sleep, so plugged in my headphones and put on Regina Spektor's 'Laughing With' ('No one's laughing at God in a war').

It turned out three rockets had hit the base that night, the first smack bang on the corner roof of Chalet 13 and the second thirty metres behind it, either a great shot or really lucky. The rocket that hit my chalet exploded upon striking the detonation roof, but didn't breach the Drehtainer. Luckily, Tony had not quite made it out of the chalet on his way to the latrines, so was not hurt. But our pet tortoise Terry, who lived in a pen outside, adjacent to Chalet 6, copped a piece of shrapnel in his back. The boys from Chalet 6 pulled the shrapnel out with pliers, dabbed some Betadine on the wound and Terry was good to go, although he did seem a little withdrawn for the next week or two, even by his standards. I was a bit edgy for a while there myself.

A week later, I had another close call. I went up to FOB Mirwais in Chora with a delegation that included Lieutenant Colonel Jason Blain, Captain Myles Conquest, and Zambetta from AusAID. We arrived late on the afternoon of 12 May and set up accommodation stretchers in a little hut on the uphill corner of the base. We awoke in fright the following morning to bursts of heavy machine-gun fire close by. Captain Conquest leaped up in his jocks, wrestling Zambetta down off her stretcher to the concrete floor, shouting, 'Get down, Zambetta, we're under attack!' It turned out the firing range was just behind the base and that the ANA had started practice early that day.

That aside, the trip was a success. We were guests of honour at a shura hosted by MDK. In the evening, MDK, his bodyguards and an assortment of district government staff joined us on base for dinner and a concert. I had a great time jamming with the local musicians, led by the mayor, Dr Azim.

I arrived back in TK tired and hungry after two nights sleeping on a stretcher and five hours in the back of the Bushmaster. As I was walking to the DFAC for lunch, a mate from the 2 Shop spotted me.

'Hey, great to see you in one piece!'

'How so?' I asked.

'We picked up some Icom chatter yesterday from Mullah Abdullah ordering his men to send a suicide bomber to your shura with MDK. They couldn't get it organised – and he got really pissed off!'

'Tell him to get a life!' I said.

Clearly, there were dangers in associating with MDK. The Taliban wanted to kill him, MK too, and there were rats in the Barakzai ranks – in particular, MDK's ne'er-do-well uncle, Shah Mohammad. When MDK's father Rozi Khan died, Shah Mohammad felt entitled to the Barakzai leadership in the province, but was denied because he was considered a little unhinged. Still, he retained some power, a small militia and a seat at the Barakzai board, for reasons Willem explained to me.

'He is not liked, but he is aggressive, and in Afghanistan this makes him useful.'

Useful to MK, it turned out; he, we understood, was funding and encouraging Shah Mohammad to undermine MDK. Shah Mohammad set up a rival militia to compete with MDK for protection work on the Road to Chora, which was finally making progress. This caused friction, and Juma weighed into this contest by seeking to confiscate weapons from both men's militias.

This issue was coming to a head when Shah Mohammad fell from grace. One late spring morning in the village, he caught a young man making eyes at a young girl and decided to punish the boy in the traditional way, by stripping him in the village square, bending him over and taking to the boy's backside with a stick. This might have been okay had he used the flat end of the stick but, not to put too fine a point on it, he used the sharp end, with a thrusting motion. This incident, which we referred to in reporting as Stickgate, was filmed by a local national and footage went viral around the province. Every time you met a local leader, he'd pull out his phone and want to show you the video. Fascinating though the incident was, even highly conservative Uruzganis felt old Shah Mohammad had gone too far this time. He became a pariah. The Afghan National Police received an order from Kabul to arrest him. MK sought to distance himself from Shah Mohammad.

This hiccup aside, MK's star continued to rise. Gizab, the far northern district of the province, had been dominated by the Taliban for six years. A handful of locals, led by a man name Lalay, had approached the Dutch and the ANA to help overthrow the Taliban district 'government', but neither were able to help. In early

April, the locals lost patience and began to take action. It seemed their little coup would fail catastrophically until MK stepped in and, combined with US and Australian special forces, went up there with firepower to help Lalay eject the Taliban from the district centre. The surviving local Taliban leaders were executed by Lalay – Russ saw their bloody bodies lying in a basement.

The Gizab Uprising gained international profile right up to the White House, cited as an example of what could be achieved by supporting local initiatives. Gizab leaders then looked to the provincial government for services, and looked to the coalition countries working in Uruzgan to help with development assistance (Tony did the paperwork to get some medical supplies up there). But when it came to security, it was MK and his men the locals up there wanted, notwithstanding that tribally they were more aligned with the Barakzai.

Holding Gizab was by no means assured and depended partly on our ability to resupply the area via the Chora to Gizab road. I called my Aussie contractor mate Barry Stevens, who had been so vitriolic about MK, to see what was going on with the road. He said things had changed, and radically.

'Mate, I've done a one-eighty on MK. He's hell-bent on getting the job done. MK's helped us to sort out contracting issues and pay the people in the villages. He said if the people in the village get paid then all will be peaceful. He was right – we've almost finished the first sixty k.'

I spoke to Russ about MK and tribal balance. 'As General McChrystal said the other day, we can exacerbate the tribal problem by fixating on it. Modern Afghans are more interested in profit, politics and access. In any case, it is not within our means to overthrow the Popalzai political dominance – you are always going to get a governor acceptable to the JMK power base. So we should work with this. MK doesn't care about tribes; he works with all of them. We should work with him.'

Not everyone was so sanguine. On 10 May, I met with Malim Habibullah and Malim Manan, two elders from the Mirabad Valley which ran east out of Tarin Kowt and up into Khas Uruzgan. A mostly Ghilzai tribal area, it had been solid Taliban country in recent years, and Habibullah explained why.

'There was no Taliban in the area in 2002,' he said. 'Everyone wanted to join the government. We even gave up our weapons. But then the government turned people into Taliban. In the second year of JMK, my nephew was killed by an ANP commander. I went to complain to the governor but he would not even meet with me. There were other crimes. One day, government forces killed four local men by driving over their heads in an ANP truck. After that, people in the valley decided to fight with the Taliban against MK and JMK. JMK and MK are responsible for bad things in the past and these things have not been resolved.'

This sort of thing seems to have happened all over Afghanistan. When international forces arrived in force in October 2001, no one wanted to have anything to do with the Taliban; they had been a disaster in government and had disintegrated in the face of the shock-and-awe combination punch of US airstrikes and special forces. By December 2001, the Taliban were broken.

But by 2005, they were back, dominating rural areas in the east and south of the country. Why did this happen? Conventional wisdom is that in 2003 the West got fixated on Iraq and left too few troops on the ground in Afghanistan to keep things sweet. But there may be another explanation.

In 2011, my father had a conversation with Governor Shirzad, who succeeded Khoday. Shirzad had fought in the Mujahedin alongside Mullah Barader; the two were close friends. But Shirzad was now in the government camp, while Barader had become a senior Taliban figure. 'Why so?' Dad asked.

'We didn't choose,' Shirzad explained. 'You made the choices for us.'

Shirzad's words and Habibullah's account of what happened in the Mirabad are consistent with the analysis of writers like Sarah Chayes and Anand Gopal. In his book, *No Good Men Among the Living*, Gopal argues that the Operation Enduring Freedom forces that remained in the country in the few years after 2002 contributed directly to the resurgence of the Taliban. In establishing themselves on the ground, they formed relationships with local powerbrokers, like Gul Agha Sherzai in Kandahar and JMK in Uruzgan, who enriched themselves by supplying foreign forces with land for their bases and logistical needs.

Avenging 9/11 was front and centre of the American agenda. As President George W. Bush said at the time: 'Either you are with us, or you are with the terrorists.' Gopal argues this mentality permeated the thinking of the military in Afghanistan, and it became a classic case of what you think is what you get. US forces were looking for an enemy, and so they found one, or rather, created one. The Operation Enduring Freedom elements operating in Afghanistan between 2001 and 2005 comprised mostly marines and US Special Forces. They were trained to break things, not fix things, and they set about doing what they were trained to do: hunt the enemy. Of course, they needed help identifying who the enemy actually were, and that's where things got messy. They took 'intelligence' from the powerbrokers. The powerbrokers identified their tribal and business rivals as Taliban.

Furthermore, Gopal argues, Hamid Karzai's modus operandi was to have a client powerbroker running the show for him in each province. Men like JMK were given governorships and became the face of government. Even if their tribal competitors wanted to join the government, they couldn't. These governors abused their positions and the corruption spread down to local officials and police; their predatory practices drove many away from the government back to the Taliban.

Gopal actually cites JMK's actions in the Mirabad as an example of how this dynamic played out. His analysis might be right – the Mirabad Valley was impenetrable to coalition forces when I arrived in Uruzgan in July 2009.

❖

I first became aware of the situation in the Mirabad on a moonless night in early August 2009 when Eric said: 'Hey, come with me down to PRT House – there's something we want you to see.'

A skinny guy with dirty feet and a long beard walked in, a farmer apparently, with a blanket worn like a shawl over his head for concealment. He sat and showed us photos on his phone of an aqueduct he'd been building. The Dutch military PRT officer with us nodded with approval and handed him ten $US100 bills, photographing him with the cash spread out like a fan in front of his face. This photo was effectively a receipt for Dutch files, a financial accountability measure in a mostly illiterate society, for these 'under the radar' projects the Dutch were running to build relationships in the Mirabad. The farmer stole back out into the night and, we hoped, made it home safe. Anyone seen working with coalition forces was at risk.

A month later on base we had a 'key leader engagement strategy' meeting focused on the question of whether we should go into the Mirabad. The Dutch intelligence officer and operations officer were against it; why stretch ourselves further and start something we couldn't finish? But the affirmative had a strong case.

'TF66 have been doing some good work there rounding up insurgents,' someone said. 'We need to follow through. People want to get rid of the Taliban.'

This was true. Mirabad elders like Habibullah were sick of Taliban bullying and wanted the development benefits that were unfolding elsewhere around the province.

What clinched it was a more political prerogative: both Aussies and Dutch were lobbying to get the 3rd Kandak of the ANA Fourth Brigade up from Kandahar into Uruzgan. To make the case, we needed to be able to argue there was a new area of operations for them to work in. With the 1st and 2nd Kandaks of the brigade ensconced in Deh Rawud District and the Baluchi–Chora Valley, respectively, this left the Mirabad.

As the discussion went on, Willem said, 'Well, if we really want peace in the Mirabad, we have to establish bases.'

This was also what the locals told us.

So the decision was taken to go in. The job fell to Australian regular forces and a plan was hatched to combine with the ANA to 'clear' the valley of insurgents, then Australian sappers would build patrol bases. Of course, the sequencing didn't work out as tidily as that and the building of Patrol Base Wali has been described by those involved as a 'hot build' – that is, they were shooting over the makeshift protection walls at the same time they were digging foundations.

My various diary entries track the progress that was made: at the BUB on the evening of 9 September 2009, the 2 Shop assessed that insurgents in the Mirabad were shifting to 'more IED-related operations because they figure they can't match us for firepower'.

Then at the meeting of provincial leaders on 12 November, Governor Hamdam announced that Taliban commander Abdul Hoy had left the area because he had lost the support of the people.

At the 4 December daily commander's update, the Dutch 2 Shop said forty-four weapons caches had been found in the Mirabad since operations began. By 9 March 2010, tribal leader Mauladad told me that people were happy with the Australians and the way they were working.

❖

And so it was that by 10 May, when those two Mirabad elders, Malim Habibullah and Malim Manan, came to see us, they felt safe enough to express their desire for more development projects in the valley. Yet they still didn't trust the provincial government. Habibullah said, 'If coalition forces come with MK's men or ANP, we will always fight them. If you come with the ANA, you can work from our homes, no problem.'

Manan agreed and said the Australian soldiers were working well with the community, collecting Taliban weapons caches, and responding calmly to IED threats.

Afghan security leaders were upbeat about the Mirabad and tended to see the Taliban's use of IEDs as a sign that the insurgents were on the back foot. But this was of little consolation to those who bore the brunt of the weapons.

On the morning of 7 June, a dismounted patrol from Mentoring Team Alpha was making its way home to Patrol Base Wali. Acting on intelligence provided by locals, they had found three separate caches of weapons and munitions, including 1600 AK-47 rounds, twenty-three RPGs and five mortar rounds – a major setback for the remnants of the Taliban in the valley, and a good morning's work.

At the front of the patrol were two young sappers, Jacob Moerland and Darren Smith, and Smith's border collie cross, Herbie. Hot and coated in dust, they were a couple of kilometres from base when Moerland spotted something on the side of the track. He pointed it out to Smith, who let Herbie off the leash. The dog strolled up to the object and began sniffing it, then stopped and stared – it was the real thing. The two sappers approached and were about to get to work when the device detonated.

It was a big bomb. Apparently the blast was heard by other patrols two and a half kilometres away, and by journalist Chris Masters, who was doing a stint at Patrol Base Wali. Moerland and Herbie were killed instantly. The guys worked hard to save Darren Smith but he died of wounds before he made it back to the Tarin Kowt Role 2.

As all this was going on, I was twenty-two kilometres away from the bomb in my office in the MTF headquarters. I heard someone in the CP down the corridor call out, 'Two category As, send choppers!' I called Maryanne and left a quick message saying the comms were about to go down, then they did. An all-stations warning popped up on the screen of my laptop: 'CLP Red – unclassified communications will be closed until further notice.' Whenever there was an incident they would close down the welfare phone lines and internet to make sure the family members of anyone killed or wounded got the news direct from a defence department notifying officer rather than Facebook or the Channel 7 news. Then a little rope went up across the entrance of the MTF headquarters chalet to send the message, 'Go away, we're busy.'

I was walking back to the office after lunch when a Dutch soldier came up to me and said, 'Sad day, I heard you lost two guys.'

At the BUB that night the room was solemn. I saw the padre, Al Lavaki, sitting in the corner looking quiet and focused. Major General Cantwell, the new Australian commander for the Middle East, was in town visiting from UAE. He sat in the CO's seat. The CO was busy making phone calls to the families of the two soldiers.

'Gentlemen,' he said, 'two fellow soldiers are now resting in peace here in the Role 2, both engineers, doing what engineers do – out the front looking for IEDs. The prime minister called to pass on deepest condolences. Until all families are notified, comms will remain down and we won't release the names until then. Their mates are still out at Wali but will come in for the ramp ceremony. Their dog Herbie will be cremated at the Role 2.'

❖

The ramp ceremony was held just before midday on 9 June. We all filed into the Apache aircraft hangar where two steel caskets sat on stands in front of the podium, surrounded by a catafalque party. Padre Lavaki spoke, then a sapper mate of one of the guys got up and spoke, followed by Lieutenant Colonel Jason Blain.

I learned that 'Snowy' Moerland was twenty-one years old. A cheeky little blond bloke, full of life and mirth, he had just become engaged. Darren Smith was twenty-six. A hell-raiser in his younger days, he had become a dedicated family man with a young son, Mason, and a wife, Angela. As he lay dying on the stretcher, he'd asked his mates to take care of them.

Major General Cantwell got up. He started speaking calmly but was weeping by the time he finished.

My emotional life is pretty submerged at the best of times. I tend not to cry at all, which can be embarrassing at funerals, when I lapse into a highly observational state of mind in which I notice details but feel like an interloper. Writing songs is probably my only emotional outlet. My diary entry describing the final stage of the ramp ceremony reflects this process at work:

When the memorial service was over, I filed out of the Apache hangar and instead of standing along the road by the Role 2, I went out to the flight line to represent DFAT in the second row of the VIP party. It was hot out there. They had two Hercules

C130s on the runway: one for the caskets, the other as backup. Padre Lavaki led the pallbearers up the ramp. They had arranged the taller pallbearers at the back of each of the heavy steel caskets in order to keep the caskets horizontal going up the ramp of the plane. Shorty Coleman's son, Angus, was standing in front of me. A young private in front of him fainted and he lunged forward and caught her before her head hit the deck . . .

The next words on the page are the first verse of my song 'Sapper's Lullaby':

> *Up from the Role 2, down past the gate, out to the flight line*
> *We stood in the sun . . .*

and then the chorus and the third verse all fell onto the page intact.

The Herc took off, as the song describes – out in to the pale summer sky, leaving us with a face full of dust. Then we turned on our heels and walked back to the rec area, Poppy's, where cake and cordial had been set up for us on trestle tables. But no one was feeling particularly chatty, so pretty soon we all drifted away and back to work. A deep and pervasive grief hung over the base. Snowy and Smithy were the first Australian soldiers killed since Ben Ranaudo, and it was the first time more than one Aussie soldier had been killed on the same day since 1971. The two sappers were well liked, and many on the base had been affected by the process of getting them home. Their bodies had lain in the base morgue, a shipping container with a refrigerator unit in the Role 2 hospital designated for the purpose. The ADF will not leave the body of a deceased soldier alone until it has been repatriated, so Snowy and Smithy's mates from Patrol Base Wali had maintained a guard of honour 24/7 outside the door of the morgue, on thirty-minute shifts – a solitary soldier standing at attention, eyes downcast under the brim of his slouch hat, rifle barrel resting on his boots, hands resting on the butt of the rifle.

Snowy and Smithy's mates also had to go through their effects with the military police officer and pack them into bags and trunks, which were painted white for identification purposes. Padre Lavaki and Regimental Sergeant Major 'Tiny' Colman had visited the morgue to identify the bodies. The medical staff in the Role 2 did the gruesome work of conducting autopsies and preparing the remains for repatriation. Bainesy, the quartermaster, was tasked to sort through the broken and bloodied body armour for decommissioning.

Bainesy was a mate of mine, an older captain, a full ranga who, prior to deploying, had secured a 'beard chit' – an army permit to grow facial hair on some spurious medical grounds. He'd taken it to the nth degree with a full Ned Kelly. He played guitar and we had formed a band along with Johnno, one of his corporals in the Q store, and Carola, a Dutch nurse who could really sing. With morale at a low ebb, we decided to chuck a Bob Hope and put on a concert at Poppy's that weekend.

We rehearsed in the shed out the back of the Q store, a dusty space with a single yellow light bulb, concrete slab floor and rifle range targets on the wall. The middle verse for 'Sapper's Lullaby' had come to me as I lay in bed the night after the ramp service. I took the finished song to the band and we rehearsed the chords and harmonies out the back of the Q store the night before the gig.

Setting up for the gig was hard going: building a makeshift stage, dragging the old PA out of the Q store and moving the heavy wooden picnic tables. By 1955 on the evening of Saturday, 12 June, we were ready to go. Poppy's was reasonably full and half a dozen of Snowy's and Smithy's mates were in from Patrol Base Wali, gathered around a vertical timber beam that ran from the concrete floor to the corrugated-iron roof. I usually hate vertical beams in music venues, but they can be forgiven in this case – they kept the roof from falling on our heads.

We played a set of my own stuff, finishing with 'Sapper's Lullaby'. There wasn't a lot of applause afterwards; it's not that kind of song, I guess. But people seemed moved by it and some of the sappers went out of their way to thank me.

After a short break, Bainesy got up and punched through some covers, backed by me and Johnno, while Mark Griffiths and Captain Conquest went around selling CDs and taking donations for the regimental trust fund. We raised $2000 for the families of soldiers killed and injured in the rotation, of which there would be many in the months to come.

❖

The summer of 2010 was full of churn and turmoil. Across Afghanistan, in terms of coalition casualties, it turned out to be the toughest fighting season in the war's thirteen years.

The Taliban didn't fare too well either. As daytime temperatures got up to 44 degrees Celsius, the fighting intensified. Between 10 and 14 June, Australian special forces were engaged in a long-running battle with a cluster of Taliban in a valley called Shah Wali Kot, south-east of Tarin Kowt. All through May, TF66 had been conducting helicopter-borne raids targeting insurgent networks in the area.

During the early hours of 10 June 2010, a company of commandoes established a fire position inside the Taliban stronghold of Chenartu. Shortly after dawn, the enemy surrounded the commandoes and attempted to overrun the position. They held their ground under heavy and sustained attack, and launched aggressive counterattacks which stunned the Taliban, who withdrew to the village of Tizak to regroup and plan another assault on the isolated commando company.

Having received intelligence that a high-level Taliban commander was now in Tizak, a troop deployed by helicopter to conduct a kill or capture mission on the morning of 11 June. Upon landing they were engaged by a maelstrom of bullets and rocket-propelled grenades from insurgents in the village and the surrounding high ground. Two men were wounded and four helicopters damaged. Though outnumbered and suppressed under a hail of machine-gun fire, the troop inched forward until they were again checked and fixed by the interlocking fire of three machine guns. But they kept fighting and regained the initiative, eventually breaking the enemy's defensive position. They cleared the remaining Taliban positions in close-quarter combat throughout the remainder of the day with the support of US Apache helicopters from Task Force No Mercy. By the evening of 14 June 2010, 'a significant number' of high-level Taliban commanders and fighters were killed (seventy, according to Wikipedia). Those left were routed and fled.

This was a great success for Task Force 66 and a real kick in the teeth for the Taliban in southern Afghanistan. But the story had a sad ending for us. On 21 June, TF66 went back into Shah Wali Kot to mop up the remnants of the Taliban. One of the Black Hawk helicopters had to make a hasty landing and crashed, killing three Australian commandoes: Scott Palmer, Benjamin Chuck and Tim Aplin.

That afternoon, back in my world, Bernard Philip arrived, sent by DFAT to lead up the new Australian–US PRT. He was a natural diplomat with an easy way with words and people, and a haircut like Tintin. He was also a ranga, and so for next two days, when I wasn't busy with the handover, I was running after him to make sure he had a hat on whenever he went outside. Having worked solo for a year, proprietorial feelings might have swelled in my chest at the arrival of the new man. But I gave him everything I had: analysis, issues, relationships and phone numbers. Mostly, I was exhausted and relieved to be handing over the reins before going on leave.

The USAID flight to Kabul, detouring south via Helmand, was horrible. I had eaten oily eggplant for lunch and threw up taking off from Lashkar Gah. The Afghan interpreters on the flight were kind, proffering paper towels, but also grateful that I had caught the payload in a plastic bag nestled in my hat.

On arrival in Kabul I went straight to the international terminal to get my flight to Dubai. In the departure lounge, I ran into Martine van Biljert, the Afghan expert I had met with Al in Kabul the year before. We swapped notes on the Gizab Uprising. She understood it was the latest turn in a long-running dispute between two sub-tribes of the Achekzai, one of which was backed by the Taliban, and the other, now, by us.

'Still,' she said, 'most people will be happy to have the out-of-area fighters dispersed back to Pakistan.'

I arrived at Sydney airport a day later and picked up a copy of *The Australian*. ISAF commander General McChrystal had been sacked. Buoyed by the hubris that seemed to come with his role, he had allowed a *Rolling Stone* reporter to ride with his entourage for a couple of weeks; the reporter had transcribed the vitriolic conversations McChrystal and his team were having about the Obama administration.

Meanwhile, Julia Gillard had pulled off a coup and we had a new prime minister. I listened to Rudd's farewell speech on the radio, arriving at the driveway of my new home just as he finished with that quirky line, 'Okay, gotta zip.'

The house was unheated in the middle of a Canberra winter; there were boxes everywhere and a lot to be done. Bernard had suggested I take as much leave as I needed. But things were changing fast back in Uruzgan and I knew that DFAT reinforcements weren't due till September. I gave myself a week and a half of leave – and it went by fast. I couldn't beat jetlag in that time so used the insomnia to finish 'Live Like an Afghan' and another song, 'Better Soldier'. I went into a studio not far from my house, run by my mate Guy Gibson, and spent five days recording those two songs, as well as 'Sapper's Lullaby'. This wasn't a rational use of my time. I was tired and needed to rest, Maryanne needed TLC, the house needed fixing up and I was in and out of DFAT main office talking about things to come. But with all that death and turmoil I felt the impulse I have always felt – to document.

In the end, we and those we love are defenceless against the march of time and fate. What else can we do but carve our stories into paper, stone, wood, compact disc or whatever is at hand?

I arrived back in TK in early July, chucked my stuff into Chalet 13 and made my way to the PRT headquarters to find Bernard. As I walked through Poppy's, I looked at that vertical timber beam around which Snowy and Smithy's mates had stood during the concert on 12 June. I saw that one of them had carved into the timber beam the words SNOWY AND SMITHY, RIP, 7/6/10.

Sapper's Lullaby

Up from the Role 2, and down past the gate, out to the flight line
We stood in the sun, slouch hat and gun
as two caskets passed us by

And followed the padre, onto the Herc.
And out into the pale summer sky
We walked back to Poppy's, and went back to work,
with the dust still in our eyes

So, soldiers, sing me a sapper's lullaby
You give it your all, knowing if you should fall
That all good things must die

These young engineers, whose job is to clear
the roads that we may pass
They're always out front, and when they bear the brunt,
man it happens fast
Sapper D. Smith had a wife and a son, the apple of his eye
Snowy Moerland was just twenty-one, way too young to die

Soldiers, sing me a sapper's lullaby
You give it your all, knowing if you should fall
That all good things must die

So go call your mother, call your old man, on the welfare line
Tell 'em you love 'em while you still can,
'cause all good things must die

Soldiers, sing me a sapper's lullaby
You give it your all, knowing if you should fall
That all good things must die
All good things must die

CHAPTER 8

NIET SWAFFELEN REVISITED

War . . . is like a monkey tryin' to fuck a football!

SERGEANT JEREMY GOODNIGHT, US ARMY

Well, Dutch friends, I've heard you're leaving,
I know you've made this plan
Because swaffelen's become illegal, here in Uruzgan
But when you're back in Holland you
can swaffel what you like . . .

FRED SMITH, *'NIET SWAFFELEN OP DE DIXI'* (ADDITIONAL VERSE)

I FOUND BERNARD IN HIS OFFICE CONTAINER IN THE NEW PRT CHALET. He was looking tired and sunburned but composed, notwithstanding the chaos reigning around him. There were Dutch 'geeks' cheerfully pulling wires out of walls while their US and Australian counterparts replaced them with US Army wiring and ITC equipment.

Bernard filled me in on things to come. There was a plan for our foreign minister, Stephen Smith, to visit on 18 July, and this would take some organising. Also, with the Dutch about to leave,

Australia would have to take on responsibility for PUCs – 'persons under custody'. The number of detainees was not small. Task Force 66 had taken more than 100 prisoners in the previous three months. Processing them was a difficult and sensitive matter, and DFAT would be involved.

Back in our container in Chalet 13, I found Tony sitting on his bunk.

'Taliban leadership are sending 450 fighters to Uruzgan,' he said. 'There have been IED strikes up in Chora and there's a suicide bomber getting around Tarin Kowt. They had a go at Khoday the other day. He survived, but his car is a wreck! Apart from that, everything's fine.'

❖

The next morning I was back in a Bushmaster bound for the weekly Provincial Security Council meeting.

Acting Governor Khoday spoke first.

'We just got back from Gizab, where we went to show support for the uprising. The people asked for help: they want more police and for MK to take responsibility for security. They liked it when he got together with coalition forces to get rid of the Taliban.'

The ANA colonel spoke next.

'General Hamid and the Dutch Minister for Defence went to Deh Rawud District yesterday and handed over the FOB to us. Security in the Deh Rawud district centre is not bad, but there are problems in the Tangi Valley north of the river, on the road that links Tarin Kowt to the district centre. Enemy have come across the border from Helmand and set up in the Tangi. They attacked a checkpoint last week.'

'Yes,' said Khoday, 'I spoke to people from Deh Rawud recently. They asked for help in securing the Tangi.'

Zachariah, the intelligence chief, confirmed this. He said that

Taliban leadership were angry at the fall of Gizab District and were looking to take it back.

'They are planting IEDs on the road from Chora through Kush Kadir to Gizab. We will need to take care of the outer districts because the enemy has plans. The big operations in Helmand and Kandahar have put pressure on the Taliban there, so many of them have moved up into Uruzgan. About 500 have come here recently.'

He advised that Mullah Sadat, who had been captured in the Mirabad two months earlier, had been released and was active again in Chenartu.

'This is a big problem: we arrest people, build the evidence, pass it up to Kabul, then they get freed. The justice system needs pay increases to make it less corrupt.'

'When we capture them we should just kill them,' said Khoday. 'They are trying to kill us!'

❖

Back on base there was much excitement. The Netherlands had made it into the World Cup soccer final. The Dutch soldiers had draped orange fabric over every available vertical and horizontal surface in anticipation of the match.

Meanwhile, US soldiers were rolling in, led by a hard-charging US colonel, Jim Creighton. The first sign of the American influx was the appearance of flat-screen TVs in the dining facility. US soldiers can't eat without a screen nearby. An endless game of baseball was playing, interspersed by broadcasts of Ultimate Fighting Championship bouts. Baseball I like, but cage fighting hampers my digestion.

I went to the daily commander's update on the morning of 9 July, where they too were talking about Chora and Gizab. There was clearly a tribal political dimension to all this, so I thought I'd better get interested in Chora. Major Justin R, the Australian officer commanding the area, was down in Tarin Kowt and in the room. I introduced myself and suggested he drop by my office for a yarn if he had time.

My bandmate Bainesy, the quartermaster, came into the office that afternoon looking a bit fragile. He asked how my leave had been.

'Brief and busy,' I said. 'What's going on for you?'

'Just got back from leave myself,' he said. 'It was all right, but my dog Max died. He was old. It was like he waited for me to get back so that he knew someone would be there to look after the girls.' His eyes were a little watery.

We spoke for a while; it was early in the afternoon and hot down in the Q store. I had air-conditioning.

'Maybe we'd better get the band cranking again,' I suggested.

'The only thing for it,' he agreed.

An hour later, Major Justin R walked into the container. JR, as he was known, was straight out of a Chesty Bonds ad: square jaw, broad shoulders, blond wavy hair like a Wallaby flanker. He had some background in special forces, and the direct, calm demeanour of a man with nothing to prove.

He got talking about his patch.

'Matiullah's boys recently passed through. They set up camp in the White Compound – provocative – and generally trod heavily on the ground in Chora. They threatened to search compounds. The locals said "no way". This was all unhelpful.'

I asked about the Baluchi Valley.

'Hard going,' he said, 'the local leaders are either dead, departed or too scared to step forward, so the Taliban has it all stitched up. COP Mashal is only eight kilometres south of Mirwais but another world. Boys there are getting into TICs [troops in contact] almost every time they step out the gate; IEDs, sniper fire, you name it.

'Anyway, the Baluchi Valley is too dangerous to pass through, so our resupply convoys travel up through the *dasht* to the east and in through the Chora saddle.'

An ops officer burst in while we were talking.

'IED strike near Mashal, sir, category A injuries not conducive to life.'

JR turned and joined the new MTF commander, Lieutenant Colonel Mark Jennings, and the operations officer, who were jogging down the corridor to the command post. Just then the dreaded CLP Red came up on the screen of my laptop, meaning there was trouble and comms were about to go down.

❖

Later that night, I was lying in my bunk when the adjutant knocked on the door and called out: 'There's been a KIA. Briefing in Poppy's at 2115.'

There must have been 200 soldiers inside Poppy's by the time Lieutenant Colonel Mark Jennings showed up with Padre Lavaki. They were ashen-faced; I guess they'd come straight from the morgue. Everyone fell silent. Jennings spoke, or rather shouted for want of a PA system, his throat already tight from the emotions of the day.

'Private Nathan Bewes was fatally wounded after stepping on a pressure plate IED during a dismounted patrol returning to COP Mashal at 1820 hours. They were 500 metres from the base on the edge of the green zone. Relatives have been notified.'

Formalities over, he continued, 'There is a clash of wills here, guys . . . today we got unlucky, but we crack on, stay professional, win the fight.'

He was choking back tears.

'Brigade Commander in Brisbane has asked that condolences be passed to men here, and to Bewesy's mates especially. A ramp ceremony will follow. Thanks, guys.'

We made our way back to the lines.

❖

On the morning of 11 July, I got up early and called Maryanne. She said that John Schumann had called to say that 'Dust of Uruzgan' was the best piece of writing about the Australian experience in conflict since 'I Was Only Nineteen'. Chocka with self-esteem, I spent the morning sorting out arrangements for the minister's visit, before bolting down to PRT House with Huip for a meeting with MDK and Ghilzai leader Mohammad Nabi Khan Tokhi (MNKT).

We had been working with Task Force 66 to broker a meeting between the two leaders and Matiullah Khan (MK). We had a date agreed, 12 July.

'Are you still good to meet with Matiullah?' I asked after the usual round of salutations.

'There are others in my tribe I have to check with,' MDK said. 'Senior men in Kabul and Kandahar – Ahmed Wali Karzai, Gul Agha Sherzai – but I think it will be okay.'

The US Department of State had invited MDK to go on a trip to America in July with a dozen other young leaders from southern Afghanistan.

'I'd like to go to America,' MDK said, 'but I don't think that Governor Khoday will let me.'

I said we would ask the Americans to talk with the Acting Governor.

Huip asked if he feared being displaced while he was away.

'Yes, I do, but Willem [the Dutch cultural adviser] said I should go anyway. I will need your support. I have heard that Karzai decided to sack me a few months ago, but your ambassador intervened. Without your support I would not last one day.'

They agreed to go ahead with the meeting with MK.

❖

That evening, Poppy's was chocka for the soccer: 300 Dutch soldiers in orange T-shirts gathered for the World Cup final. I get interested in soccer about once every four years. It was late, I was tired, and tomorrow was going to be a big day, but I decided to stick around and support my Dutch colleagues.

As any expat knows, patriotic feelings expand exponentially in the company of fellow countrymen gathered a long way from home, especially when viewing a sporting contest. So the atmosphere in Poppy's was charged. The Dutch soldiers had set up a makeshift stadium facing a big white screen. Their IT geeks did not let us down and the final against Spain came beaming through the projector onto the big screen from Johannesburg.

It was an intense and bitter affair all the way. Fourteen yellow cards were awarded over the course of the match. The first half was a scoreless war of attrition. In the sixty-sixth minute, Netherlands winger Arjen Robben narrowly missed a chance; 300 Dutch stood and roared, then sat and sighed as the shot sprayed wide.

The match reached full-time with the score nil-all. The prospect of a penalty shootout loomed. Early in extra time, the ball deflected off a Spanish defender and over the backline. It should have been a Dutch corner but a goal kick was awarded and the Spanish centre, Jesús Navas, began a series of passes that ended up on the right foot of Andrés Iniesta, who drilled a volley low to the goalkeeper's right to score. Game over.

I have never seen so many heartbroken blond giants. Their grief was tangible. They trudged away from Poppy's at 3 am, weeping into their orange T-shirts.

❖

The morning of 12 July was Bewesy's ramp ceremony. A dozen of the guys from COP Mashal were down for the ceremony. They stood together on the little podium by the coffin, clutching one another's shoulders like footy players before a match. One of their number stepped forward to the microphone and, holding back tears, read a eulogy they had prepared.

Early that afternoon, I went with Hamidi, the cultural adviser, down to the front gate to collect MDK and MNKT for the meeting with MK. The two leaders sat silently in the back of the Hilux. Given the association between MK and Task Force 66, driving into Camp Russell must have felt like entering the belly of the beast for them.

We walked into the TF66 shura room. Colonel Jim Creighton and the Task Force 66 commander were already seated. Matiullah Khan was there in the prime spot, along with five of his closest mates, senior Popalzai figures from Tarin Kowt; I had understood it was going to be a one-on-one with MK, and had the feeling we had walked into some kind of ambush. MDK and MNKT evidently had the same thought; they looked apprehensive and irritable as they sat down.

Colonel Creighton opened proceedings.

'There are many great leaders in Uruzgan. The key to success is getting them to work together for security. Working together we can identify and eliminate the insurgency. Let's open the lines of communication, for the benefit of the province.'

'I agree with you, Colonel,' replied MK, 'but ask Commander Tokhi what is the difficulty between us.'

'I don't feel good about this,' MNKT responded. 'We are old enough and wise enough to have organised this meeting without ISAF holding our hands.

'We have been left behind by this government. In the Taliban times I was imprisoned in Kandahar with JMK. Matiullah used to come and visit. We were equals and friends, but ever since then I have been having difficulty. We have no share in this government. The government should not be run by one tribe.'

'When my father died,' MDK said, 'Karzai made me district chief of Chora, but since then I have had trouble with the chief of police, the governor and the Taliban. The police chief has been bothering me and beating up my soldiers. Now the Taliban say about me, "Daoud is an infidel," the coalition forces say, "Daoud is Taliban." I am neither and if I have enough support, I could help defend this place!'

It was his usual line, and probably true, but it reminded me that we were the prime audience. It was us they were trying to 'message', not each other.

'Matiullah is my big brother,' he continued. 'We've got to work together, but we want a share of support from the government, the coalition forces – and more development funds.'

He turned to MK. 'Why did you bring these people?' he asked. 'I was told it would just be you.'

'Witnesses,' said Matiullah. 'What did I ever do to you, little brother? When you were young and in trouble and made mistakes, I helped you out, gave you money.'

'Yeah, what did he do to you?' one of MK's goons echoed.

Another of Matiullah's silver-haired mates weighed in.

'I'm not a woman, I won't hide. I'll speak my mind: when you were in trouble in Kandahar, I called your dad and we came to get you.'

'I'm not denying this,' said MDK. 'When my father was alive I was a crazy teenager just seeking pleasure.'

'I was in Kabul when I heard you were in trouble,' said Matiullah. 'I told you if you straightened up you could work with me.'

'I don't deny this,' said MDK.

Matiullah and his cronies continued patronising MDK, mainly, I guess, to diminish him in our eyes. MDK responded by denying nothing.

One of Matiullah's mates spoke about the great job MK was doing up in Gizab. Another very dark-skinned elder, known as Toor Mullah ('Black Priest') chimed in. 'God bring peace between the tribes of Uruzgan. Unity is everything.'

The meeting ended amicably enough. There was a group photo and a few reluctant hugs. These blokes had grown up in the same sandpit, even fought together as teens against the Russians in the Mujahedin. So their love–hate relationship was deep and complicated, though in recent years weighted more heavily towards the hate side of the equation.

In the Hilux, MDK and MNKT laughed and joked in what were clearly sarcastic tones. I asked for a translation. Hamidi obliged.

'They are saying, "We talked, but in reality there was nothing going on."'

In the wash-up, there were differing views about the value of the meeting we had hosted. TF66 were fairly upbeat about it, but Commander Creighton, prone to sporting analogies, recognised that Matiullah had 'fouled' by bringing his friends. Bernard and I were not convinced it heralded the beginning of a new era of conciliation. Getting them together was worth a try, but it confirmed that rivalry and mutual suspicion ran deep in their blood – 'win-win' was an alien concept to them.

I suppose it is hard to shake the suspicion that your rival wants to kill you, when he does.

❖

The next few days were busy. I was running around knocking off tasks for the minister's visit from a to-do list in my diary:

- book MTF briefing room
- line up Commander CTU for a meeting
- organise lunch with the DFAC

- brief Governor Khoday
- get scissors and ribbon for Shit Truck.

The last item was a little unusual. AusAID and the ADF had pooled funds to acquire a truck to help the Tarin Kowt municipality with its woeful effluence management. The 'Shit Truck', as we called it, looked like a petrol tanker. And just as a vacuum cleaner hoovers up dust into a bag, so the Shit Truck was to suck its target material into its tank and remove it to someplace I never asked about or wanted to visit. As part of the minister's visit, we would ceremonially hand over this 'Shit Truck' to the governor. In the Western world, a cheap bottle of champagne dashed across the bonnet would have sufficed for such a ceremony. But in deference to Islamic culture, we decided a ribbon and a large pair of scissors would be more appropriate. I ran around the base trying to procure same, some 3000 kilometres from the nearest newsagent.

As usual, a dozen drafts of the visit program went back and forth to the embassy in Kabul, who were liaising with the minister's office in Canberra, and a dozen other stakeholders in between. It was always a messy process.

In the evenings I rehearsed with the band. We decided to play a farewell concert for the Dutch; many Dutch soldiers were actually disappointed with that failure of their political masters to extend the mission, and besides we figured they needed some cheering up after the World Cup loss. We locked in 17 July, the night before the minister's visit. Any diplomat will tell you that a minister's visit requires intensive last-minute organisation and can make or break a career. But art prevailed over reason, and posters went up in the DFAC advertising Fred Smith and the Tarin Kowt Musicians' Union, playing at 2000 hours, 17 July, Poppy's.

We rehearsed behind the Q store. The band had expanded and so had the set list. The instrumental core comprised Bainesy, Johnno and me on guitar – it was hard to get a bass player, let alone a drummer in Tarin Kowt. Carola had left but we had others on happy claps and backing vocals, including Chris Way, the Dutch legal officer, a young Aussie sergeant named Amy, an American woman called Charlotte and Jeremy Goodnight, a US sergeant.

A Texan, Goodnight was like a character out of *The A-Team*, the last of the tumbleweed soldier philosophers. Good-looking in spite of his recently departed youth, he spoke in a stream of loud and proud pronouncements, chewing the wad of tobacco permanently nestled in the corner of his mouth. He had recorded an album in Nashville and could sing country songs like he owned them. And he was full of down-home wisdom from ten years of deployments in the Middle East: 'These little bases are like small towns – what goes around comes around, quick! Do people favours whenever you can.'

Goodnight and I were dining together on the evening of 16 July when a faraway look came into his eyes. I sensed a monologue coming on, and his monologues were worth listening to.

'Iraq, Somalia, Afghanistan, I've been to all these wars, and everyone one of them is just the same: War . . . is like a monkey tryin' to fuck a football!'

I stopped chewing, and nodded slowly as if I'd understood the profundity of what he'd just said. I spent the rest of the meal attempting to visualise the monkey and the football, and to compare and contrast their unviable union with my experiences in the field of human conflict.

I was still pondering this when Bernard tapped me on the shoulder.

'Julia has called an election. The minister isn't coming.'

'Oh, great!' I said. 'I mean bugger!'

'The visit is still on,' he said, 'but your dad will lead the delegation.'

'Okay. And the Shit Truck?'

'He will launch it.'

I opened my diary and scrawled 'camera' at the bottom of the to-do list. In the course of his illustrious diplomatic career, Dad had presided over ceremonies numerous and tedious, but to my knowledge he had never launched a Shit Truck.

After dinner, Goodnight and I headed down in the direction of the Q store for rehearsals. As I ducked into a Dixi, an extra final verse for 'Niet Swaffelen op de Dixi' came in to my head. At rehearsal I asked Chris Way a question or two about Dutch geography to complete a rhyme, and scrawled the verse into my notebook.

❖

I spent the morning of Saturday, 17 July, preparing for the visit with Bernard and the ambassador, Paul Foley, who had come down from Kabul. Dad and a couple of senior officers, who were now on the manifest, had all been at embassies on the receiving end of visits; they were not in the business of making life hard for those on the ground. The pressure was off.

By late afternoon I was able to cut away to get ready for the gig. We started loading into Poppy's at about 1530. Roger the Dutch PsyOps guy had gone to great lengths to set up a sizeable stage, made mostly of trestle tables fastened onto timber forklift pallets. We started soundcheck at 1700, and it was a shitfight all the way trying to wrestle a decent sound out of the crap PA on a concrete floor.

Fortunately, one of Bainesy's boys from the Q store, known to all as La La, had once had the misfortune of being married to a singer and had some experience with PAs. He tweaked knobs and shuffled wires and two hours later we had something workable.

But I was sweaty and dishevelled so I went back to Chalet 13 for a clean shirt.

By the time I got back to Poppy's the joint was packed with about 250 people. A large group of Dutch soldiers sat to the left of the stage. The rest of the room was populated by Aussies and a few newly arrived US soldiers who'd come to see what the fuss was about.

The gig started rough, with sound issues and the crowd talking. I got pissed off and snapped, telling them to shut up or leave. Not my style, but I guess I was exhausted. Goodnight walked over and said, 'Just pay attention to the people who are listening.'

Good advice. I ploughed on through the opening songs.

Mark Griffiths and Captain Conquest were selling sports shorts featuring inbuilt mesh underwear and the Mentoring Task Force logo. We were raising more funds for the 6 RAR Foundation. I improvised a jingle for the shorts:

> MTF shorts, MTF shorts,
> Good to wear when you're playing sports,
> Heading to the gym and the tennis courts,
> in my MTF shorts ...
>
> The shorts are baggy but the undies are strong,
> keep your lefty and your righty where they belong,
> no fruit salad like old King Kong,
> in your MTF shorts ... etc.

When I broke into the opening harmonica solo to 'Dust of Uruzgan' the room started to settle. The song went down well; by now people were listening. I followed with 'Sapper's Lullaby', which seemed to further subdue the gathering, many of whom had been at the ramp ceremony for Snowy and Smithy. I turned to the Dutch soldiers and made a short speech thanking them and their predecessors for their contribution to the province.

'It's been great working with you guys, but we know what you've been up to in those Dixis, and I have an important message for you.'

We broke into *'Niet Swaffelen'*, running through all the five verses as per the original recording. Then I threw in another verse that I had omitted from the recording:

> Niet Swaffelen op de Dixi, listen well to this
> There are lots of people in Kamp Holland you could swaffel with
> You could swaffel with the Slovaks, down at the Slovak gate
> You could swaffel with the Aussies but be sure to call them 'mate'
> You could swaffel with the chef, you could swaffel with Two
> You could swaffel with Dick on Arm if he doesn't swaffel you
> but niet swaffelen op de Dixi . . .

Then straight into the instrumental, with everyone singing along: *'Niet, niet, niet, niet, niet, niet, niet, niet, niet, niet, niet, niet, niet, niet swaffelen op de Dixi, niet, niet, niet!'*

I dropped the volume, turned to the Dutch corner, and went into the verse that had come to me in the Dixi the night before.

> Well, Dutch friends, I've heard you're leaving, I know you've
>   made this plan
> Because swaffelen's become illegal, here in Uruzgan
> But when you're back in Holland you can swaffel what you like
> You can swaffelen a windmill, you can swaffelen a dyke,
> You can swaffelen a hash pipe, in Leiden or Kherlain
> But you can't swaffel the World Cup
> Because the fucking thing's in Spain . . .

The room exploded. Aussies whooped and clapped, Dutchies hooted in feigned indignation – and they all sang along with the final '*niet swaffelen op de dixi, niet, niet, niieeeet!*'

The Dutch were totally up for that sort of humour. They were piss-takers, just like us. At the end of a busy week in the middle of a tough summer it was a nice moment, a thunderbolt of mirth shared by a little community gathered in a dusty camp in a forlorn Afghan province.

I stepped back and played guitar while Bainesy and Amy and Johnno and Chris and Jeremy Goodnight knocked out covers. It was a good night and we raised a couple more grand for the 6 RAR Foundation.

❖

Being a Sunday, the morning of 18 July should have been 'low ops', but with the delegation coming to town that wasn't going to happen. Dad got off the bird in full body armour, along with two other senior officials from Canberra. They were tired but relatively relaxed as we filed into the MTF briefing room.

The Dutch commander and civilian representative arrived.

'We as a military are sorry to be leaving and will hand over everything we can,' said the Dutch commander.

The CivRep said the Netherlands would stay focused on development in Uruzgan through to 2013, and were particularly keen to finish the Road to Chora. He emphasised the importance of the districts; the war would be won or lost in the countryside. He said the Dutch approach of shunning Matiullah Khan had won a lot of support for ISAF among the wider population, but acknowledged we would need an ongoing relationship with the guy. He concluded: 'The last challenge is to get this camp speaking with one voice.'

We acknowledged all this and said we would do what we could to help finish the road.

We broke for lunch before wriggling into body armour and heading down to the stables, where Bushmasters and Australian Light Armoured Vehicles (ASLAVs) were lined up along with the Shit Truck. Military protocols required an increased security posture proportionate to the rank of the 'principal'. They had Dad pegged as a four-star general equivalent, so he had a couple of Close Personal Protection guys by his side at all times, and the convoy was double the size it would ordinarily have been.

As we set off towards the gate, I looked down at my clipboard and noticed with amazement that the visit was running on time. I was pointing this out to Bernard when the Bushmaster ground to a halt. Five minutes passed and I started to get anxious. The governor had summoned every senior official in town to meet the esteemed delegation; it would be disrespectful to leave them waiting. I tuned into the Icom conversation between the drivers to see what was going on. The Shit Truck, it turned out, had swung a little wide around the corner and its rear fender had collected the razor wire spindled along the side of the dirt road. Along with a couple of gunners, I spent the next ten minutes kicking at the wire, then we pulled out some bolt cutters and, finally, liberated the Shit Truck. I ran back to the Bushmaster, hopped in and the convoy rolled.

We arrived at the governor's compound just as the sting was leaving the mid-afternoon sun. The rose garden was in full bloom and there were peacocks milling around the downward-facing rifle butts of the Uzbek security guards. About seventy provincial government officials had gathered in the meeting room; a podium and a microphone had been set up in front of a large picture of President Karzai. Speeches followed; Afghan leaders pleaded for ongoing commitment. We promised business as usual – for the next little while at least.

Dad had taught in schools in Kalgoorlie and Albany in the late 1960s before joining the Department of External Affairs, as it was called in 1969. With Hamidi interpreting, he and Acting Governor Khoday, also a former teacher, covered some business on our relationship with the provincial government before conversing amiably over shared experiences in front of the far-flung chalkboards of their respective homelands. Then we went off to the courtyard and launched the Shit Truck, handing the keys to the governor with suitable solemnity.

Governor Khoday was so pleased he invited us onto the roof of the residence to view the fields of the Tarin Kowt bowl. Dad's security detachment went into a huddle, then got the okay from the sniper they already had positioned up there. We walked up two flights of stairs to a landing where there was a makeshift cane ladder propped up against the roof of the third storey. Khoday shot up the ladder like a mountain goat – seventy years of dirt trails, gardening and squat toilets had kept him limber. For Dad, forty years of twelve-hour days behind a desk had only increased his gravitational affinity with the earth. The ladder creaked as he made his way to the top with the CPP boys arrayed below like a cordon of upwards-facing, heavily armed slips fieldsmen. The rest of us followed.

In the late afternoon sun, the view was all bucolic serenity. We could see out to the mountains concealing Deh Rahwud, due north across the Tarin Kowt bowl to the mouth of the Baluchi Valley, and west out into the Mirabad. In the foreground were green fields with a smattering of workers labouring waist-deep in vegetation. Beyond these fields was the Dorafshan River, running north–south to the intersection with the Tiri Rud River. Dad had read hundreds of briefing packs, cables, talking points and cabinet submissions with the word 'Uruzgan' in every paragraph. This *was* Uruzgan.

After some happy snaps, Governor Khoday shot back down the cane ladder forward. Dad, meanwhile, edged his way backwards over the gutter then downwards by a process I could only describe as incremental, the CPP guys offering unwelcome advice at every rung. The rest of us then piled down the ladder and out to the front gate, where we farewelled a buoyant Khoday and clambered into the Bushmasters. We dropped off Dad and the entourage at the flight line, then made our way to Russ's place for dinner as the sun set over Deh Rawud. Russ was to leave the following week. I remember his parting words of advice: 'Take it easy, guys, we're just here to move the ball two yards down the field. Just a little progress, that's all we can achieve.'

❖

I was typing away on my laptop the following morning when Bernard walked in. 'How would you feel about leading a district engagement team up to Chora?' he asked.

I had become pretty comfortable on the MNBTK, and the band was humming along, but I firmly believed that district-level engagement was critical to the work of a PRT. We needed a credible presence in the districts, particularly in Chora, where locals were reportedly anxious about the 'vacuum' the Dutch would leave. The Taliban was already making the most of this uncertainty. We needed to get out there and quickly. Chora was a natural spot for me – I was good mates with the district chief, MDK.

'Okay,' I replied. 'When?'

'The Dutch mission team are pulling up stumps on 27 July. Maybe you'd better get up there and catch a handover. The US PRT guys started arriving this morning. You could meet them tomorrow morning, and head up to Chora on Wednesday.'

'Yep,' I said, and with that began a two-month journey to the outer edges of my comfort zone.

CHAPTER 9

AUGUST 20 (FOB MIRWAIS)

An August summer's day, a morning clear and bright . . .
FRED SMITH, 'AUGUST 20'

IN THE 2009–2010 'SURGE', 4500 TROOPS FROM THE US ARMY'S
Stryker Regiment poured into southern Afghanistan. The Stryker
Regiment was so named not in honour of some Christian metal
band but in recognition of the vehicle they got around in: an
eight-wheel gun car/troop carrier with a steel fence attached to
its flanks to deflect rocket-propelled grenades. It's fair to say that
these soldiers were not the touchy-feely types. About 1000 of them
came to Uruzgan that summer and were assigned to partner with
the Afghan National Police, who were more like a ramshackle
light infantry than Sergeant Plod.

The PRT work – the governance, development and relationship-
building stuff at the heart of the counterinsurgency strategies in
Iraq and Afghanistan – generally fell to men and women from the
US Navy, Air Force and National Guard. A hundred or so of these
types arrived at the same time as the Strykers to join a handful of
Australian and US diplomats and aid workers in the new Uruzgan

PRT. Led by naval pilot Commander Kyle Higgins, the US PRT soldiers had already been in Afghanistan eight months. They had four months to go, and by the time they got to Uruzgan were not bursting with enthusiasm. To be fair, they'd been jerked around. They'd started in the relative comfort of Bagram Air Base, reputed to have thirty-one different flavours of Baskin-Robbins. From there they had been shunted up to Parwan Province. Then, with two weeks' notice, they were sent south to Uruzgan, where they found themselves foraging around for office and living accommodation on a hot lunar landscape.

From this larger contingent, Commander Higgins picked fifteen soldiers to form a team led by Lieutenant Willard Cooper. They were to escort me up to FOB Mirwais and form the logistical and security backbone of a district engagement team.

We all gathered together in the old Dutch PRT briefing room on the morning of 22 July. Commander Higgins gave them riding instructions. Their job, he said, was to protect me.

'Without you, Fred can't go outside the wire. Without Fred, you've got no reason to go outside the wire. That's your job and nothing else. No fighting patrols, no kitchen work, no tower duty. Any questions?'

There were none.

'Okay, form up at the trucks tomorrow morning at 1000 hours with the Aussie resupply convoy.'

The convoy that left on the morning of 23 July was larger than the usual resupply convoy. In addition to the Australian elements, there were five US Mine Resistant Ambush Protected (MRAP) vehicles carrying my PRT contingent and a couple of Stryker vehicles carrying a forward party from the new police mentoring team assigned to Chora. I was in a Bushmaster with a couple of diggers and the pugnacious young captain who ran the base at COP Mashal. He was teasing the other diggers in the Bushmaster because the day before the guys up at Mashal had got into a TIC – a battle – while the diggers down in Tarin Kowt had missed out.

'Every time we step out the gate, I say, "This could be the last day, boys!"' he told me.

The sun was setting by the time our convoy rolled out of the *dasht* and into the Chora Valley through a gap between two mountains known as the Chora saddle.

Everything on FOB Mirwais was on a slope running from the east down to the west. On the north side of the base, on the uphill corner, there was a row of a dozen or so large brown tents. These 'lines' were home to the enlisted men.

Dutch captain Adrian Ham met me as we arrived. He took me and the PRT guys to the Dutch PRT accommodation tent in the middle of the lines. There was a tent full of Australian infantry to our right and a dozen or so sappers in the tent to our left. Lieutenant Willie Cooper and I and some of the older guys took bunks in this tent; the others went to a second tent down at the end of the lines.

I was stuffing my clothes away when an angry US sergeant barged into the tent. He identified himself as 'The Sarg' and then barked, 'Who's running the PRT unit?!'

'I am,' I said.

'Well, you're going to have to move your guys from that tent down there. I got thirty more men coming in next week and we're staying here for a fuckin' year!'

Willie turned from his bunk and said, 'We'll deal with this when your men arrive, Sergeant.'

The Sarg saw the lieutenant rank on Willie's shoulder, mumbled, 'Yes, sir,' and slunk out of the tent.

Captain Ham gave me the bad news.

'I think you're going to have to share an office with that guy.'

'Excellent.' I shrugged. 'Maybe we'd better go and claim some real estate there!'

Captain Ham showed Willie and me the single Drehtainer that was to be our office. Like everything else on the FOB, it was on an incline. A single long desk was positioned against the uphill wall and a huge map of the district on the downhill wall. It had sticky notes on it covering various locations with things written on them like 'HEProject', 'Akhtar Mohammad, 'Brown Eyes' and 'IED Strike 13/6/09'. Over an area to the south-west of the base called Pay Kelah someone had stuck a picture of a chiefly figure with an annotation that read: 'Haji Loylala, RIP 131209, of NATURAL CAUSES!' – as if it was astonishing that a tribal leader could be so indolent as to die a peaceful death.

I spent a couple of hours copping the beginning of a handover from Captain Ham and getting to know Willie. A six-foot-plus African American in his late-thirties, Willie had initially struck me as sombre and serious, carrying though he was the weight of responsibility for shifting his team around and settling them here on the dark side of the moon. But as we spoke he started joking a bit, and whenever he laughed a massive smile cracked across his face. I warmed to him.

He said he'd grown up in the projects of New Jersey, had his first son at sixteen and first daughter at seventeen, and joined the army the following year just to stabilise things a bit. He'd had a couple more kids since but had not seen much of them in recent years. Although a reservist, he'd done five rotations of Iraq and Afghanistan.

'I'm done, man,' he admitted. 'When I get back home I'm quitting. They can take their health insurance and stick it!'

❖

When I awoke the next morning, the tent was already hot. I slipped on thongs and began the long walk to the 'pissaphone', a standard piece of military sanitation equipment. Located in the middle of the base, it comprised a waist-high piece of PVC pipe jutting out of the ground at a forty-five-degree angle with the other end buried deep. Looking around me, I was struck again by the majesty of the area. The Chora Valley was like a bowl, about six kilometres at its widest, defined by craggy brown mountains, snow-capped in the winter. It was beautiful.

The agricultural strip – the green zone, as we called it – ran a couple of hundred metres either side of a river that snaked through the valley and watered the fields that sustained life in the valley. Beyond the green zone was the *dasht* that marked the perimeter of the valley – dusty rocky desert terrain that ran up steep hills. I could hear goats bleating from the fields; locals made their way along the dirt road adjacent to the base on foot, motorcycles, donkeys and bicycles.

It all seemed peaceful, but Chora had some lively history. In June 2007, the Taliban had launched their largest offensive of the year in Chora, reflecting the strategic importance of its location at the meeting point of three valleys. They had sent in several hundred men, who began taking over police checkpoints and asserting themselves in residential areas of the district capital, the town of Ali Sherzai. Some of the local tribal leaders escaped down to Tarin Kowt and pleaded for help. The fifty Dutch soldiers stationed in the area at the time had retreated to the district government centre and were surrounded on all sides. Rather than extract them, the Dutch commander in TK ordered them to fight and dispatched a supporting force of Dutch and Australians. Rozi Khan had chipped in about 150 of his militia, and the ANA and Matiullah each threw in fifty guys.

A three-day battle ensued that has since become known as the Battle of Chora. Dutch F-16 fighters weighed in and the Dutch used their Panzer Howitzer, a large artillery-piece firing 155mm high-explosive rounds all the way from Tarin Kowt, forty kilometres to the south, pulverising designated grid squares one kilometre wide.

All this firepower in concert with a unified local community drove out the Taliban. According to Afghan government estimates, seventy-one Taliban were killed. President Karzai was so pleased he appointed Rozi Khan district governor, despite centuries of animosity with the Barakzai. Rozi presided over the area until his death in September 2008, when his son MDK was appointed district governor.

The Dutch invested heavily in the Chora District during the following three years. They had rebuilt the damaged district government offices and worked with Aussie engineers to build a base (FOB Mirwais, also known as FOB Locke) on the southern edge of Ali Sherzai, on the slopes of a steep rocky hill overlooking the valley.

❖

FOB Mirwais was blokey – an oasis of preposterone, porn and protein powder in a desert of bucolic poverty. On the base were sixty to eighty Australian soldiers from Mentoring Team Charlie (MT-C), mostly guys from 6 RAR at Enoggera Barracks. Afghan soldiers had a tendency to use Western-style porcelain toilets in the squatting position, leaving, among other things, boot marks around the rim of the toilet bowl. So the Aussie soldiers had a padlock on the door of their designated toilet container. The combination was 4051 – the postcode for Enoggera.

These soldiers rotated from FOB Mirwais in and out of the combat outposts down in the Baluchi Valley: COPs Qudus, Buman and Mashal. They had been out there in the dust for six months already, so were not particularly in the mood for making new friends. There were some serious hair experiments going on in August that year – porn-style moustaches, grizzly beards and wavy hair were all the go.

Major Justin R (JR) ran a focused and cohesive command post with an informal feel. The intelligence officer was a thoughtful captain named Nick. Every afternoon at 1700 he would go up to the same spot in the central guard tower and take a photograph of the valley, as he built an archive of photos documenting the changes in season. Then there was the young operations officer, known as Mod. He had a forceful belligerent manner about him.

Mod ran Willie and me through the normal framework of operations: there were fighting patrols, community engagement patrols, reconnaissance patrols and search patrols for weapons caches. All of these were conducted with ANA soldiers. The role of Mentoring Team Charlie was to build the capacity of the 2nd Kandak of the ANA Fourth Brigade, of which there were around 180 members on base. They lived in a separate walled area on the upslope of the compound, but their kitchen, a brown earth building with burn marks on the outside wall from the wood smoke that poured out the window, was down near the command post.

The Kandak were a mix of Tajiks and Uzbeks from Afghanistan's north, most of them not particularly thrilled to be living on a remote base in the middle of the Pashtun south. They were loath to take risks, seeing no point in dying this far from home. Every evening they'd play volleyball on a rocky court that also served as a parade ground. Their ball would often run down the slope to our little alfresco dining area. We'd boot it back up the hill to them; they'd grin and nod in thanks. That many Afghan soldiers was enough to warrant their own mullah, who, while I never actually met him, I heard five times a day as he delivered his call to prayer through a crappy old megaphone. The first call was at 0400 every morning and would set the roosters of the valley a-crowing. The occupants of the infantry tent next door to mine would wake and say, 'Thank you, Mr Mullah, thank you for letting us know it's four am' – or words to that effect!

The Dutch PRT team up in Chora had things pretty well set up. They had been paying the district chief, MDK, a monthly stipend to cover the running costs of the White Compound (the district office) and provided phone cards and diesel for the generator. We lacked their resources, which made things difficult. Initially, Commander Higgins had directed that our guys were not to do 'tower duty' – rostered 24/7 pickets in the watchtowers to make sure baddies did not come over the wall. But it was obvious to Willie and me that this community on FOB Mirwais was pretty small; 'mucking in' was the culture, there was no other way to make it work. Willie related this to Higgins by phone. The commander was not happy but accepted the logic, and our soldiers went on the tower duty roster.

The Dutch PRT mission team had a great interpreter named Zia. He was a polite, diligent, intelligent guy in his mid-twenties, spoke good English and understood the local politics. I wanted to keep him up there with us but there was some uncertainty as to where his next assignment would be.

Over the next couple of days, I set about gauging the political and security landscape of the district. A consistent thread was that politics was security and the successes of the last three years were largely a result of key local leaders supporting the district government and wielding their militias to keep the Taliban at bay. The role of our military presence was to support this. The PRT could help by channelling projects through the district government to the key tribal leaders.

But the situation was not stable; there were threats. MK was taking a zero-sum approach to stability of an area that was predominantly run by an affiliation of the Barakzai and Achekzai tribes. He was using money and influence to activate a handful of troublemakers with grudges against MDK. As well, the Dutch project pipeline had dried up as their PRT drew down, and the rest of us, lacking both resources and forewarning of the Dutch withdrawal, had not made arrangements to fill this void. A third, more immediate, problem was that MDK was in the US on the State Department tour, and his enemies were getting active in his absence.

Captain Ham offered the Dutch point of view on the Chora District: the tribal leaders were divided between those who did and did not support MDK. Many in the latter camp had been refused funding for some project or other, and/or were on MK's payroll. The main powerbrokers of the valley were on MDK's side – the so-called Barakzai triangle: Malim Sadiq, Mohammad Akbar Khan (whom we called MAK) and Akhtar Mohammad (referred to by all as 'Brown Eyes', more because of the colour of his eyes than any behavioural proclivities). Sadiq was the most powerful, with a militia of around sixty men. But he was not easy to deal with. A surly old bastard, he had seen foreigners come and go – he had a pot plant in his compound growing out of the back end of an old Russian missile. And with the almond crop afflicted by disease, he was doing it tough.

The former district chief of police had been killed in an IED strike and replaced by Mohammad Gul. Some seek greatness, others have it thrust upon them. Gul, by all accounts, had not ascended to the position through talent and application; rather, his predecessors had met with violent deaths. I had met Gul before, on my trip to Chora in May 2010. He had a nice sense of comedy about him. Thin as a rake, he wore a green police cap like a French gendarme, with his pants pulled high and tucked into knee-high socks. This ensemble was augmented by a round bearded face framing a foolish grin, and a red leather bandolier of 9mm pistol rounds slung diagonally across his chest – it was as though Thin Arthur from *The Aunty Jack Show* had stumbled onto the set of *The Good, the Bad and the Ugly*.

Mohammad Gul knew me to be a musician and so whenever we met he would embrace me, and with his right arm around my waist, his left hand clasping mine, would draw us together cheek to cheek, pelvis to pelvis, and lead me in a tango before we sat down to the business at hand. I hadn't experienced this kind of affection from police officers in Australia.

In the valley there was also a network of semi- and non-government organisations working on various projects, mostly related to irrigation. Life in rural Afghanistan is all about water, and using gravity to move it through mud aqueducts and sluices to irrigate crops. There was a long-running water dispute in the Chora Valley between Brown Eyes and other leaders further down the river.

Captain Ham explained that part of a typical day's work was receiving visitors. To this end, the Dutch had a shipping container down in the north corner of the base, which they called PRT House. It was stocked with water bottles, Afghan sweets and nuts, some wind-up radios and a cardboard box full of black-rimmed adjustable eyeglasses. The glasses were the brainwave of some previous rotation of the Dutch PRT and had led to the proliferation of Afghan Buddy Holly lookalikes around the Chora Valley.

FOB Mirwais had a battle rhythm that culminated every day, just before dinner, in a battle update brief in the command post (CP). The senior staff, twenty or so men, would file into the CP, a room about the size of a Sydney suburban bedroom. There wasn't a lot of space – it was a catastrophe if someone farted. At 1730 on my second day there, Captain Ham brought Willie and me into our first FOB Mirwais BUB. I took a position on the floor at the front, something I'd continue to do for the following two months.

'The resupply convoy made it to Mashal,' Nick reported, 'but found three IEDs along the way. While dealing with one of them, they were engaged by RPGs from the green zone. ANA cited insurgents to the west and engaged with small arms fire. I assess the RPGs were likely a "come on" to draw coalition forces into the green zone. We obviously didn't bite. No casualties that we know of, but it's a sign that these guys are getting more confident around Nyazi.'

Nick added that there'd been a suicide IED at the Sajawal crossing.

'One ANA and one civilian KIA.'

Each unit in Mentoring Team Charlie had a call sign. The infantry team in the tent next door to ours was India 36. When Nick finished, Mod rattled off the next day's plans for each of these call signs.

JR then summarised. 'Okay, keep the guard up – things are getting tough with the fighting season now in full swing. This is the first time they've had a go at one of our convoys accompanied by a protection party. So keep moving – if you stay still more than a few minutes you become a target. Also, we will need to show sensitivity with the ANA boys. Colonel Gul Agha told me the guy killed down in Sajawal was due to go home three days ago. Their supply lines and leave flights don't work as well as ours.'

We filed out and dined al fresco at picnic tables that sloped up the hill. It was pleasant out there on a summer's evening as the day cooled and the sun set over the hill behind us, with the noise of the never-ending Afghan volleyball match providing the soundtrack to the evening's meal.

After dinner, Willie got the guys together in the little vestibule outside our tent for what would be a nightly brief, covering the day's events and the plans for the next day, which usually involved escorting 'Mr Fred' (as they called me) to visit the White Compound or a local tribal leader. These nightly debriefs were conducted in US Army English – a mixture of acronyms and ghetto slang that took me a couple of weeks to understand.

Later, I found Captain Ham in the office tidying up some files. I asked about Nyazi. He told me the area was difficult due to weak local leadership. But it was important.

'We had hoped to start the Road to Chora up here and run it south to meet the northbound roadworks. If we can't get through the Nyazi area we'll never finish the road.'

Just then we heard gunfire from the direction of Ali Sherzai. Captain Ham pricked up his ears to discern its direction, then shrugged his shoulders and went on.

'Then there's the Chora courthouse, which our embassy funded and built. We launched it ten days ago. At this point it's an empty shell; there's just one judge, with three teeth.'

❖

The next morning we formed up into a 'packet' for a foot move down to the White Compound, where a shura was to be hosted by the deputy district chief to formally farewell the Dutch and welcome the new Aussie/US PRT contingent. It was a mixed security packet, with the Aussie soldiers showing the shooters from my PRT team how to forge their way through the streets of Ali Sherzai – how to signal motorcyclists to stop, wave pedestrians around the packet, when to search people who came too close. It was important that my guys used the same methods; locals like to know what to expect around a rolling entourage of twelve heavily armed men. In some ways, consistency was a virtue.

On the other hand, although there were only three ways to get to the White Compound, we had to try to take a different route every day so as not to 'set patterns'. The insurgents had spotters who observed our patterns by watching patrols as soon as they left the base; this was how IED strikes and ambushes were organised.

We arrived at the White Compound to find seventy elders had gathered. We sat on cushions as various tribal leaders took it in turns to talk, thanking the Dutch for their support and asking the new PRT to exercise the same sensitivity towards tribes and culture.

Captain Ham got up and spoke about the Dutch involvement; he was sad to be leaving. I spoke, making it clear we understood the competitive tribal dynamics of the province and would be supporting the district chief, MDK. At this point a couple of elders scowled and left. But the main leaders – Malim Sadiq, Brown Eyes and MAK – all grunted approvingly and we broke for lunch.

As we prepared to leave, I took a photo of Captain Ham and Zia at the gate of the compound, which I subsequently emailed to Captain Ham. The subject heading read: 'The Last Dutchman in Chora.'

❖

Captain Ham was set to fly out on 30 July but was told to bring his departure forward to correspond with a southbound convoy departing three days earlier. I had hoped to have a full week with him up there at FOB Mirwais to learn the ropes, but five days in I already had a list of logistical challenges that needed to be addressed – such essentials as comms, terps allowances, travel, food, accommodation and fuel. I felt a sense of responsibility for the motley crew that had been sent to protect me. They were uncomfortable and weary. Decent mattresses would be a good start, I figured. I needed to tackle these problems down in Tarin Kowt, so I signed up for the same convoy.

I was in a purposeful frame of mind when I got to TK, but my intentions were soon blunted by the churn created by the Dutch withdrawal and US arrival. Everyone seemed to be moving office containers; the Aussie and US geeks were still getting around with clipboards and cables, trying to set up the IT. Patience was in short supply. We had five new AusAid officers, plus Bernard, me and Mark Griffiths sharing one office container because all the other computers were shut down. The new American headquarters team was bedding down, trying to find a rhythm. Bernard was busy trying to smooth things over and getting stuck into the political and tribal engagement work.

I agreed to stick around in Tarin Kowt for the Dutch US Transfer of Authority ceremony on the Sunday, which was nice enough, although hot in the midday sun. Jim Creighton tried to do the first half of his speech in Pashtun, which amused the nationals no end. And the Dutch were chucking parties all over the base to celebrate their departure.

A week later, on 3 August, I hopped on a convoy back to FOB Mirwais with an AusAID officer named John Morley who was joining the team to get some projects going. My diary from the following morning reads:

> Back in Mirwais now. The boys on the base are preparing for a big and risky op tomorrow into the Central Baluchi Valley in the area around COP Mashal. They are keen to get it done before Ramadan sets in and it becomes hard to motivate the ANA. I went to a meeting this morning on the operation. We tried to put together a list of local leaders we could work with in the Baluchi, but the list was thin. The Dutch PRT had an officer down there who had built an under-the-radar relationship with a local guy called Hashim Khan. The insurgents found out and went looking for him.

They found him praying in the local mosque and shot him three times in the back of head.

So the people in the area are reluctant to talk to us. We need the local leaders, though, because in JR's words the 'in order to' is development – it's all about clearing the insurgents so that we can engage the local community by offering something they want: development projects, and in particular to drive the Road to Chora through the valley. So their mission is to go down there, hold the ground and generally pick fights with and kill insurgents.

Apart from the IED threat, there had been a sniper getting around the area with an old World War II vintage .303, and apparently he knew how to use it. He hit one of our guys from a range of 500 metres. Luckily the soldier was wearing body armour. He was knocked forward onto his face – a .303 is a big round – but got up and, after a change of underpants, was good to go. Body armour was heavy – twenty-three kilos – but it saved lives.

Meanwhile, in my absence, there had been some fiddling with the infrastructure on the base. Zia was kicked out of his accommodation and moved into much lesser circumstances, while the second half of my team was moved to another tent closer to mine. They needed to make room for The Sarge's forty Strykers for the police mentoring team, who now had a lieutenant they all called LT (US Army speak for 'lieutenant'). Young and solidly built, he had a nice manner and seemed like a sensible guy.

Some genius had decided to move our meeting facility out of the PRT House container, now wanted for storage, to a shack upslope of the ANA quarters. Although bigger, it had no aircon, was not easily accessible and was surrounded by the remains of IED-smashed ANA Ford Rangers in which, according to the ANA commander, eight of his men were killed. It was not a very positive atmospheric for local leaders to have to walk past these ghoulish wrecks to meet us.

It turned out there was another problem with this new PRT meeting venue – specifically, its proximity to the landing zone. I had a meeting in there with the venerable but surly Malim Sadiq. Initially, the meeting was pretty stiff. I said, 'We would like to do some projects with you.' He said, 'Bugger the projects, just give me weapons and ammunition.' I said, 'We can't do that, but how about a nice new well or another aqueduct?' The conversation was going back and forth in this manner when a great big Chinook chopper landed thirty metres away. The door of the new meeting room was blown open by the downwash and a massive dust storm swept in. I ran at the door and slammed it shut with a shoulder charge. Sadiq sat there with his turban wrapped around his face laughing as I leaned against the door coughing dust. The meeting loosened up a bit after that.

I had other, smaller problems. I'd set up my desk but needed to find a way to balance my chair on the sloping floor. I now had a short length of four-by-two propping up the rear legs, but they kept slipping off it. Not ideal, ergonomically speaking, but this clearly wasn't Canberra.

❖

On 5 August, John Morley and I had a long yarn with the assistant district chief as well as the district's chief of police, Mohammad Gul, and MDK's chief of staff, LK. They were despairing. That morning two ANP officers had been kidnapped by the Taliban just south of the Chora crossing and taken out to Nuri, an insurgent stronghold in the valley to the north-east of Ali Sherzai. It was the first time ANP had been kidnapped in broad daylight. They, in turn, had detained some uncles of the Taliban guys who had pulled off the kidnapping to give themselves a bargaining chip.

Meanwhile, JR and most of Mentoring Team Charlie were down in the central Baluchi. They'd found two IEDs on the way and detonated them. They reckoned they'd probably get a whole lot more on the way back. Mod calculated the insurgents would just slide north, so he wanted to run an operation around Nyazi to pick off any northbound Taliban. They looked for the action, these boys.

❖

On the morning of 7 August, Bernard called from TK and asked me to organise a visit on 9 August for him, Commander Jim Creighton, Juma, Governor Khoday and General Hamid, as part of a broader strategy to bring the government out to the people. It was a good initiative, but I had a bad feeling about the timing.

'The guys will have just got back from the central Baluchi,' I said. 'Besides, if the strategy is to support and be seen supporting MDK, we should wait until he gets back.'

Bernard replied, 'It's not a monarchy up there, and Jim is not convinced MDK is the man for the job. In any case, we've got a schedule and the choppers are all lined up.'

I acquiesced.

8 August

Mentoring Team Charlie came back in from Mashal this morning after the four-day op. It seemed to go well. They found a heap of weapons and IEDs and by the end of it nationals were talking to them.

Found out this evening that the ANP men held hostage up at Nuri were released. Great news – we thought they were doomed. Apparently, some Haji from the Awi Mountains went over there and said let 'em go or you will never pass our way again.

9 August

The imminent visit inspired a spate of grooming, some of it more successful than others. LT got one of his corporals to cut his hair and wound up looking like a pineapple.

Last night, before the visit, a chopper was due in at 0330, bringing some Independent Electoral Commission reps. It kicked up so much dust the pilot couldn't see the ground, finally landing on the fourth pass. In the end they turned off all the lights in the camp and the pilot was able to use his night-vision goggles to land the bird. The result was that we all woke up at 0400 - and stayed awake.

Then the visiting party rolled in on two Chinooks at about 1000 hours. It started with twelve persons but then all the local ANA and ANP showed up in force, looking more alert, and numerous, than I've ever seen them. I guess that's what happens when the bosses come to town. We started with a brief in the old Dutch rec area. Then we rolled down to the White Compound with a packet that must have numbered 100 with the ANA and ANP.

When we got there, there were about 120 local elders to greet us - a huge turnout for Chora. Everything was swell for the first half hour, with various speakers mouthing platitudes. An old joker named Khaksar - apparently the local pharmacist, poet and historian — got up and raved for ten minutes about the place of Chora in global history, referring at various points to the fall of the Berlin Wall, the 1969 moon landing and a number of other historical events that the terps did not condescend to relate to us. He finished, and folks applauded politely.

Then a man the locals all call 'Thin Sadiq' proclaimed that MDK needed to be sacked and the whole shura exploded. Someone yelled back. A little old man got up and started abusing them all. Shoes went flying across the room, then boots. Then some pushing and shoving and shouting and yelling and a few ANP guys stepped into the fray. A rabble of them spilled out onto the landing, where there was more pushing and shoving and abusive language, a few slaps, then some punches thrown. Juma Gul punched somebody so hard he hurt his knuckles. The ANP guys belonging to Malim Sadiq and MDK cocked their weapons. My PRT soldiers made to wade in but Willie held them back.

This went on for five minutes or so before the White Compound's caretaker Shah Wali and his boys rolled out the dining cloths and started bringing out platters of mutton and saffron rice. Seeing the food arrive put things into perspective in a country in which you never know when you are going to get your next hit of protein. The belligerents and the rest of us all sat down to eat like nothing had happened.

After lunch, the packet rolled out of the White Compound. Strolling gaily back to FOB Mirwais surrounded by their minions, both Khoday and

Juma were jubilant. It had all gone very well from their point of view. I took Bernard and Higgins around the base and tried to sensitise them to the logistical needs before escorting them up to the landing zone.

My diary entry on 10 August contains two sentences of self-reproach:

That horrible feeling when your instincts become clear after the event. The payoff for not trusting your instincts in favour of other people's arguments is that you can blame them when things go wrong.

I should have been more insistent about delaying the shura. Sure, we should be supporting the district government and not the personality cult of MDK, but we were there to promote harmony between the locals and minimise the opportunity for insurgents to exploit fractures in the community. And this 'fighting shura' only inflamed those fractures. And besides, a shura of that size was a once-in-a-year opportunity to bring the government to the people – and it had been a disaster.

The following day we had a post-mortem with LK.

'It was planned,' he said, 'a kind of ambush.'

Gulum Hazrat also dropped around for a post-mortem. Head of the local office of the Afghan National Re-Construction Coordination department, responsible for implementing the reasonably successful National Solidarity Program through a network of community development councils, he had been in Chora six years and seen it all.

'The same thing happens with all the district chiefs, including MDK's father when he was alive. They can't keep everybody happy.'

He said he worked closely with the White Compound and found MDK easy to deal with. Hazrat explained that most of the tribal leaders had gained prominence fighting the Russians, when they had earned their title 'Commander'.

'Some are better than others. The one they call 'Thin Sadiq', who was yelling yesterday at the shura, he wanted to be chair of his local community development council, but he only got one vote – from his son!

'People in Chora have two faces. They support one leader one day and another the next. I am lucky – I get support from both MK and MDK, so no one can touch me. People here understand that MK is against MDK, so some of them feel confident to speak against MDK for that reason. As for the struggle between those two, I don't wish to discuss this.'

Several of MDK's enemies came into the FOB in the weeks that followed. The most articulate was Abdul Ramin, who was known as 'the Colonel'. He had land and money and sons studying in Kabul. He would list complaints against MDK in a fairly structured sort of way, citing figures and statistics.

Then there were the two Sadiqs: Thin Sadiq and Fat Sadiq, as they were referred to by locals in the valley. Neither were related to or liked by Malim Sadiq. They showed up at the gate every few days asking to see me, such as on 11 August, when, in the early afternoon, Zia popped his head into the office.

'Sadiq is here, sir.'

'Which one?'

'Fat Sadiq,' he lamented.

My heart sank.

Fat Sadiq seldom bathed and sat on the couch with his legs spread wide, stuffing nuts and sweets into his gob, bits of which would fly out onto the coffee table as he enumerated his complaints about the district chief.

'MDK is your enemy,' he'd tell me. 'He hates you because you killed his father. He wants to lay IEDs against your vehicles and kill fifty Australians.'

Pretty unsophisticated stuff. On the way out the door he asked for another wind-up radio. Ever courteous, Zia apologised and told him we were all out, even though there was a box of them visible in the corner.

12 August

Ramadan started yesterday. Things should slow down a bit now. The Afghans can't drink water or eat from sunup to sundown. So in the heat of the summer we can't take the terps out past about 10 am and the ANA boys won't go out patrolling any later than that either. Hopefully the Taliban will take a break too. We'll see.

I'm up sitting in the aircon of the office and don't intend to move much till around 5 pm. It's chaos out there. Forty degrees Celsius. The camp is full of boys relaxing from the ops around Mashal so we are chocka - about 150 pax not counting the Afghans. And now the shitters on the east side of the camp are blocked and the internet doesn't work.

The last two days we've been integrating a couple of new people who arrived with Bernard, including a second terp - an older guy with a pot belly, a Stalinesque moustache and a proclivity for gallant pronouncements.

'I am happy to patrol and be shot by insurgents,' he said in our first meeting in the office.

I said I hoped that wouldn't be necessary.

'I am not afraid,' he replied. 'I have already been shot twice.'

He lifted his shirt to show the scars; his belly looked like a relief map of the Hindu Kush.

Bernard also brought in Corporal Torres from Brooklyn, designated as a civil affairs officer. Shortish, solidly built, tattoos on his arms, bald and with a quick, streetwise mouth - there's something astute and winning about him. We took him out on patrol this morning and his pants split. This has been a problem for the US police mentoring guys: there is something wrong with the manufacture of their uniforms. The Police Mentoring Team Stryker guys went down the bazaar with sixteen pairs of pants to be repaired. They left the pants at the sewing shop and came back with fifteen big watermelons. Then they sat in the sun eating them. I haven't seen them so happy since they got here.

On the morning of 13 August a young guy in his late teens came in and knocked on the side gate wanting to see us. He was from Pay Kelah, south-east of FOB Mirwais on the northern banks of the Chora River that ran down from Sarab in the north-east. Torres and I went down to the PRT House container to meet him.

He told us that his father used to work with Gulam Hazrat on the National Solidarity Program but was killed by insurgents ten months ago. He said there were no leaders in Pay Kelah who could stand up to the insurgents.

'Now they are getting stronger day by day and moving more confidently around Pay Kelah,' he said. 'Insurgents are stashing weapons in the green zone on the other side of the river in

AusAID development adviser Kate Elliott doing business with engineers Hashim and Kabir from Uruzgan's Ministry for Rural Rehabilitation and Development. LORRIE GRAHAM

This is a stickup! Dutch political adviser Eric Peterson demonstrates, at close range, an RPG launcher captured from the Taliban by Dutch forces.

Paul Warren and Ben Ranaudo chilling out in the back of a Bushmaster, early July 2009. COURTESY OF RACHEL INGRAM

Playing '*Niet Swaffelen op de Dixi*' for Dutch special forces at a Task Force 55 end of rotation party, Poppy's, 15 November 2009. JAN-KEES DE MEESTER, COURTESY OF NETHERLANDS ARMED FORCES

Afghan and Australian soldiers on patrol in the Baluchi Valley. AUSTRALIAN GOVERNMENT DEPARTMENT OF DEFENCE

A Bushmaster cuts its way through the main street bazaar on the road north out of Tarin Kowt – the beginning of the Road to Chora. AUSTRALIAN GOVERNMENT DEPARTMENT OF DEFENCE

Barakzai tribal leader and Chora District chief Mohammad Daoud Khan (MDK) talking to Australian soldiers. AUSTRALIAN GOVERNMENT DEPARTMENT OF DEFENCE

The neighbourhood warlord, Matiullah Khan (MK). A complex and charismatic figure. Protector, provider and predator. Monopolist and man of the people. Or some of them anyway. KATE GERAGHTY/FAIRFAX PHOTOS

'The Communist' and Rassoud rehearsing together in March 2010. DR KHOSHAL
MOKAMEL

Playing with Dr Farouk's band from Kandahar, Afghan New Year's celebration
at PRT House, 20 March 2010. SERGEANT MICK DAVIS, AUSTRALIAN GOVERNMENT
DEPARTMENT OF DEFENCE

Sappers at work. AUSTRALIAN GOVERNMENT DEPARTMENT OF DEFENCE

A soldier stands vigil outside the refrigerated shipping container that functioned as a morgue in the Tarin Kowt Role 2 hospital, 8 June 2010. It is ADF practice not to leave the body of a fallen soldier alone until it has been returned to Australia. FRED SMITH

Padre Al Lavaki leads the funeral procession for Darren Smith and 'Snowy' Moerland past the Role 2 hospital, 9 June 2010. AUSTRALIAN GOVERNMENT DEPARTMENT OF DEFENCE

Pallbearers carry the caskets of Privates Timothy Aplin, Scott Palmer and Benjamin Chuck on to the Hercules aircraft for repatriation to Australia, 24 June 2010. AUSTRALIAN GOVERNMENT DEPARTMENT OF DEFENCE

Concert to farewell the Dutch, Poppy's, 17 July 2010. From left to right: Johnno, Major Chris Way, Amy, Charlotte, me and Bainesy, in his best pair of shorts. SERGEANT EVA KLIJN, COURTESY OF NETHERLANDS ARMED FORCES

An Australian delegation leaving the provincial governor's compound, 18 July 2010. The civilians from left to right are: me, Bernard Philip (Director, PRT), Ric Smith (Special Envoy, Afghanistan and Pakistan), Peter Baxter (Director General, AusAID), Jon Merrill (Assistant Secretary, Afghanistan and Pakistan Branch, DFAT), Paul Foley (Australian Ambassador to Afghanistan) and Khoday Rahim (Acting Governor of Uruzgan). AUSTRALIAN GOVERNMENT DEPARTMENT OF DEFENCE

Australian and US soldiers dining al fresco at FOB Mirwais, August 2010. FRED SMITH

Meeting with the village leader in Pay Kelah, Chora District, 14 September 2010. Clockwise from top left are: JR; Zia; me; MDK and his chief of staff LK; MDK's bodyguard; Mayor Azim; and a village elder. JOHN MORLEY

Angry mob approaching from Ali Sherzai at the beginning of the Chora Rock Show, 16 September 2010. Photographed from the FOB Mirwais guard tower by infantry signaller Jordan Graue, Mentoring Team Charlie.

MDK (right) and a couple of his shooters in the back of the CH-47 Chinook en route to Chora, following the assassination of Malim Sadiq, 16 November 2010. This was the first time I'd seen MDK carrying an automatic weapon. FRED SMITH

Omar Sherzad (the tall man in the front row, at right) arrives on the Tarin Kowt airstrip in the company of Jan Mohammad Khan (JMK, in traditional dress, at left) to take up his appointment as Uruzgan provincial governor, 13 December 2010.

AUSTRALIAN GOVERNMENT DEPARTMENT OF DEFENCE

The Boxing Day Test, 26 December 2010. We had them 5 for 20, then this guy came in!

AUSTRALIAN GOVERNMENT DEPARTMENT OF DEFENCE

A Little Eid celebration, marking the end of Ramadan, with the interpreters, 12 August 2013. CORPORAL MARK DORAN, AUSTRALIAN GOVERNMENT DEPARTMENT OF DEFENCE

In concert out the front of Green Beans, 27 August 2013. As I launched forward into a heroic guitar solo, the lead got caught on something, yanking the guitar back. In the band, from left to right, are: Debbie Xinos; Mark Correa; 'Corky', a US soldier whose name I've forgotten; and Glenn Treasure. Alex Tompkins is playing drums but you can only see his boot on the kick pedal. AUSTRALIAN GOVERNMENT DEPARTMENT OF DEFENCE

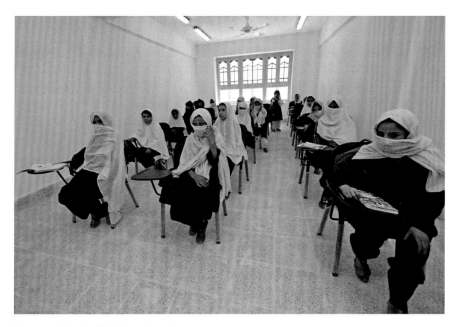

The Malalai Girls' School in Tarin Kowt. AUSTRALIAN GOVERNMENT DEPARTMENT OF DEFENCE

The Road to Chora. AUSTRALIAN GOVERNMENT DEPARTMENT OF DEFENCE

The Transfer of Authority ceremony, 28 October 2013. In the front row (from left to right) are, *inter alia*: Opposition Leader Bill Shorten, Uruzgan Chief Justice Maulawi Mohammad Jan, the Dutch ambassador Han Peters (orange tie), the Australian Ambassador HE Jon Philp, the then Defence Minister David Johnston, the then Prime Minister Tony Abbott, Brigadier Hamid and provincial Chief of Police Matiullah Khan. CORPORAL MARK DORAN, AUSTRALIAN GOVERNMENT DEPARTMENT OF DEFENCE

The remnants of the Uruzgan PRT, at the flight line, preparing to leave, 31 October 2013. Left to right are: David Windsor, Stacey Greene and Rohan Titus. SAMAD ALI REZA

Playing 'Dust of Uruzgan' with Private Glenn Treasure (left) and Lieutenant Alex Tompkins at the Commemoration Ceremony, 2 November 2013. CORPORAL MARK DORAN, AUSTRALIAN GOVERNMENT DEPARTMENT OF DEFENCE

Me and Captain Kristin Gardiner in front of the last Dixis in Tarin Kowt. 'Movember' had kicked in. MAJOR HAYDN BARLOW

Maryanne and Olympia, 17 January 2014.

The *Dust of Uruzgan* show, on stage at the Burnie Civic Theatre in Tasmania, 3 June 2014, with Liz Frencham on double bass and Dean Stevenson on drums (Carl Pannuzzo usually plays but he couldn't make that trip). NEIL PLAIN

preparation for ops in Ali Sherzai against ANP headquarters, the White Compound or FOB Mirwais.'

He named four of them, mullahs each commanding a dozen or so guys.

'Would it be useful if the ANP patrolled in the daytime?' I asked.

He said they needed protection at night, which was when the Taliban moved around freely, placing IEDs and kidnapping people.

'We don't have any way to call you guys at night,' he said. 'The insurgents make Afghan Wireless Network turn off the telephone tower after 6 pm. If we had satellite phones or radios, we could call you. I've got three or four men in my household so we can protect ourselves. But we can't look after the rest of the area. These people killed my father last year. I want to fight them face to face.'

'I've lost friends to the same enemy,' said Torres.

The young man continued: 'They want to control more area during Ramadan. They plan to make checkpoints and lay more IEDs. When they see police they try to kill them and take their weapons. If you guys don't help, they will come across the river soon. You guys should train local informers and give me a satellite phone. I take risks to come here and we don't receive anything.'

Later that afternoon, we received a visit from the mayor of Ali Sherzai, Dr Azim, an affable fellow in his early thirties. Mostly bald, he always wore eyeliner. He wasn't a doctor, but his father had been, which in Afghan culture entitled him to the title. By his own account he was the pre-eminent musician in town. He also had an endearing tendency to pose as a military leader, harmless enough since no one else took him seriously.

'If all of us were determined to remove insurgents from this area it would not be a difficult job,' he said. He added that if nothing was done now, the insurgents would be firing RPGs at Ali Sherzai and laying IEDs around the base and the White Compound. We had to act soon.

❖

On the morning of 14 August, waiting to head out the gate for the weekly NGO meeting, we were held up because the ANP got notice of a couple of IEDs in town. The meeting was thinly attended on account of Ramadan, the mood at the White Compound languid in that Ramadan sort of way. We spoke a bit about the situation in Pay Kelah, which I had been reporting on for the last three days.

As we were spilling out of the White Compound, MDK and LK rocked up in an ANP vehicle. MDK looked tired but happy and freer after his trip to the US, as if three weeks in another world had temporarily liberated him from the pressures of being a tribal leader in the Uruzgan snakepit. I invited MDK down to Mirwais, and he and LK showed up shortly afterwards. Justin joined the meeting and we had a good yarn.

'I've heard reports of increasing insurgent activity in Pay Kelah,' said MDK.

'We've called for a security meeting tomorrow,' JR replied. 'We're looking to mount an operation in the area early next week.'

'And what about the people of the area?' I asked. 'Are they supporting insurgents?'

'If locals see us doing things against insurgents, they will support us,' said MDK. 'But if they don't see us doing anything, they won't have the confidence.'

In the early evening, I went to the BUB. Jason Brown, an Australian SAS soldier, had been killed down south. A bad summer was getting worse. Also, a couple of focused-looking young journos and a cameraman from Channel 10 had shown up, looking for 'digger stories'.

Zia came into the office at 2100. I offered him the phone to call his fiancée. At one point, she had to hang up because her brother had walked in. As he waited to call her back, he came over all sad and said, 'Sir, about my salary, sir. Would I be able to set up a separate contract to increase my salary?'

I told him the truth: I'd asked my boss at the embassy two weeks back, but hadn't heard anything. He was receiving $600 a month from his original contract transferred from the Dutch to US armies.

'I owe my uncle some money, and my fiancée's family said that the time has come for us to marry.'

I asked about his fiancée; had he met her yet?

'Sure, she is my cousin.'

'Do you like her?'

'Oh yes, we like each other, but she is in Peshawar and I don't think I can live there. Many ISAF terps have been kidnapped by Taliban.'

He said he hoped to live with her in Jalalabad.

'So when do you want to get married?'

'Well, that depends on my salary, sir.'

❖

My diary entries over the days leading up to 20 August reflect a growing sense of pressure. The Taliban were getting more active it seemed, despite Ramadan, while life on the base was becoming uncomfortable.

15 August

The shitters on the north side of the camp were shut down a couple of days ago. North-side residents have been walking 150 metres to shit and shower. Concurrently, there have been six cases of gastro in the camp. I was sitting outside the tent this morning pulling my boots on when Sergeant Sands reeled out of the tent and chundered in front of me.

'Morning, Michael,' I said.

'Morning, Mister Fred.'

The good news is that they have diagnosed the problem with the shitters. One of the pipes to the septic tank has been running uphill at an angle of ten degrees rather than downhill at ten degrees. We have been literally pushing shit uphill.

As part of their program to support MDK, the Dutch gave his little brother, Khoshal, the contract to remove the effluence from the shitters. We've continued this contract. Khoshal, like MDK, is small of frame and squeaky of voice. But whereas MDK swings between being effervescent and morose, Khoshal is consistently morose. Khoshal prefers to liaise with me because I'm polite and he wants to be seen as a political player. So every few days, a digger will come from the guard tower, knock on the door of my office and say, 'Hey, Fred, Shit Man is here to see you!' A little unkind, perhaps, but I know who they're referring to.

This morning we had a security meeting with MDK, ANP, ANA – even the local intelligence chief showed up. We discussed what to do in Pay Kelah and decided to patrol out there tomorrow with MDK; get him talking to the locals. A fighting patrol was supposed to go out there tonight to clear the area, but the ANP checkpoint at Kala Kala got hit at around 1800 and needed support. Reports are one ANP KIA and one insurgent KIA, although Zia asked if anyone had actually seen the body of the insurgent, sceptical that the ANP actually returned fire. Anyway, this means the patrol is now going to Kala Kala at 0400. We will set off at 0615, too early for MDK's liking but too late for the ANA, who like to get home by 0900 during Ramadan.

16 August

This morning's patrol to Pay Kelah was pretty benign and even comical at times. We gathered at the picnic tables at 0600 and rolled out of the gate pretty heavy. With a couple of platoons of ANA, my PRT boys, two platoons of MT-C [Mentoring Team Charlie], a good number of ANP, plus MDK and LK carrying AKs, we flooded Pay Kelah with acronyms. Dr Azim was the highlight of the morning. Made up with eyeliner and red nail polish, dressed in an ANP uniform his mother had ironed, he walked at the front of the patrol with a megaphone, calling out something like, 'Come out, you scoundrels.' They didn't. We did, however, enjoy a walk through the countryside and conversations with local elders – and were home by ten, before the ANA got too thirsty and stroppy.

The night of 17 August was rough. Just before dinner, Zia asked whether I had any news from the embassy about money. I was embarrassed to say I didn't.

Morale among the soldiers in my PRT team was low. There was an aircon in the tent but it didn't work very well, and with daytime temperatures reaching 45 degrees Celsius, the guys had nowhere comfortable to hang out.

At 2100 the camp sergeant major, Damien Perdon, walked in and asked if I could play the 'Last Post' and 'Reveille' on the harmonica at a Long Tan service in the morning. Long Tan was a 6 RAR battle and these guys make a point of marking the day wherever they are. I downloaded the music from the Veterans' Affairs website and learned the two tunes.

The following morning I played at the solemn little service out there near the picnic tables, in front of the memorial made of corrugated iron and rocks. It was a nice ceremony.

19 August, 1930 hours
Our new second-string interpreter just came in and asked me about his work for tomorrow. I've been lending him to LT's police mentoring guys, who lost their terp recently – he just went home and didn't come back. LT came back from his meeting at police headquarters this afternoon saying that the new terp wasn't bad but had a tendency to say his own piece in the course of the conversation, which is the last thing you want an interpreter to do.

According to LT, 'I was having an argument with Mohammad Gul. He was asking for more resources. I said, "It's up to Juma Gul to supply these." Mohammad said, "Yeah, but Juma won't help." The terp said, "He's right, Juma won't help – can't you see that?"'

I asked our new terp if he wouldn't mind going out with the police mentoring team again tomorrow and he launched into more bold declarations: 'This is life; we must do the work. Show me the insurgents, I will shoot them first shot, not second shot, first shot. I won't miss!'

'That's wonderful,' I said, 'but perhaps in the meantime if you could just translate what LT says, I would be very happy with that.'

'No problem,' he declared. 'What LT says, I will say!'

I asked if he was happy here. He said it was okay, he had friends in the camp. He added: 'The valley it is very beautiful, but the people – they are stupid!'

19 August, 2120 hours

I had Zia in the office writing up a meeting report and went down to the command post to check the timing of tomorrow's meeting. I was walking back past the kitchen when I heard a crack, then a thud and an explosion. I looked up to see machine-gun tracer rounds flying about five metres above my head. I ran for cover into the cook's quarters and a bunch of diggers ran out in battle dress with rifles poised. I had been sitting there for ten minutes talking to the cook when Willie came running in with weapon and body armour, naked above the waist, fly down and bootlaces undone. Catching his breath, he said, 'Man, I didn't know where you was!'

Apparently he'd been lying in his bed in a state of undress when he heard the rounds come in. His first responsibility is to make sure I don't get killed, so he leaped out of bed, pulled on his pants and boots, threw his body armour over his bare torso, and ran around the base looking for me.

'Sorry, mate,' I said. 'I figured I'd stay here and keep my head down.'

It turns out the insurgents got pretty close to the base and fired a couple of RPGs at us from the *green zone. The grenades crashed harmlessly into the hill behind the base, but it's a sign of their growing confidence.*

The morning of 20 August began like any other, the tent warming up at 0800. In my diary for the day, I'd listed nine items I wanted to discuss with MDK, ranging from the previous day's rocket attacks to White Compound sustainment. We had planned to meet in the command post to get Mod, Nick and JR involved. As I walked into the CP to touch base with Mod, I heard the crackle of the Icom as a call came in:

'*Zero Alpha, this is India 36.*'

'*India 36, this is Zero Alpha, send.*'

'*Troops in contact. Two category As.*'

Mod went into action, taking the 'nine liner' and calling in a medivac from TK. I realised I was no use in there and that the CP was about to get busy; I cleared out and went up to the office container. I had Zia call MDK and postpone the meeting, then we got on with writing up a report of a meeting we'd had the day before. At around 1100 Willie came in to call his wife, but found the line had been cut, a bad sign.

'Have you heard?' he said. 'Some dudes from Mentoring Team Charlie were killed down south.'

'No,' I replied, though I had walked out of the CP suspecting the worst. Then I turned to my laptop to see the CLP Red come up on the screen, and a few minutes later there was an email from Tarin Kowt saying there would be a muster for personnel down there at 1400 at Poppy's.

It turned out two guys from the infantry tent next door to ours had been killed. They'd been doing a spell down at COP Mashal.

In the early afternoon I was hanging my laundry on the line

when I saw two Chinooks come in through the Chora saddle and circle around the valley in towards our landing zone. I pulled my laundry off the line to protect it from the imminent downwash dust storm.

The choppers had come to collect a handful of soldiers to reinforce Mashal while the mates of the dead men went down to TK with the bodies. I watched Captain Ben Williams, the MP, get off before a team of five men (known as a 'brick') got on in full battle rig to reinforce Mashal.

Later in the afternoon I could hear Ben in the tent next to ours, working with the guys' mates to get their stuff ready to send home.

20 August, 1730 hours
Just walked past the picnic tables outside the kitchen and the boys were sitting around quietly, heads down, bummed out. Now I'm sitting on the floor in the CP waiting for the BUB to start. The room is hushed except for Dukesy, sitting in the corner there smack-talking about 'Killing the c%#*'.

Then my meeting notes from the BUB, fragmentary as always:

Engineers cleared the overwatch position for the op ... ASLAV was in position on the overwatch ... Dale and Kirby got out to do PT on the other side of the vehicle and stepped on pressure plate ... Killed instantly ... Kirby has two young daughters ... MP Ben Williams here to gather effects ... other members of India 36 currently helping with inventory ... family not yet notified so don't speak to media reps here on base ...

JR said he thought they hadn't been to that overwatch hill before, but it turned out they had, a couple of years and several rotations earlier; this was enough to set a pattern.

'We need to work on data capture,' he said. 'Also, guys, this was a twenty-kilo YPOC [yellow palm oil container]; there will be some traumatised lads from clearing up the battle scene, and India 36 will be short for the next two months. They're unlikely to get topped up before we go home.'

JR went on, speaking in that detached way soldiers are trained to in the face of victory or defeat. 'So they outplayed us this time. We need to be more vigilant. But we crack on. We don't treat the local nationals any differently. And we don't deflect blame. Okay, thanks, guys.'

And we all went off for dinner.

❖

August 20

An August summer's day, a morning clear and bright
A week after Ramadan, the lines were nice and quiet
The sappers were away and from the tent next door
Some boys were down in the valley on an op at COP Mashal

I stumbled from my tent, towards the pissaphone
Down past the genny where the camp dog chewed a bone
I went to find my terp to call the district chief
Walked past the Afghan's kitchen stuck my head in the CP
I heard a call come in from India 36
Through the static of the Icom saying something about a TIC
Another IED a couple of category As
Mod called in a medivac and I got out of the way

Went up to my desk to type up a report
Of a conversation I had the day before
Willie wandered in to call his missus dear
Found that the phones were cut confirming what I'd feared

Two choppers circled in, from Tarin Kowt they said
Through the Chora saddle, to our dirt and stone LZ
The MP got off first, he'd done all this before
A brick of boys got on the bird to reinforce Mashal

When the MP came around, by then it was half past three
Those who'd stayed from the tent next door helped with
        the inventories
Packed all their effects, less pornos and their fags
Ready for Sunday's chopper in white-painted Echelon bags

I went back to the CP for the 1730 brief
The staff were sitting quietly, the room was thick with grief
Till Dukesy arced up red, saying, 'Let's go settle scores'
The OC said, 'We keep our heads and crack on like before'

And all through dinner time and that evening warm and still
Quiet speculation about what happened on that hill
Till Willie briefed the team, laid the facts out cold
Then went through the orders for the next day's foot patrol

CHAPTER 10

TALIBAN FIGHTING MAN

When she gets on the phone saying how's it goin',
man I don't wanna get her all stressed
But how to explain that the two-way range
can put a boy a little on edge . . .

FRED SMITH, 'TALIBAN FIGHTING MAN'

AFTER DINNER THAT NIGHT OF 20 AUGUST, THE PRT TEAM GATHERED in the vestibule outside our tent for the nightly patrol orders. We were a motley bunch, an assortment of young tearaways and older guys reflecting the diversity of American society: whites, African Americans, Hispanics and a couple of office workers on National Guard duty from their usual jobs back in California or South Carolina. Everyone had heard that something had happened; they'd seen the MP in there with the guys from the tent next door, packing up Kirby and Dale's effects. The mood was solemn as Willie spoke.

'Okay, guys, two Aussies were KIA down south today by an IED on an overwatch position.' He explained what had happened, careful to get it right. Then he gave the guys a lecture about complacency. 'So, two months to go, okay – we don't want nobody dying out here.'

He ran us through the orders for the foot patrol to get us to a weekly meeting, scheduled the following morning at the White Compound, then we all cut away.

I got back to the office and found The Sarge downloading to LT about his marriage. His wife said she felt distant; and there was some other dude on the scene. LT handled himself with a lot of maturity for a guy of twenty-five; he spoke of how his own parents had split up and were now 'very unhappy and living with weirdos'.

I woke at around 0300 on account of having eaten the sugary American spareribs, still a little wound up from the RPG attacks. I went to call Maryanne but the phone lines were still down.

I was regretting not telling her what was going on. This was a common dilemma for soldiers in the era of modern communications, as my middle-of-the-night diary scribble reflected:

> I should have told Maryanne about the RPG incident when we spoke on Monday. It's the dilemma that Willie identified when we were talking the other night: 'Do you tell your wife about the incident or wait till she finds out in the news? If you tell her she starts to get worried; if you don't, she gets worried and then pissed off that you didn't tell her.'

My diary entry from that night suggests I was starting to think like a FOB soldier in other ways:

> Being attacked on the base where you live increases your sense of vulnerability. There's comfort when you're feeling under threat in knowing you can fight

back. I'm starting to feel it would be good to learn
to shoot.

I had always figured that a civilian's best defence lay in his non-combatant status. But the primal impulse to grab a rock when feeling threatened was tangible.

At the next day's BUB there was more bad news for Mentoring Team Charlie. Two men down at Patrol Base Qudus, Clarkie and Goose, were badly wounded when their vehicle hit a low-metal-signature IED during a road move. Clarkie was about to go into surgery. It seemed likely they'd both survive.

Bernard had asked me to come down to Tarin Kowt, so on the afternoon of Sunday, 22 August, I loaded my bags and guitar on the bird alongside the white-painted Echelon bags and trunks containing Kirby and Dale's stuff. I was feeling bad about leaving Willie and the team, but relieved to be heading back to the relative comfort and safety of TK.

On the morning of 24 August, I went to Kirby and Dale's ramp ceremony, which was sad as ramp ceremonies always were, only more so for me since I knew the guys on the podium talking about their lost friends. I noticed the commanding officer, Lieutenant Colonel Mark Jennings, looked particularly stressed. It turned out there had been another death that morning during a complex and extended battle sixty kilometres west of Tarin Kowt.

I got back to the office from the ramp ceremony at 1230 to find the CLP Red warning was up on the screen of the laptop. Then my mate Bainesy, the quartermaster, walked in looking pretty shaken.

'Fark!' he said. 'There was a TIC this morning out west. A lance corporal took a round through the shoulder. I've just been down at the morgue recovering the body armour . . . exit wounds all through the chest!'

Three days later we were at another ramp ceremony, this time for Lance Corporal Jared MacKinney. He was a keen athlete apparently, known to his mates as 'Crash' because he was a little accident-prone. So was his memorial service, which featured a couple of slapstick moments. As they were running the photos of him through PowerPoint, a rogue photo of someone's hairy bum appeared. Then, after the 'Last Post' was played, the iPod jammed and soldiers were left with their arms up in a salute for a couple of minutes while the digger at the mixing desk pressed every button to try to make 'Reveille' play. One of Crash's mates got up and told some funny stories about the larrikin ranga, but broke into a sob when he said how much he'd miss Crash.

The new MRTF commanding officer, Lieutenant Colonel Mark Jennings also spoke: 'Jared MacKinney died a soldier's death, chest towards the enemy while trying to help a mate.' From Mark's brief description of the battle, I couldn't quite work out what had happened, but I remember walking away from that ramp ceremony with a clear feeling that I needed to write a song about this guy Crash MacKinney. Then life got busy and I didn't get a chance to make a start on it.

Back at the office in the PRT, we now had two more DFAT staff, Damian Donavan and John Cavanagh. As we prepared to go to yet another ramp ceremony, for a US soldier who had been killed in a separate incident in Deh Rawud, we got talking about why there had been so many deaths in Uruzgan that summer. There were a few theories: the battlegroup was operating on a wider area of operations; coalition soldiers were doing more partnered patrols with Afghan forces; insurgents had been pushed up into Uruzgan by the US surges in adjacent Helmand and Kandahar provinces; the enemy was getting better with IEDs. There was an equally plausible theory: our luck had simply run out.

The base in Tarin Kowt was still recovering from the chaos of the Dutch withdrawal. But there were positive signs: the US contingent came to town with money to spend and began hiring local contractors in a massive project to turn the pebble walkways on Kamp Holland to concrete, a project we all called 'OEF' (Operation Enduring Footpath, a pisstake on the original Afghanistan mission 'Operation Enduring Freedom'). I wished I had a skateboard – and figured it was only a matter of time before a US military policeman showed up on a Segway.

I tuned into some bigger picture intelligence on the war and the province. Taliban leader Mullah Omar had given his fighters the green light to target local civilian leaders, which they had been doing anyway prior to that, but with mixed feelings. Meanwhile, Bernard had further developed the political strategy so now we had a defined approach to dealing with each of the main players in the province. The strategy included plans for influencing and containing Matiullah Khan, encouraging him to be more accountable, inclusive and generally more statesmanlike, while protecting and supporting those he perceived to be his rivals, including MDK, MNKT and the provincial governor.

We managed to keep MK out of a new security arrangement that had been struck between the contractors and local leaders in Dorafshan to continue the Road to Chora project established by the Dutch. The Baluchi Valley still looked impenetrable though.

I also got clarification from the Independent Electoral Commission of the intended whereabouts of polling centres in the Chora District, which was of interest to the guys in the FOB Mirwais command post, where I returned on the evening of 30 August.

It has always been understood that interventions by the international community in problematic countries will only work where there is a political solution – a viable path to an accord that can bind the country's disparate and fractious political strands. Ahead of the international community's interventions in Iraq and Afghanistan, perhaps there had been a lazy assumption that democracy would automatically provide this political solution. We have come to realise that democracy, though the best option in the long run, can create as many problems as it solves. Elections are hard work for a fledgling bureaucracy to run, and a fledgling security force to protect. They can exacerbate instability by inflaming ethnic political divisions, and if perceived to be corrupt, they diminish the credibility of the state. The constitution agreed in Bonn in November 2001 set up a constant schedule of elections for Afghanistan. The 2009 presidential elections were to be followed just a year later by the Wolesi Jirga (lower house) elections.

All this political science theory was far from the minds of the FOB Mirwais command post staff when I got back. They just wanted to know where the polling stations were going to be so they could prepare to go out and defend them if they were attacked on 18 September, election day.

The next three weeks for us were all about trying to create a positive security environment for the vote. The Taliban's job, on the other hand, was to scare people off voting. At the security meeting on FOB Mirwais on 31 August, the head of the local intelligence unit said that the Taliban were getting around certain villages threatening to cut off the thumbs of anyone who voted. The police chief, Mohammad Gul, said he had information that two suicide IED waistcoats had been brought into Ali Sherzai. He suggested LT's police mentoring team combine with his officers to conduct a thorough search of the bazaar.

Meanwhile, three Independent Electoral Commission represen-tatives were in town, distributing voting cards and hiring people to run the polling booths. They parked on our base at nights to keep the ballot boxes and their cars safe from interference.

The base was now in better shape. One of the sappers had stripped the canvas from the old Dutch toilets, draped it over some bedframes and built a swimming pool! His colleagues had stuck pictures of bikini-clad women on the wall. Someone sourced a beach ball and an inflatable palm tree. It was a great thing to come back sweaty from a patrol, strip down and lounge in the pool.

That's where I was on the afternoon of 1 September, after returning from a difficult meeting with MDK. I'd had to explain that a local national taken to the Role 2 hospital in Tarin Kowt a few days earlier had died of sepsis. The meeting went further downhill when MDK complained about phone cards and ammunition, and other things we couldn't give him. I had just got out of the pool when Zia told me he'd received a call to say that Abdullah, son of Haji Loylala (the Pay Kelah area tribal leader who had died of natural causes), had just been shot in the Ali Sherzai bazaar by an ANP officer named Kareem. Abdullah had sworn at Kareem, who had just finished his shift but was still in uniform. Kareem had replied, 'You will never curse at me again,' and unloaded a full magazine into Abdullah's chest. We had had hopes that Abdullah would grow into a leadership role in Pay Kelah. So much for that.

On 5 September, we went out to Mohammad Akbar Khan's property to look at a proposed polling centre location. He showed us the new house he was building and his mini hydroelectric generator, as well as the aqueducts and sluices he used to move water around. It was a thing of beauty, if you're into hydraulics.

We stopped at the White Compound on the way back, where I spoke with MDK; he was keen to go ahead with the planned search for suicide vests in the Ali Sherzai bazaar. He recalled the suicide attack two days before the presidential elections the year before. Zia chipped in with his account of that event.

'After the explosion,' he said, 'vehicles went out from FOB Mirwais to bring back the dead and wounded ANA soldiers. When they returned, the ANA colonel smelled the hot rifle barrels of his men and struck two of them with the butt of his rifle as punishment for firing indiscriminately after the explosion.'

Zia remembered that they brought the suicide bomber's charred head back to FOB Mirwais. He had had nightmares for the next month.

Later, I was relaxing in the pool when Zia told me that Fat Sadiq was here.

'It's okay, sir, he wants to see Torres.'

'Beautiful.'

Torres was trained in active listening skills, which had backfired on him. Fat Sadiq had found a friend for life.

That evening, LT asked Willie and me for the loan of five of our PRT soldiers for a patrol to Kala Kala the next day. I said that as a US Army resource it was Willie's call to make, and Willie gave them the green light. The guys were keen, but were probably just looking for action.

I was working in the office at 1100 hours the following morning when The Sarge and our civil affairs sergeant Gary burst in, highly excited. They had just got into a TIC and were buzzing with adrenaline. They'd been to a place called Qal'eh-ye Ragh to do some 'atmospherics testing'. There they had met a local national who told them, 'Things are fine here, Malim Sadiq and his boys keep things pretty quiet, but if you walk five minutes that way and cross that aqueduct you will get shot at!' Soldiers being soldiers, they walked five minutes that way, crossed the aqueduct and sure enough . . .

As Gary explained, 'The whole hillside across the river lit up with muzzle flashes from 200 yards away! Man, there were rounds zippin' and fizzin' all around us. We had no cover so we ran behind a little hill and returned fire. Then we went into a flanking manoeuvre to get closer. Then we got shot at again, so we fired back – like, I mean we raked the whole goddamn hill with gunfire. Then we went after them but they ran away!'

I had never seen him so happy, but it also reminded me of what Al Sweetman said: 'War is great fun until it isn't.' If one of those rounds that was 'zippin and fizzin' around had hit its mark, the mood would have been very different. The only casualty was Torres's pants, which he split again leaping around in the fray.

Half an hour later, The Sarge intercepted an email from his wife to her new lover. I spent the rest of the day trying to create enough space for him to make an endless number of calls to her. These calls were brutal, but there's no privacy in a FOB. In any case, he didn't seem to care who overheard him. I guess soldiers get used to the idea of having no privacy.

The disruption was actually a problem, as we were trying to make a serious decision about the search for the suicide vests.

My diary from 2200 on 6 September records:

What a day. I'm watching a James Bond film here in the recreation room because The Sarge is arguing with his wife and her boyfriend on the phone. Meanwhile, there are suicide vests floating around the bazaar. They were going to do the operation tomorrow but couldn't get Mohammad Gul on the phone so are thinking they will postpone until Wednesday. Zia said it would be better to do it tomorrow because people will flood to the markets on Wednesday buying food for Eid. With more people around it will be harder to search the markets and more dangerous.

Mohammad Gul came in to the FOB at 8 pm. After the mandatory tango, we talked about the timing of the search operation. Gul said tomorrow was possible and probably the best option, but LT said, 'We're not ready – you've seen the kind of day we've had.' The timing of any military operation is affected by various factors, but here the dalliances of a woman in a military town in Germany was affecting operations forty kilometres up the Baluchi in the middle of southern Afghanistan. Let's just hope this doesn't end badly.

The search went ahead on Wednesday. They didn't find any vests, nobody got hurt and it was a good show of force and cooperation with the ANP ten days out from the election. It was also my wife's fortieth birthday and a party was going on back in Canberra. I called just as the speeches were about to begin and hung up feeling a long way from home.

I had dinner that evening with Zia and his interpreter mates in their room, which made me feel better. They were in a good mood because the following day was likely to be Little Eid, the end of Ramadan, subject to the proclamation of some high priest in Saudi Arabia based on his evaluation of the state of the forthcoming moon. MDK was organising a feast and we were invited.

I returned to the office after dinner to find The Sarge in a bad way. He had been checking bank accounts online. Then I heard one side of a tough phone call. 'How we gonna manage the kids if you're in Germany and I'm posted wherever? Are we gonna tell your parents what's goin' on now just as they're about to go on holiday? What am I gonna do about my life insurance? If I step on an IED tomorrow half a million bucks goes to you and your new boyfriend! I keep breaking down in tears in front of LT, now he's keeping me from patrolling – I'm supposed be leading these kids but I can't keep my mind on the job.'

I spoke with him afterwards. Whereas our soldiers did eight-month rotations broken by three weeks' leave, US soldiers did year-long rotations with two weeks' leave. There was no way you could reconnect with family in two weeks. The Sarge, like many of his mates, was on his fifth rotation in ten years. US soldiers traditionally put on a metal wristband whenever they lose a 'brother'. The Sarge wore three of these, each etched with the name of a fallen comrade. He was a man in a world of hurt.

The following morning, we were milling around getting ready to patrol down to the White Compound. We skipped breakfast in anticipation of some serious Eid eating. I went to check with Zia.

'Sorry, sir,' he told me, 'we have received news from Mecca. The moon has not appeared and Eid will not be until tomorrow.'

I told the team. The younger privates thought this was hilarious.

'Mr Fred, you sayin' the mission is cancelled because the moon didn't show up?!'

'Yep.'

'Hey, Connor! Mission cancelled – the moon didn't show!'

10 September, 0300 hours

. . . ended up feeling shit yesterday for a number of reasons mostly relating to my thin-skinned sensitivity to what other people want from me: Maryanne was upset because I'd missed her birthday. Then the NDS [intelligence] representative came in to say the insurgents are holding a shura at 3 pm in Nuri to discuss how to disrupt the elections, and was pissed off because we couldn't arrange airstrikes. Then the embassy gave me a hard time because my travel arrangements weren't in place and said they could see no way of putting Zia on a separate contract *to get him decent money. In a land where push always comes to shove, you need a big wall around your home. I guess that's why they all live behind compound walls.*

I awoke the following morning ready for an Eid party. We were about to step out the gate for the trip to the White Compound when we saw a huge crowd coming towards us from Ali Sherzai. There looked to be around 300 people with black banners and a guy with a megaphone in a pickup truck in the middle. We thought better of leaving.

As the mob neared the base, Aussie and US soldiers kitted up and went into the guard towers, their rifles poised. The crowd stopped about ten metres from the FOB wall. They were shouting and yelling but didn't seem to have violent intentions. With JR away, Mod was in charge and he made an interesting call for a young captain. 'De-escalate!' he commanded, ordering half of the men in the guard towers to come down. Soon after, the crowd headed back to Ali Sherzai.

Willie and our two sergeants were a little shaken. We had almost walked right into the middle of the angry mob. That afternoon, MDK explained what all the fuss was about.

'They are angry about an insult to the Koran.'

It turned out that Pastor Terry Jones from the Dove World Outreach Centre, a Christian church in Gainesville, Florida, had announced he would burn 200 Korans on the anniversary of the September 11 attacks. It had been a slow news week in the US and the press had fixated on this obscure pastor with a congregation of fifty. The matter had gone right up to the White House; President Obama had sought to stop Jones from going ahead. But not before news of it had reached the Chora Valley.

'They came to me first,' MDK said. 'I told them you can protest but it must be peaceful. There was one mullah from Kush Kadir who was trying to make them get violent but the other mullahs told him to go away.'

MDK called back an hour later with an interesting proposition.

'I have been talking to the mullahs. They want to speak with you. I told them to come in to the White Compound at 4 pm so you can talk to them.'

After what had just happened, it felt counterintuitive to leave the safety of the base. Willie was understandably nervous. But I went down to the command post and explained to JR that, from a political perspective, there would be value in being seen to support MDK on this – and, more importantly, we needed to build a dialogue with the mullahs.

He saw it from a military perspective – we needed to signal we weren't intimidated and were prepared to get out and dominate the space. He assigned me two 'bricks' from Mentoring Team Charlie and we rallied up a dozen of my own guys. We rolled out of the gate double the usual strength at 1545. The streets of Ali Sherzai were empty and quiet. It was eerie. The only sound was our boots on the gravel as we made our way to the White Compound. We walked into the shura room and found MDK sitting in the prime position – back to the rear wall – and flanked on each side by twenty men, all wearing turbans and scowls on their faces. We sat against the wall near the door.

'Thanks for coming,' MDK began. 'These mullahs asked me to bring you here to hear them.'

Gary started taking photos, but the mullahs signalled they were not happy with this. We took this as a sign that some of them were Taliban. Zia seemed nervous and translated as carefully as he could.

The senior mullah spoke. 'We are mullahs from the mosques of Chora. We have heard there will be an act of disrespect for our holy book. When we hear someone intends to do this intentionally, we are ready to do anything to stop it: we would lay down our lives, sell our property, we would even sell our wives to buy weapons to prevent this.

'All the people you saw gathered today were very angry. They wanted to enter your base and fight. We mullahs tried to calm them down and promised that we would give this message to you and ask you to prevent this violation of our holy book. If this burning of the Koran happens tomorrow, these people will be beyond our control and the consequences will be very dangerous for you. You will not be able to leave your base. But first, please explain to us why this is happening. Why does this man want to burn the Koran?'

'Thank you for your message,' I said. 'We have heard of this man in Florida and his plans to burn the Koran. We share your disgust. This morning, our men were scared and not sure what would happen so they got their weapons and went up into the guard towers. Thanks to your leadership, the people were peaceful and this was not necessary. And now we understand from you that people only wanted to pass on this message. So this morning there were people on the streets with anger in their hearts, while our guards in the towers were full of uncertainty. But the thing is, men on both sides of the wall felt the same way about this man in Florida. Our men on the base do not support what he is doing.'

'Today was Eid,' the head mullah said. 'It was supposed to be a happy day, but instead we were sitting in the hot sun on the ground throwing dirt on our heads. This book is from God; if someone is insulting our book, they are insulting us.'

'This is one crazy man in a country of 350 million,' I said. 'He is not supported by the US government.'

'In our country, if there is a crazy guy we put him in chains and keep him in hospital to stop him doing stupid things. This is not the first time. We have heard stories of US soldiers putting Korans in the toilet.'

'That behaviour is not legal for American troops,' I said. 'There are crazy people in every country and we can't control every one of them. President Obama supports what you think and if this man burns the Koran tomorrow he will be breaking the law. He will be arrested.'

'The American government is the most powerful in the world,' said the mullah. 'We cannot believe they cannot stop one man from burning a Koran!'

MDK chimed in, diplomatic as ever. 'Please help send a message to your commanders to prevent this. I am very happy that these mullahs were able to keep this protest peaceful. You guys make great sacrifices here to provide security, but if this happens it will take a lot of work to restore security.'

'Please tell your people that we heard them today,' I said, 'and their message has been passed on to our leaders. ISAF has great respect for Islam. We are building a mosque in Sorkh Morghab in memory of Rozi Khan. The US Army has thousands of Muslims and all of them would be disgusted with this action.'

I continued: 'This man in Florida is crazy. The media here made this man bigger than he should be. If you watched American TV you would think that all Afghans are terrorists, and if you watch TV here you would think that all Americans are like this man in Florida. But of course neither is true. MDK knows this, he has been to America. He has seen mosques; he has seen Muslims praying on the lawns of the White House. So I hope you enjoy your Eid and do not let this stupid man ruin your celebrations.'

'We will try to do so,' said the head mullah, and they all got up and left.

MDK look pleased and a little relieved.

'That was a good conversation,' he said. 'It was worth listening to them. Come to the White Compound tonight; we will have that feast I promised you.'

That evening, as the sun set over the valley, we had a splendid feast with the district government staff at the White Compound. There was music afterwards, me jamming on my guitar with Dr Azim's band. The younger US soldiers were amused to see 'Mr Fred' playing and dancing with the local nationals. I suppose it never occurred to them to engage with Afghans in that way.

❖

Election tensions were mounting. Our young friend from Pay Kelah came in and told us insurgents were talking to people at night, using the 'Burn the Koran' protest to dissuade voters.

A candidate named Obaidullah Barakzai dropped in to see me. He was an evil-looking guy who had done bad things as district chief of Khas Uruzgan seven years earlier. He was running against Abdul Khaliq – the mainstream Barakzai candidate and Malim Sadiq's brother – probably with support from Matiullah. He raised his concerns that Khaliq's mob would attempt to fiddle with the ballot boxes, but was also worried about the insurgents.

'Each moment I feel at risk,' he said.

Meanwhile, Juma Gul was seeking to send fifty ANP officers up to Chora for the elections. MDK was resisting, fearing they would interfere in the voting in JMK's interests. Then the Colonel came in and complained about MDK's weakness and failure to stop the protests. The games never ended. I was getting tired.

15 September
Four days till I go on leave and I didn't do well today. Elections on the 18th and we haven't been

patrolling, partly because of Eid and partly because of rumours of the suicide bomber. It's been a long summer but the weather is starting to cool. I'm losing my appetite for reaching out and meeting new people. Maybe it's been too long without the intimacy of loved ones and I've just put a shell around myself. Haven't written any songs since 'Sapper's Lullaby'. At the moment, I feel as if that fertile person was another man. No conspicuous acts of violence around the elections yet, though someone brought in a Taliban night letter this morning which warned people not to vote. Zia was scornful of the awful grammar and spelling in the letter.

The following morning life got interesting again – a bit too interesting. We were meeting with all the players to discuss election security. At 1000 hours the ANA intel officer got a call from one of his contacts down the valley.

'The Taliban has spread a rumour that coalition forces at COP Mashal have burned a Koran. There are around 600 men coming towards the base from the south-west Nyazi direction. Some of them are insurgents. They are carrying shovels, sticks and spears, and a burned copy of the Koran on a funeral stretcher.'

Ten minutes later, MDK got a call from a friend in town saying there was a mob of around 400 gathered in Ali Sherzai. Mullah Naim was telling them a Koran had been burned in the Baluchi.

At 1034, Mohammad Gul got a call from the Nyazi ANP checkpoint; the crowd from the south-west was getting closer and were armed.

The calls kept coming. There was a tsunami of men coming our way from two directions and they were angry. We were informed that the guys at COP Mashal had burned some notebooks the day before but the interpreter made sure they weren't Korans. The insurgents were clearly distorting the facts and peddling rumours to fan the flames of revulsion over the 'Burn a Koran Day'. We clarified all this with MDK, and he left the base to talk to the mob.

JR, ever mindful of his brief to keep the Afghans running the show, asked the ANA operations officer what he thought we should do. He replied, 'Let's just wait it out, let it run its course. That's what happened the other day.'

MDK called. He had tried to explain the situation to the mob in Ali Sherzai, but they had moved on him. His men had cocked their weapons, at which point the mob had turned around and started heading towards FOB Mirwais. He told us to get ready for anything. The protesters had at least ten AK-47s and intended to use them. He had secured himself in the White Compound.

JR had his men rig up in body armour and head into the guard towers. I got up on the roof of my office Drehtainer and saw a sea of men coming towards the base from Ali Sherzai – and another converging from the west. There must've been about 1000 all up. Mod saw me up there and suggested it would be a good idea if I stayed inside the office. This seemed sound advice.

Zia and I were sitting in there at 1145 when The Sarge came in and placed a call to Germany to talk to his wife (for chrissakes!). From outside, we could hear the crowd shouting and drawing nearer. At 1154, we heard what sounded like the beginning of a hailstorm. It turned into a full-on hailstorm as 1000 protesters began throwing rocks. Rocks were literally raining on the base. Zia and I were frightened and apprehensive, but giggling, as I recall. Meanwhile, the guys up in the guard towers were lying flat below the parapet to avoid being struck. This went on for a few minutes.

Then we heard a single shot, followed by bursts of automatic gunfire. It sounded like AK-47s. Then some heavier guns. The ANA guys, it turned out, were shooting 'Beirut style', rifles over the wall, head below, with no idea where the rounds were going. Then a couple of American M4s chimed in. The protesters dispersed, some of them through Ali Sherzai, where they trashed and looted the bazaar on their way to the White Compound.

MDK called at 1241 to say the protesters had come at the White Compound and that he and the mayor and his guards opened fire. The shots had killed two and wounded two others. The protesters had gone to the mosque near the bazaar, where the mullah was winding them up to get their weapons and embark on jihad.

Zia and I walked out of the office container; the base was a mess. Rocks the size of golf balls and apples carpeted the ground. The front and side gates were dented and riddled with bullet holes. No one on the base had been seriously hurt but there were cuts and bruises. The mood was one of hilarity and relief, a sort of astonishment at the biblical spectacle that had just unfolded.

Soldiers were swapping accounts of what they had just seen, trying to piece it all together. JR said that when the ANA intelligence officer saw the hordes breaking into the ANA storage container out the front of the compound, he ran outside with pistol drawn, shooting it Hollywood style (sideways) over the heads of the 'rioters' to stop them stealing ANA uniforms. But he ran out of ammo and had to beat a hasty retreat. He was pelted with rocks and nearly consumed by the swarming mass. JR had dragged him back into the compound and slammed the gate shut.

Corporal Torres came into the office with one of our privates and explained to Willie and me that the young soldier had seen a protester raise his weapon towards the guard tower, had gained permission to fire, then fired a single round through the man's clavicle. He guessed the man died but the body disappeared into the crowd, leaving only bloodstains in the dirt outside the gate.

I wrote up the incident in a single-paragraph report and emailed it to the PRT headquarters. These kind of incidents were often investigated; the paper trail needed to be in order.

That afternoon, many of the protesters regathered in the local mosque. We heard one of the mullahs was trying to incite them to rally again, but they seemed to have lost their enthusiasm. At the end of the day, five lay dead. For many practical reasons, Muslims bury their dead quickly, so preparations needed to be made.

The following morning a couple of NGO workers came in to talk about the previous day's events – the Chora Rock Show, as the staff in the command post were calling it.

'Only twenty or so of the protesters were insurgents,' said one of the men. 'The rest were just local guys deceived in the name of Islam. Their real aim was to disrupt the elections. It was well planned.

'We think that, in the end, three men were killed and four wounded outside your base, and two more were killed outside the White Compound. Your soldiers and the ANA were very patient. In the end, it was good that you opened fire when you did; otherwise more would have been killed.'

He explained that some mullahs would use today's burial as an opportunity to preach against the government.

'Malim Sadiq has been talking to people, trying to calm them down. He is very much in favour of the government; if we lose him, this area will fall to insurgents.'

Later in the morning, MDK dropped by.

'Mullah Mohammad Hassan is preaching in public in Konji. Mullah Nooradin is driving around with a loudspeaker in Pay Kelah saying the usual stuff. I think people are tired of it. They're looking at yesterday and wondering whether it was worth the deaths. It was he who moved the people up from the Baluchi yesterday.

'We talked to them back on 10 September, and showed them respect, but they didn't understand. We need to get better at working with the mullahs. Let's work on this after the elections.'

I asked if he knew of any insurgent plans for election day.

He said he had heard there was a plan to fire rockets and mortars from Nyazi.

'I will get together with Malim Sadiq and patrol out there to try to encourage people to vote. With my thirty guys, if you can get me ten coalition soldiers and some ANA, we will go out there this afternoon. If we can take them on, good; if they run and hide, well, at least it will give the local nationals confidence to vote tomorrow.'

I went to JR with this suggestion. After some cajoling of the ANA colonel, it was agreed and we sent out two bricks plus ANA. They went through the Achekzai area with MDK's men that afternoon. Nothing happened. The insurgents just melted away. They were bound to come out again at night.

That evening at 1730, they fired a rocket from Nyazi in the direction of the base, but it landed in the valley without detonating.

❖

And so it was that we limped into election day. I woke early on account of having eaten too much. It was a beautiful morning, a little cool, with a slight breeze; all was quiet. At 0900 the guys at the tower called for Zia and me. There was a national at the gate wanting to see 'the PRT'. We went down to meet a tired-looking man in his mid-thirties accompanied by his two sons: a robust little boy of about five and his younger brother, who looked to be in a bad way. I went and found 'Doc', the corporal trained as a medic who ran the regimental aid post.

'They're always fuckin' coming around wanting pharmaceut-
icals,' he snapped. 'I suppose I'd better see them.' Doc was actually
a softy and had saved the lives of a number of local nationals during
his tour.

Zia and I brought the man and his boys up to the RAP, then
I got on with my day.

MDK dropped in at 1200. He said Malim Sadiq had asked him
to get voters mobilised in the Achekzai area. He asked JR for a
little firepower for a patrol.

By 1330, it was hot and I was tired, so I went for a nap in the
tent. Corporal Torres had the same idea. As I was drifting off to
sleep, I heard the angry scream and whistle of an incoming rocket.
I threw myself out of bed and flat on the floor as the thing flew
overhead and landed somewhere, elsewhere. Torres had done
the same; there was a moment of comedy as he and I exchanged
foolish grins while lying there side by side in our underwear.
Rockets are funny – when they miss.

Later in the afternoon I went down to the command post to
see what was going on. They said that apart from the rockets, all
was quiet. There was such a concentration of Afghan National
Security Forces around the polling stations that the insurgents
weren't going to risk taking them on directly. The turnout was
looking modest but not completely embarrassing.

I was walking up towards the shitters near the RAP when I
ran into the Doc.

'How's that little kid who came in this morning?'

'Ah, they always bring 'em in too fuckin' late. I did what I
could.' He shook his head and walked away.

I turned to see the man and his older son walking towards me
down the slope from the aid post. He was pushing a wheelbarrow,
the contents covered with a hessian sack, the younger boy's hat on
top. I put my hand on my heart and bowed my head in an Afghan

gesture of respect. He nodded faintly enough to acknowledge me and kept going down the hill to the gate, head up, eyes forward, the older son walking by his side, one hand on the handle of the barrow. I watched as the guard opened the gate for them, bowing his head to the man as he made his way out and home to bury the child.

'They just get on with it,' I thought to myself.

❖

19 September, 1120 hours

In the back of a Bushmaster leaving Chora en route for decompression leave via Tarin Kowt, Kandahar, Kabul, Dubai and Sydney. As I got in the Bushy this morning the vehicle commander said, 'This time no spewy spewy!' The last time I took a ride down south in a convoy I had eaten oily peanuts before I got on board, and ended up chundering in my helmet just before we reached COP Buman. Legend of this has clearly got around. Anyway, my shins are dusty and itchy, fingernails are split, my tennis elbow is hurting, I'm still constipated and my left boot is fucked – the sole is coming off the leather. My guitar is dried out, warped and untunable. I'm ready for a break.

It's a big convoy including the ANA. We're chaperoning the ballot boxes back south to Tarin Kowt. We stopped at the Chora crossing because the ANA spotted the chassis of the rocket fired yesterday and wanted to check it out. Now we are stopped again on the outskirts of TK because a report is coming in of a TIC at the governor's compound.

By the time the convoy got to MNBTK I was running late for the flight to Kandahar. I had them drop me at the flight line and got straight on the bird without touching base with Bernard. I landed at Kandahar Airfield and went to Camp Baker, where I slept for a couple of hours. I woke in the late afternoon, then bought a watch to replace the one that had disintegrated in the sweat and dust of a summer at FOB Mirwais. I was in such a daze, and in awe of retail, that I left my credit card in the shop. I ate and went back to sleep and woke late the next morning and had to hustle out to Taliban Last Stand Terminal. The flight to Kabul was to be a circuitous one, via Lashkar Gah, Herat and Mazar-e-Sharif – and it was delayed. 'Hurry up and wait,' as they say in the military. A marine dropped his duffle bag near mine and sat down. He looked exhausted. We got talking for want of anything else to do. He was about to go out on two weeks' leave after eight months at a FOB. We swapped stories of FOB life. It was another world out there.

On the five flights it took me to get home, I wrote most of this song.

Taliban Fighting Man

There's no airport bar in Kandahar where the C-130s land
It was hot as hell and in that concrete shell where the Taliban took
    a last stand
I was staring at the screen of the Coke machine with a weariness
    deep in my bones
Waiting out there for a bird to take me home

Onto the scene came a big marine and sat down next to me
He said, 'The name is Roy and I'm here deployed with the
    Delta Company

We had just got back from northern Iraq when the general got on
the phone
Now I've got two weeks' leave up my sleeve and I'm waiting for
the bird back home

'Well I fought this year from Khush Khadir down to Kandahar
A lotta fighting patrols but as far as I know I ain't been killed so far
Gotta trust in fate but I step out of the gate with my M4 clean
and honed
Man, so much fun, who the hell would want to go home?

'Us boys go strange living down range no women there to keep
you tame
You shit in a bag, gotta read your dog tag to remember your own
first name
And sharing a tent with fifteen men means you never have to
feel alone
Man, so many friends, who the hell would want to go home

'But when the rounds come in and the fifty-cals spin and your
bowels move with the fear
You learn to depend on those new best friends 'cause your
mother cannot help you here
And if you come to harm it's those brothers in arms who gonna
pack your toothbrush and comb
Into a box, with your iPod and socks when they send your busted
body back home

'I got a pissed-off wife but I guess that's life for a Taliban
fighting man
She's got her hands full putting kids through school, God I do my
best to understand

When she gets on the phone saying how's it goin', man I don't
　　wanna get her all stressed
But how to explain that the two-way range can put a boy a little
　　on edge

'Home on leave brings some reprieve but the couple weeks can
　　leave you cold
Get a new tattoo, jetlagged and confused, not to mention
　　my six-year-old
Who knows his dad from a photograph and a voice on the end of
　　the phone
Saying, 'Pretty soon, son, your daddy'll be coming on home'

'Still this ain't no blues, it's the life that I choose of a Taliban
　　fighting man
Some days it's a joy being out here with the boys hanging with
　　my brotherly band
I do my best and I don't forget it was them who threw the
　　first stone
Man, so much fun, who the hell would want to go home
So much fun, who the hell would want to go home'

Then his flight got called and he stood up tall and said, 'I'd best be
　　on my way'
I said good luck because I know it could suck being home for just
　　fourteen days
There's war and peace but the war don't cease when you're back
　　in the domestic zone
So much fun, who the hell would want to go home?!
So much fun, who the hell would want to go home?!

I wrote this rap to a riff I came up with on the banjo while
rehearsing with the Spooky Men's Chorale a year beforehand.

After recording the banjo part and the rhythm section, I sent an MP3 of the mix to US songwriter Jonathan Byrd, whom I gigged with a little in the US in 2007, to sing the part of the US marine. He recorded the vocal take in a friend's bedroom studio while on tour in Toronto. Jonathan did some time in the US Army before getting into music, and generally does a good line in 'ornery', so I had a feeling he would nail the part of 'Roy'.

Truth to tell, only a few verses of this song actually came out of that conversation at Kandahar airfield. 'Roy' is a composite character made up of that marine, The Sarge, Willie Cooper and a dozen other US soldiers I met. A few lines came from Jeremy Goodnight, in particular the term 'spinning the fifty-cals', which I heard him use to describe the way the rear gunner of an MRAP vehicle worked the mounted machine gun when a supply convoy he'd led in Iraq was busting through an ambush. They didn't know where the incoming rounds were coming from so they just 'spun the fifty-cals' around, firing in all directions.

The song is set in a single conversation. Why? Because, as Leonard Cohen puts it, 'In songwriting, the most specific solution is the most universal.' But friends I worked with over there reckon they met this guy a hundred times. There are themes in the song common to the experience of US soldiers.

My mate Mike Gisick joined the US Army in 1999, then got out and worked as a journalist embedded with US troops in Iraq and Afghanistan at a number of FOBs. He met an Australian diplomat on his travels and now lives with her in Canberra while writing a PhD thesis on Iraq and Afghanistan veterans. With easy access to telephones and social media, he talks about the 'collapse of the distance between war and home. For the World War II guys it was a much more enclosed experience. They went away, did what they did, and never talked much about it when they got home.' I'm sure there are psychological problems with this approach in terms of the isolation that generation of veterans felt for never sharing their experiences with family. On the other hand, it might have been an easier way to fight a war – there was a practical logic behind the old school approach.

More broadly, the engagements in Iraq and Afghanistan have taken their toll on people and their families in the US Army. Divorce rates in the US military went up 42 per cent between 2001 and 2011, according to US defence department figures. Nearly four in ten (37 per cent) of post-9/11 veterans say that, whether or not they were formally diagnosed, they believe they have suffered from post-traumatic stress. Among veterans who served prior to 9/11, just 16 per cent say the same.

And yet, for all this, soldiers enjoy soldiering. The same study revealed that 96 per cent of veterans who served on active duty in the post-9/11 era were proud of their service. The bonds of friendship formed out on the FOBs are like no other. War correspondent Dexter Filkins argued in a recent article on post-traumatic stress disorder that part of the problem for soldiers coming home was leaving the camaraderie of their wolf pack for the relative isolation of suburban homes. In a recent Australian documentary screened on ABC TV, Warrant Officer 'R' was quoted as saying that, after twenty days of solid fighting, 'We learned to be a family of blokes, each loyal to each other. And I think there were guys who, all of a sudden, realised they liked this shit!'

CHAPTER 11

ZEEBRUGGE FOB

*The death of a mate sharpens your fighting urge. You really
want to take it to the people who did this to your friends.*

CAPTAIN JAMES FANNING, 6 RAR,
IN *AFGHANISTAN: INSIDE AUSTRALIA'S WAR* (ABC-TV)

*So when I've had enough and can't take any
more and home is where I want to be
I go clean my weapon and back up for more . . .*

FRED SMITH, 'ZEEBRUGGE FOB'

THE PROCESS OF WRITING A SONG ALWAYS STARTS SOMEWHERE;
it doesn't seem to matter where. A horse appears in front of you:
a melody, guitar riff, phrase or character drifts into your brain.
You get on that horse, leave the stable, keep your hands loose on
the reins and see where you wind up.

The song 'Zeebrugge FOB' had its genesis in a fingerpicked
guitar riff that came to me around 2007. Then, in October 2010,
the title 'Helmand PRT' began appearing in my notebooks.
The sketches that followed described the hardships of the work

environment as I imagined it to be for the Helmand Provincial Reconstruction Team, the civil–military team doing the same political and development work as us, but in neighbouring Helmand Province.

Helmand Province abuts the western border of Uruzgan. Some evenings in Tarin Kowt I would get up on the roof of the office container to watch the sun set over the mountains. I'd wonder what was going on out west in the province that lay beyond Deh Rawud District. Then, at the following morning's briefing, I would find out. The 2 Shop would kick off every DCU with a quick sweep of events around Regional Command South, mostly unhappy. My notes for the day often began, as they did on 22 March, with 'Helmand . . . IED . . . 12 CivCas', or 24 March: 'Helmand . . . 1xUSMC KIA'.

At the Provincial Security Council meetings, the local leaders often complained about the impossibility of preventing insurgent leaders from coming across the border from Helmand. They said it would always be hard to secure Uruzgan while Helmand remained an insurgent stronghold. And it was.

In 2005, the Taliban was making a comeback across Afghanistan, particularly in rural areas in the south. In response to this resurgence, ISAF muscled up under NATO leadership. US troop numbers grew, and coalition members, including the UK, France, Germany, Denmark, New Zealand and Canada – the latter two conscious that, having sat out Iraq, they were a bit exposed with Washington – offered to take on specific provinces.

In the south, the Canadians took the lead in Kandahar Province. Their mission in the province was controversial at home and tough on the ground. In this, the spiritual homeland of the Taliban, Canada lost 155 soldiers, one media reporter, one diplomat and two aid workers before withdrawing in accordance with a pre-agreed timetable in 2011.

The story of how we came to be in Uruzgan is an interesting one. Dad was Secretary of the Department of Defence in 2005, and his account of the decision-making process reflects the combination of strategic policy thinking, coalition negotiations and circumstances that got us into the province.

'By mid-2005, with the Taliban resurgent, ISAF coalition members had begun deploying forces and aid teams into key provinces. The UK, Germany, France, Denmark, Canada and New Zealand, among others, had already joined the United States in the field, and so the Netherlands and Australia began considering what they should do as members of the coalition. It wasn't so much a matter of direct "pressure" from the United States or NATO, more a judgement that as members of a community with a continuing shared interest in Afghanistan we needed to join the others and do more to help meet the challenge.

'The Dutch were prepared to accept leadership of a province, but wanted a "tier one" partner to share the load. Australia was still in Iraq and, with ADF and civilian agencies now in the Solomon Islands as well, we didn't want to take on a province on our own, but we were prepared to join a "tier one" partner. And so, with the Brits and Americans encouraging the union, and the Afghan government pleased to have another base covered, the Netherlands and Australia found each other in Uruzgan.'

Specifically, the Australian government agreed to send in a 300-strong Reconstruction Task Force, mostly military engineers focused on building schools, hospitals and roads, to work alongside 2000 Dutch soldiers in Task Force Uruzgan.

Meanwhile, the Brits took on Helmand. It was an unhappy marriage from the start. The British had a 'reputational problem' across southern Afghanistan which went back to the nineteenth century: in July 1880, a battle took place at the village of Maiwand in Kandahar Province, just east of the Helmand border, in which

Afghan forces defeated two brigades of British soldiers, losing 2500 fighters in the process. The Battle of Maiwand is legendary in Afghanistan partly for the role the poets ascribe to a woman named Malalai. There to tend to the wounded, she saw the battle turning against the Afghans, picked up a flag from a slain standard-bearer, removed her veil and rallied the troops to an improbable victory. The battle is seen as emblematic of Afghan resilience against the dreaded British, and in Helmand Province, 'son of an Englishman' is the most grievous insult.

Greybeards in Helmand had fonder memories of the Americans. In the early years of the Cold War, the US and Soviet Union were competing for influence in Afghanistan. The Russians were mostly active in the north, while the Americans focused on the south, engaging in big infrastructure projects and irrigation. The Kajaki Dam, built by USAID in 1953, was reasonably functional in providing electricity to Kandahar and much of Helmand. The irrigation projects were less successful as the soil in the Helmand River Valley proved unsuitable for vegetables but pretty good for opium poppies. The Helmand opium trade developed, mostly in the hands of such evil geniuses as the Akhundzada family.

When the Communists came to power in Kabul in 1978, they implemented a land reform campaign that unsettled the dominance of the wealthy landowners, the khans, who had kept things stitched up for centuries. The power vacuum was filled by mullahs and upstart warlords who became 'commanders' in the fight against the Russian occupation. In Helmand, Mullah Nasim Akhundzada emerged to become leader of the Alizai tribe by rallying conservative Helmandis resentful of the modernist reforms of the government, and by killing off rivals for the position. Opium was the perfect cash crop to fund his militia, and he monopolised the trade. He issued a religious decree saying it was permissible for farmers to grow poppies. He paid farmers to plant it and then bought the crop at a low price. He set up a network of processing laboratories driven by electricity from the dam.

After Nasim was shot in Pakistan in 1990, his nephew, Sher Mohammad Akhundzada (SMA), took over the family business. SMA forged an alliance with the Karzai family. In 2001, when Hamid Karzai became interim president of Afghanistan, SMA was appointed governor of Helmand.

Helmand was the last province to be surrendered by the Taliban. When they left, SMA moved into the provincial capital, Lashkar Gah, and built a ruling alliance with two other tribes. He appointed the head of Noorzai tribe as police chief and the leader of the Alikozai as chief of intelligence, and all government positions, including police, went to members of those three tribes. This trinity was fiercely anti-Taliban, so the smattering of US Special Forces in the province saw them as perfect partners in getting the bad guys. This was not good news for SMA's enemies, principally from the Ishaqzai and Noorzai tribes, which had been left out of this arrangement. SMA used the relationship to monopolise the Helmand drug trade, which by then was providing 40 per cent of the world's opium supply.

In 2002, Taliban leaders were working to infiltrate southern Afghanistan. They had no joy in Kandahar but got immediate traction in Helmand, particularly among young men from the Ishaqzai and Noorzai tribes and others who had been preyed on by the new Helmand trinity. By 2005, Helmand had become a problem, with the Taliban holding districts in the north of the province and conducting regular large-scale attacks on local police.

From their experiences from Malaya through to Iraq, the British had written the proverbial manual on counterinsurgency, and read it too. It said the key to counterinsurgency was having a credible local government to work with. SMA clearly didn't fit the bill, so when they agreed to take on Helmand Province it was on the condition that he be removed from the governorship. President Karzai reluctantly agreed and shifted SMA to a senate sinecure. SMA was displeased and, according to one account, sent 3000 of his militia to join the Taliban, giving them an entree to the drug trade. The UK had also very publicly agreed to be the ISAF lead on counter-narcotics, a fact the Taliban propaganda machine used to convince Helmand farmers that the Brits were their enemies. So with numbers and narrative on their side, the Taliban launched a massive offensive in Helmand, just as the Brits were arriving.

British defence secretary John Reid was famously quoted as saying, 'If we came for three years here to accomplish our mission, and had not fired a shot by the end of that, we would be very happy indeed.' It didn't work out that way. In their first year in Helmand, British forces fired four million rounds, mostly just defending themselves. Their original strategy had been to concentrate on the provincial capital, Lashkar Gah, and create an 'inkspot' of security and prosperity that would spread. But under pressure from Karzai and the Americans, the British quickly abandoned this in favour of a 'platoon house strategy' with soldiers spread thinly across police stations and government buildings around the province. Low in numbers and equipped only with open-top vehicles, they were unable to get out and dominate the terrain. They soon became the prey, not the predator, hunkered down behind sandbags, eating rations, defecating into plastic bags and fighting for days on end just to avoid being overrun.

Defending the Kajaki Dam was a priority for the British and ISAF. By 2008, the dam was badly run down but still producing electricity. USAID lined up a Chinese contractor to provide a third turbine to get electricity production up for Kandahar and Helmand. In September that year, 4000 British troops were pulled off-line to support a massive operation: a convoy to haul a thirty-tonne turbine 100 kilometres across Taliban-infested desert to Kajaki.

That turbine was never properly installed, but two extant turbines were refurbished and running successfully enough to antagonise the Taliban. So the Brits set up a forward operating base called Zeebrugge to defend the dam from hostile local insurgents.

In early 2010, 10,000 US Marines poured into Helmand Province as part of President Obama's '30,000-man surge', taking over FOB Zeebrugge. It brought to mind a comment from Pink Floyd's Oxford-educated manager Peter Jenner, whose touring philosophy for the band was: 'Go where the love is, man!' It seemed to me that the love was not in Helmand.

Some perverse mechanisms lead to this heavy investment in Helmand: the Marines had been released from Iraq, and 10,000 of them were ready and available to populate President Obama's promised surge. But the Marines don't like working in the same sandpit as other kids, and demanded their own patch. Helmand was the only available battle space big enough and the Brits were willing to hand it over. So the Marines rolled en masse into this hostile province. In the autumn of 2010, in the Sangin District alone, home to the Kajaki Dam, twenty-nine marines were killed and thirty lost both legs.

❖

Flying overnight to Kandahar from Istanbul, all this history was on my mind as I looked out the window down at the Helmand River Valley, sparkling in the early morning light. I was returning from a few weeks off, initially spent in Canberra recovering from FOB Mirwais, followed by a week-long tour of cafes and military bases in the Netherlands, where 'the Dixi song' had earned me some minor celebrity.

I wasted no time in getting onto a bird to TK. I was looking forward to getting back into it. It wasn't certain whether I would be based in Tarin Kowt or Chora, but I was hopeful it would be the latter as I was missing the country air.

I arrived in TK on the morning of 16 November 2010, dropped off my bag in Chalet 13, and made my way to the PRT. I found Bernard in his office container. He looked tired.

'So, you want me up in Chora?' I asked hopefully.

'You're not going anywhere! It's flat strap here. John Cavanagh is out in Deh Rawud, I'm going on leave in a week and the re-inforcements I was expecting from Canberra haven't arrived.'

Four hours later, I was on a chopper to Chora. This would be funny, if it weren't for the backstory: a suicide bomber had killed Malim Sadiq. Sadiq had been hosting an Eid celebration, and the bomber had somehow got in through the side gate. Sadiq had apparently turned to welcome the young visitor just as he detonated his vest.

MDK was staying in his compound near Tarin Kowt at the time. He asked to be flown up to Chora immediately, so we lined him up a ride on a Chinook that was servicing the province that afternoon.

'There might be value in having me chaperon MDK up to Mirwais,' I said to Bernard, 'to facilitate and keep an eye on things.'

'Okay, but you are not to leave the FOB!' he said.

By mid-afternoon I was clambering onto the back of a Chinook with MDK and three of his bodyguards, all armed with AKs.

The loadmaster was wearing a pimped-up helmet and a facemask with ghoulish skeleton teeth. Over the throb of the twin rotors he yelled: 'Kandahar?'

'No!' I yelled back, 'Chora, FOB Mirwais!'

'We just been there!'

'We gotta go back. Suicide IED – these guys need to get there.'

He checked with his pilots through his headset, turned and gave me the thumbs-up, and we took off. The rear gunner had the back ramp down and was sitting with his legs astride his mounted machine gun, his feet dangling in thin air. We chugged up through the Baluchi Valley, through the Chora saddle and around the bowl, landing at FOB Mirwais twenty minutes later.

I walked MDK and his shooters down to the command post, where we met the new commanding officer, then proceeded straight to the front gate, where a crowd of Barakzai tribesmen was waiting. They took MDK away.

I went up to the PRT office. Willie Cooper and the team had apparently all made it home unharmed. John Ward, a smart young lieutenant, a reservist and lawyer from Baltimore, was now leading the PRT contingent. My AusAID mate, John Morley, was getting up there every couple of weeks; he and Ward seemed to be getting some traction in the district. In addition to assisting in the completion of a number of Dutch projects, they had a dozen or so new ones, continuing to spend the abundant and flexible US military money with the benefit of John Morley's development experience – ensuring, for example, that the projects were evenly spread across factions in the valley. Politics is everything.

A new lieutenant had replaced LT running the police mentoring team, but The Sarge was still around. They'd lost a man in an IED strike near Nyazi a month before. Apparently The Sarge had been out front of the patrol and had stepped right over the concealed bomb, but the man behind him stepped right on it and was 'demolished'. The Sarge had been bowled over by the blast. He seemed okay to me, actually better than before, but LT was apparently pretty affected by the death and was licking his wounds in Tarin Kowt.

Just before dinner, I was meeting with the old ANA commander, Colonel Gul Agha, when the ANA intelligence officer walked in and said they had brought the head and legs of the suicide bomber onto the base. 'Chuck it in the bin!' said Gul Agha. He seemed unusually shaken by events. He had been in Chora two years and understood the death of Sadiq was a serious blow: who was going to pay and command Sadiq's militia? Who would inherit his land? He knew these questions of political economy would have implications for security in the valley.

The new PRT team treated me well and had set aside my old bedspace. Some positive word seemed to have spread about me, which was gratifying. Following the after-dinner brief, Lieutenant Ward and I went to the office and yarned a bit about Chora politics. As we were talking, his sergeant came in and said, 'Hey, boss, I got some photographs of the suicide bomber's head!'

He handed Ward his digital camera and John took a look.

'Ooh gross. You wanna see, Mr Fred?'

'No, thank you.'

Some people get by in a war zone by being tough, others by knowing their limits.

At 1100 the following morning, Colonel Gul Agha came back from Malim Sadiq's place, where a couple of hundred people were gathered for prayers and condolences. He said the family had decided to bury the body last night just before sunset; now would be the right time to convey condolences. Our weapons inspection team was keen to go over the bombsite for forensics and intelligence before too much changed. A mission was ready to go within half an hour.

I was torn. Bernard's last words were fresh in my ears: 'You are not to leave the FOB!' But according to Gul Agha, Sadiq's militia had the place all locked down. I knew I'd count my manhood cheaply if I didn't go. So I put on my body armour and joined a twenty-strong packet that rolled out the gate just before midday.

It was a beautiful autumn morning, the sun shining down on the valley and that crystal-clear light for which Chora is legendary. It felt good to be out in the countryside with the guys again.

We arrived at Sadiq's compound to find eighty men in turbans sitting quietly at lunch. We went into a small room and talked to MDK. He said the suicide bomber was a young man from Chora. This was unusual. Suicide bombers were always young men, but usually sent from Pakistan. He said they would wait until Abdul Khaliq arrived before trying to think their way forward through the bigger issues. We had lunch while the inspection team did its work, then headed home.

I spent the next couple of days kicking around FOB Mirwais. 'Movember' was in full swing and there were some filthy moustaches loitering beneath the noses of many of the Aussie soldiers. The FOB had become a more social place; the fresh rotation of Australians seemed to be getting on well with the Americans. On Thursday night, social events in the recreation room featured the final of a US vs Australia ping-pong tournament, followed by the 'tough guy competition'. An Aussie corporal was pushed forward and pitted against a muscular American private. Two bottles of maple syrup materialised and the parameters of the contest became clear.

'Three! Two! One! SKOL!'

It was all over in five seconds. The young digger slammed the bottle down on the table, his face at once displaying triumph and nausea. He punched the air, the boys went nuts, then he reeled out of the recreation room to chunder on the rocks.

The following morning, I flew out of FOB Mirwais, never to return.

❖

Back in TK there was some follow-up to the killing of Sadiq. There were rumours that the guard who should have been at the gate had a brother who worked for MK, so he might have been influenced. There were reports the insurgent leader from the area had claimed responsibility for the killing. But, as was often the case with assassinations in Afghanistan, we never got to the bottom of it.

Sadiq's death aside, I have fond memories of my last two months working in the PRT in Tarin Kowt. For my first year in Uruzgan I had worked alone, something of an outsider, with no formal position in the Dutch or Australian food chains. But now I was part of the PRT team and, in relative terms, a veteran campaigner. I was comfortable and secure in the role and had developed a good knowledge of the province, as well as some sound instincts.

Bernard, who had been there since June, left on extended leave in mid-November. Luke, an AusAID officer, took over leadership of the PRT. We got along well, although he was still working out his relationship with the commander of Combined Team – Uruzgan, US Colonel Jim Creighton.

Jim was everything an American colonel should be: square-shouldered, square-jawed, straight talking. He wanted to fix the province yesterday. 'Get 'er done' was his motto, and he often did. Our role was to encourage him to be patient. Though forceful, he was approachable and open to discussion and debate up to the point at which he made his decision, usually informed by an American football analogy. After all, life in Afghanistan was a contest.

Within the DFAT team in the PRT, I focused on some basic office logistical matters that no one else had had time to attend to. At the time we were still borrowing terps from the ADF on an ad hoc basis. We needed our own interpreters and they needed to be good. We were having daily conversations with ranking officials and tribal leaders on sensitive political issues which required strong language skills and a capacity for handling nuance, as well as a level of decorum and savoir faire. Zia came back from leave in late November and we kept him down in Tarin Kowt for this reason.

The PsyOps team were a friendly bunch and let us use the printer in their office on the other side of the headquarters complex. One day, I had to print a translation of a meeting report in a hurry. I grabbed Zia and we ran out the back gate and past the Dixis, only to realise I had forgotten the thumb drive with the document on it. As I turned back to the office, Zia said: 'Hastee makes wastee, sir.'

'What?'

'Hastee makes wastee,' he repeated.

'Oh, haste makes waste – very true, thank you,' I said, realising he had absorbed this piece of wisdom by reading the words, not hearing them spoken.

The PsyOps office staff didn't respond when I rang the buzzer, so I began climbing the gate.

'Sir,' said Zia, 'I do not think this is very good idea.'

'It's okay,' I said. 'I used to climb trees all the time when I was a boy, Zia.' Then 'Aargh . . . thud!'

As I went to leap down, my trouser leg got caught in the barbed wire and I fell a couple of metres face first onto the gravel.

'Are you okay, sir?' I heard Zia say from the other side of the gate.

A good interpreter was an adviser as well as a translator.

After that, I got serious with the embassy and they sent me three printers, five smart office chairs and some laptops. And I focused on building a small cadre of interpreters for the PRT. I was pretty familiar with the pool of terps around the base from the concerts at PRT House. I identified Zia and three others who had the chops. I negotiated their release from army contracts, set up a contract with the embassy through a third-party supplier, trebled their wages and got them working for the PRT. They remained with the PRT until the end of the mission and were valued as translators, advisers and friends by my successors.

Logistics aside, there was meaty political work to be done. Back in the capitals, Dad – when he wasn't being quoted in WikiLeaks – and his coterie of special representatives from participating nations were busy encouraging and finding funds for an Afghan-led reconciliation and reintegration program. In the early phase of the war there had been no deliberate approach to bringing former Taliban into the government and the political process. As a result, many of them who might have liked to join the government remained out in the cold – the enemy – simply because they saw no other option. And it didn't take long for the battle lines to harden again.

Some in Afghanistan, and in Washington, argued we should simply keep a foot on the throat of the Taliban until they disintegrated or surrendered. But it was becoming increasingly clear that we couldn't kill them all, and that they weren't going away. So November and December 2010 were full of meetings about the establishment of a provincial secretariat for the Afghan Peace and Reintegration Program, and discussions on low-key approaches for bringing fighters down from the mountains back into their villages and communities.

There was also the ongoing work of implementing the political strategy. Of the Popalzai warlords, JMK's influence seemed to be waning as he spent more time in Kabul. MK's influence continued to rise. Colonel Creighton and Task Force 66's commander met with him regularly, so at the very least, he knew what behaviours we wanted to hear and see. There was debate on base as to whether we should promote the possibility of MK being made the provincial chief of police.

Meanwhile, we were engaging intensively with the non-Popalzai leaders to keep the relationships we'd inherited from the Dutch in good order. It seemed to be working. None had defected to the Taliban and our conversations with MDK, MNKT and other tribal leaders in the Dorafshan/Baluchi Valley seemed to be improving prospects for completion of the Road to Chora.

Overall, the security situation in the province also seemed to be improving. With Task Force 66's successes in 'counter-leadership' and Aussie regular forces partnering with the ANA and pushing the FOBs out into the valleys, insurgents were generally having a hard time of it. The American elements were working well with the ANP.

A new area of work for DFAT officers was detainee monitoring. The Dutch had managed the problem of handling PUCs (persons under custody – prisoners), but when they left, the Australian government had to take this on. The Abu Ghraib torture scandal in Iraq had reminded us just how sensitive this stuff could be, so the government went for a gold standard approach, building a first-world-standard remand centre, bringing in ten military police officers and getting DFAT involved to provide an additional and independent layer of accountability.

When our soldiers captured suspected Taliban, legally we could only hold them for seventy-two hours before passing them on to Afghan authorities for prosecution. We were only able to assemble a decent evidence brief on a small portion of those 'PUCked'; the rest we had no choice but to let go. We took responsibility for those we passed on to the Afghan justice system, setting up Excel spreadsheets on which to track their progress from the Tarin Kowt prison up to Kabul and visiting them regularly.

Every week I would get together with the Task Force 66 legal officer (TF66 did most of the PUCking) and we'd go out to the prison in town. The prison warden would bring in the handcuffed prisoner. He would sit on the bed in the prison warden's office and I'd sit on a chair in front of him. I would ask a series of questions: Is the food okay? Are you being allowed to pray and wash? Have you been mistreated? Do you understand what you are being charged with? Most of them had no complaints but pleaded their innocence: 'I'm just a farmer, I don't know why I've been detained.' It wasn't my job to judge their innocence or otherwise, only to make sure they were being treated according to standards.

As part of a plan to bring the government to the people, Colonel Creighton hit on the notion of a province-wide meeting of tribal leaders in Tarin Kowt, a 'super shura'. He wanted to get it done before the end of the year. Acting Governor Khoday was broadly supportive but seemed to have reservations about the timing. We in the PRT thought it was a good idea but that we ought to wait until spring. It was too cold to have people camping and sitting outside the governor's compound and, in any case, we had heard via contacts that Khoday would soon be replaced. A new governor would need time to find his feet before embarking on a project like this.

Sure enough, on 1 December, a man named Omar Sherzad was named the new governor. I got hold of his phone number through UN contacts and put him in touch with our ambassador in Kabul, who had him over to dinner.

A week later, Sherzad arrived on the TK airstrip with an entourage of twenty. They weren't all his people; front and centre was JMK, obviously eager to be seen as the kingmaker. We all rolled down to the compound and into the governor's office; local officials and line directors were gathered to meet their new boss. JMK bustled in and made a great show of drawing back the chair behind the governor's desk and inviting Sherzad to sit. It was old school theatre of power, but one had the sense the ageing warlord was clutching at straws as his real power waned.

Sherzad turned out to be a sensible, thoughtful man with a quiet air of authority. He understood English better than he spoke it. He eschewed the turban, instead getting around bareheaded in a shalwar kameez teamed with a beige sports jacket, from the left shoulder of which dangled a beige rubber arm, the original having been forfeited in a battle against the Russians with the Mujahedin. Sherzad came from a wealthy family, which meant he could be independent from the powerbrokers in Uruzgan. The word on the street was that as he only had one arm, Uruzganis felt he would be less able to steal.

In his team was a young guy called Fazal, whose phone number I secured at the first opportunity and called regularly throughout the rest of December. We spent a lot of time working to help Sherzad settle into the job and offering him the benefit of our views on provincial politics, including the viability or otherwise of various incumbents in the district governor roles around the province. He was wise enough to know there was a lot he didn't know about Uruzgan politics and took time to reach his own conclusions. He told Luke and me that he wanted the super shura postponed until he had his kitchen organised, so the shura was delayed accordingly.

❖

December rolled on, busy but professionally rewarding. There was snow on the mountaintops surrounding the Tarin Kowt bowl, but still no rain. I was supposed leave before Christmas, but with Bernard still away and a new governor on board I thought it best to stick around until the New Year.

We had a great Christmas in Tarin Kowt. I put together a band for a concert. I found a couple of guitar players from the US Camp Cole, and we rehearsed with Zahir, the driver of the Dixi shit-sucking truck, on tabla percussion. I also found a backing vocalist called George, a grey-moustachioed, semi-senior citizen from Illinois, working on paving the TK airstrip and other infrastructure projects with the US Army Corps of Engineers. He had an endearing habit of bragging – of the twenty-nine dancing competition trophies he had won, his achievements in minor league baseball, the huge fish he caught in Alaska. The only way to stop him was to get him singing – that, or talking about Matiullah Khan. He regaled me with a detailed account of how MK had 'made his millions' providing 'security' for the road to Kandahar.

The ADF cooks made a great Christmas roast lunch. The gig that evening went nicely. Base Command chipped in with a couple of space heaters, which didn't really work on the concrete floor of Poppy's, so both audience and band were dressed in puffer jackets and beanies; it looked like a *South Park* convention. Rocky and I did an English/Pashtun version of 'Those Were the Days'. Twenty of the terps showed up and danced around. It was a nice way to bring the disparate elements of the base together on Christmas night. As the gig wound up, Colonel Creighton got up on stage and wished everyone Merry Christmas and said nice things about me being the heart and soul of the base.

The following day, a Boxing Day Test had been arranged on the newly paved airstrip: Aussies vs 5th Kandak of the ANA. We fielded first and I kept wicket. We had them 5 for 20 when the young captain, wearing a smart Afghan cricket tracksuit, smacked eleven sixes and took their total to 132 off twenty overs. I batted first drop and chipped the ball around in close for about ten overs, running singles. This was easy to do as the Afghans had set their field deep, believing everyone battled the way they did: *Allah Akhbar!* I was eventually run out. Having glanced the ball down to fine leg, the other batsmen called yes, then no, but by the time I got back to my crease the fieldsman had thrown the stumps down from forty metres away. (Afghans have great throwing arms; I remembered that from the Chora Rock Show.) Eventually we needed three runs off the last three balls. With the sun sinking over Deh Rawud and the temperature dropping, the padre went out to bat and by the grace of God (ours, not theirs) scored the winning runs off the second-last ball. The rowdy, 100-strong Afghan National Army supporters went very quiet, but at the end of the day, cricket was the winner.

❖

During my last five days in TK, I somehow got engaged in Deh Rawud district politics. Hamidi drew me into it. He said there was a smooth flow of insurgent leaders from Helmand through Deh Rawud to the Tangi Valley, in particular a talented bomb-maker living in the Tangi, who was active in the Deh Rawud district centre. I remembered my plan to write a song about Crash MacKinney, who'd perished in the Tangi five months beforehand at that battle in Derapet, but I really wasn't ready to write it and there was a lot to do in preparation for my final departure from Uruzgan.

On 31 December, I put Zia on a chopper back to Chora. It had been a little selfish keeping him down south for the month, but he had been helpful in building the relationship with the new governor.

The following morning, John Morley and Hamidi took me out to the flight line. I took one last glance at my beloved mountains and got on the Herc to Kabul.

The CPP guys picked me up from the airport and took me to the hostel where they lived. I went straight to bed, but awoke at 0230 and began hooking into my parting-shot cables, the subjects being the first month of Governor Sherzad; MK's business practices (drawing on my conversations with George and others); and MDK and Chora. This latter cable argued that there was a good chance MDK would be dismissed from the district governor position, and also a good chance he would be assassinated. We could do what we could in Kabul to protect his tenure, but there was not much we could do to prevent him being killed, short of putting him in cotton wool on the base, which would undermine his leadership role.

My last day in Kabul was 3 January. I scrambled around the embassy trying to sort out travel and leave arrangements before heading back to the hostel in the late afternoon for a meeting with MDK, who was in town. He arrived with MNKT and the ever-morose Senator Abdul Khaliq, who now had even more reason to be morose given the recent death of his brother, Malim Sadiq. There was a kerfuffle trying to get them in past the Gurkhas at the gate, resolved only when Khaliq surrendered the pistol he had wrapped in a pink handkerchief.

We were having a useful conversation about the security situation for the Baluchi when Bernard walked in, fresh from leave. We talked a little longer, then I escorted the leaders down to the gate. As we reached the inner gate, MDK turned and said, 'Okay, Farid, see you in TK.'

'I am leaving tomorrow,' I said.

'Leaving? For how long?'

'Forever.'

He shook his head. 'You guys always leave so fast.'

I had been there six months longer than most of my contemporaries and eight months longer than the military tours, but understood why he would see it that way.

We embraced in that Afghan way, and I watched him and his two friends walk down the chute to the front gate and out into the streets of Kabul. That was the last time I saw MDK.

Bernard and I got a lift to the embassy, which by now felt like a real embassy: a four-storey building with fifteen Australians and about as many Afghan staff. There was a recreation area/ dining hall on the ground floor, and the ambassador, Paul Foley, had been kind enough to organise a concert for me. About eighty people showed up from various embassies and ISAF headquarters, including some familiar folk like Hugh, who came with me to Afghanistan eighteen months earlier; he was now working in ISAF headquarters. Craig Coleman joined me on guitar and Lauren Patmore from the political section laid on some backing vocals.

By the time I finished playing it had blown up into a full-on party. Having gone for a couple of months without a drink, the temptation was to get amongst it, but I had work to finish so I ducked upstairs and spent an hour tidying up those three cables. Then Bernard grabbed me and we went back to the hostel for a drink in his room. We were joined by the journalist Bette Dam, a tall, intrepid Dutchwoman who got around Uruzgan in a Toyota Corolla. She and Bernard teased me for my dedication, referring to those last-minute cables.

'Well, that's Uruzgan,' I said. 'We get caught up in this little province only a mother could love. We start to care about it.'

'Most Afghans don't,' said Bernard. He recalled a visit he had made with the senior AusAID officer to an Afghan official in Kabul. On their arrival the local bureaucrat had sighed and said: 'You are Australian? You must be here to talk about Uruzgan.'

'Zia only knew Uruzgan existed because it was the final question in his high school geography exam to sort out the wheat from the chaff,' I chipped in. 'Knowing where Uruzgan is can win you a trivia competition in Afghanistan.'

'Not entirely true,' said Bette. 'Uruzgan is important in Afghan history. Mullah Omar grew up there, and of course Karzai began his rise to power in Uruzgan.' She had written a book on the topic.

'Well, we would never have been there if it wasn't for you Dutch,' I said.

She laughed. 'You could have done worse. You could have gone to Helmand!'

❖

The next morning at the airport my little bag of harmonicas was deemed suspicious by the baggage-scanning machine: on its screen the mouth harps resembled ammunition. The official asked me to open the little bag. I pulled out the D harp and blew a version of 'Oh, Susanna' while stomping my foot in an exaggerated country hick kind of way. The young officer was suitably impressed; he took the harmonica, blew on it, held it up and asked, 'Geeft?'

'No gift, mine!' I said and took it off him, smiling. Also smiling, he subjected me to a gratuitously sensual pat-down body search. In my hungover state, I took it as one would a massage and we parted on good terms. You don't get that kind of service in Australian airports.

In the passport line at Dubai I got talking to a Turk who had migrated to the US. He said he was now running a district development team in Helmand, but that it was getting too scary. Travelling to a shura the week before, he said his convoy hit six IEDs along the way.

'I already done four and a half years in Iraq. You can't keep pushing your luck! Still, nothing happening in Detroit right now. The economy is tanking.'

I played a little concert at the Australian headquarters on my last night in Dubai before boarding an Emirates flight back to Australia. Arriving at Sydney airport at dawn, exhausted, the brash light and heat of an Australian summer slapped me in the face.

Back home I turned inwards for a couple of weeks, adjusting quietly, grieving the loss of that world without even knowing it. Three performances at the Cygnet Folk Festival in mid-January got me out of my shell in the way that standing on stage in front of 400 people can do. I played a set of my Uruzgan songs, backed by a PowerPoint presentation featuring some of the extraordinary photos taken by ADF photographers, who patrolled alongside our soldiers throughout the Uruzgan mission. The audience response was overwhelming. No one had seen these photos before, and the songs and stories felt like they came straight from the front – because they did. The show felt immediate and important – and I was pioneering the use of PowerPoint in rock 'n' roll.

A week later, I was having dinner with my dad when he asked a difficult question.

'So what now? The good news, and the bad news, is that the department will probably give you whatever you want.'

AusAID officers recently returned from Uruzgan had been rewarded with interesting postings; it would have made professional sense for me to move on to greener pastures than the dust of Uruzgan. But I wasn't ready to let go.

As usual, I let myself be led around by my own songs. Indeed, I went chasing them. There was a handful I hadn't finished, among them the Helmand PRT song I had started in October. I realised there was a fundamental problem with the way I was approaching the song: the guitar riff had an American bluegrass feel, but the Helmand PRT was run and staffed by the British. It just wasn't going to work as 'Helmand PRT'.

I knew there were things I did not know but needed to in order to finish the song, so I went online and looked up 'Helmand Province' and eventually the Kajaki Dam. This led me to an online photomontage by a Chicago photographer, Scott Olson, who in October 2010 had been embedded with India Battery, 3rd Battalion of the 12th Marine Regiment, fighting to defend Kajaki from the FOB Zeebrugge. The series of photos and captions described a horrendous week that began with them medivacing a young Afghan boy wounded in the fighting, and ended on 19 October when Marine Lance Corporal Francisco Jackson stepped on an IED. The photos showed his damaged boot, his grief-stricken comrades and a photo of his son, a week later, receiving the folded flag as his body landed at Dover Air Force Base in Delaware. Heartbreaking!

I never knew Francisco Jackson, or his fellow marine, Corporal Ryan Yeaton, through whose eyes I wrote this song, but I knew what it was like to be on a FOB when a comrade was killed. Men were devastated, yet stepped out the gate the next day all the more resolute to get the job done.

Francisco Jackson's death was one of 90,000 in this war so far, but no less a tragedy for that. The early verses of the song cover the creeping scepticism and doubt soldiers can feel when confronted with the toxic politics and drug lords of Afghanistan. The middle verses touch on the imperative for soldiers at the FOBs to be aggressive – it was what the Afghans expected of us, and the reality was that if you didn't dominate the terrain, the enemy would, and rockets and rounds would start coming over the fence. The final verse reflects the fighting spirit that emerges from despair as a band of men on a FOB respond to the death of a brother.

Zeebrugge FOB

My name is Ryan Yeaton, I'm from Maryland Heights
Born and raised in Missouri and I came out here to fight
With the India Battery, 3rd Battalion, 12th Marines
Now deployed in Kajaki at Zebrugge FOB

This broken little province that I find I'm fighting for
Sends more opium than Burma to the ports of Baltimore
And the Taliban and the drug lords keep the place a goddamn mess
Well I swear I am a fighter but right now I must confess that . . .

I've had enough, I can't take anymore, right now I just want to be
Home far away from this forsaken war, not fighting from
   Zeebrugge FOB

USAID built the dam here back in 1953
To tame the Helmand River for the electricity
We were sent to Kajaki and it's here we take our stand
To defend the plant and turbine from an angry Taliban

But if we stayed inside the FOB we would become a sitting duck
So we get out on patrol and trust our mettle and our luck
I got a sweet little daughter to a woman that I love
When a man's got a family feeling lucky ain't enough and now

I've had enough, I can't take anymore, right now I just want to be
Home far away from this forsaken war, not fighting from
    Zeebrugge FOB

We were out there patrolling on October 19
When they killed Francisco Jackson with another IED
Sent his body back to Dover and the sacrificial flame
Man, I loved him as a brother, now I fight on in his name

So when I've had enough and can't take anymore and home is
    where I want to be
I go clean my weapon and back up for more
Still fighting from Zeebrugge FOB

The guitar riff had initially come to me as a delicate fingerpicking thing but we ended up with a more strident recording. The recording engineer, Peter Kennard, had a previous incarnation as a lead guitarist in a country band, and he laid down the heavy Gatling-gun Fender Telecaster for the final touches.

The Marines who were stationed at Zeebrugge in October 2010 are now based in San Diego. They have heard this song and I occasionally get emails and Facebook messages from them.

CHAPTER 12

DUST OF URUZGAN REVISITED

Never let the facts get in the way of the truth

NASHVILLE SONGWRITERS' EXPRESSION

We'd been static there for hours when I shifted slightly back,
My foot tripped an AP mine, and everything went black . . .

FRED SMITH, 'DUST OF URUZGAN' (REVISITED VERSION)

IN FEBRUARY 2011, I SHOWED UP AGAIN IN THE REAL WORLD. I PULLED my suit out of the cupboard, ironed a shirt and went back into DFAT central, working part time, four days a week, in the International Security Division. My work was focused on what we call Civil Military, which is all about preparing Defence and civilian agencies to work together in stabilisation missions like Uruzgan or Bougainville, or in responding to natural disasters overseas. It was work I knew about and believed in, so I was happy enough to be doing it, but my heart and mind that year were bent in service of song.

I had six songs already recorded, three more written and finished, and a handful of works in progress. I've always felt twelve songs are about right for an album – any more and it becomes unwieldy. Through the autumn of 2011, I assembled the songs 'August 20', 'Taliban Fighting Man' and 'A Thousand Splendid Suns' from my notes and scrawls. I polished them up and set about recording them, along with 'Zeebrugge FOB', 'Woman in a War' and 'Trembling Sky', a song from the perspective of an Afghan refugee. I did the tracking and mixing in a range of studios, depending on the whereabouts of the talent needed. I worked with Peter Kennard in the Blue Mountains to track the initial 'beds' for 'Trembling Sky' and 'Taliban Fighting Man', and with Liz Frencham in her studio in Trentham, Victoria, where we did 'A Thousand Splendid Suns' and the vocal on 'Trembling Sky'. Jonathan Byrd, who was touring in Canada at the time, dropped a vocal for the marine part of 'Taliban Fighting Man' in Toronto. My friend Carola van Houwert, the Dutch nurse from Role 2, sang the female part to 'Woman in a War' in a studio near The Hague. It was a haphazard way to make an album, but I figured the cohesion of the recording would be thematic rather than sonic.

There were songs I couldn't seem to finish, notably the one I wanted to write about Jared 'Crash' MacKinney. It was not so much that I couldn't finish it; more that I couldn't get started.

I spent May and early June booking the tour for the album – tedious work, but I am self-managed – while mixing and mastering the CD, getting the artwork together and resolving the track order. Track order – i.e. the sequence in which songs appear on the album, is important and always takes a few weeks to bed down. You fiddle with different combinations and permutations until it feels right. Outside perspectives can be helpful, and I sent a demo to Melbourne songwriter and film scorer David Bridie, who gave me a couple of useful insights: that 'Live Like an Afghan' was strong and would provide useful variety up the batting order, and also that 'Trembling Sky' had an air of finality about it so should probably end the album. So I put 'Dust of Uruzgan' at track one, 'Live Like an Afghan' at number two and 'Trembling Sky' last. The rest of the songs seemed to settle nicely in between.

I also sent John Schumann a demo, and he was kind enough to write some flattering quotes that I could use in the media release. He gave me some advice on contacts in record companies, but none of them offered me anything worthwhile. I decided to go ahead and release it myself, with a company called Inertia Records distributing it to shops.

My publicist, Christine Taylor, sent CDs out to journalists in mid-June with a 1 August release date. She did a great job, but a little luck also came my way. I went out one evening to the pub to meet my AusAID mate Luke, just back from Uruzgan. I found him on a bender with his mate Stephen Fitzpatrick from *The Australian*. We went back to Luke's place for a drink in front of the gas heater in his living room. Luke brought out his twelve-string and insisted I play some of my Uruzgan songs to Stephen, who was taken by them and sensed there was an interesting backstory. We did an interview and he ran the story and some photos of me on the front cover of the *Weekend Australian Review* on 30 July.

Overall, the media response was overwhelming. I had already put out seven albums, most of which had been reviewed kindly, but *Dust of Uruzgan* was getting full-page spreads in the mainstream broadsheets.

Sydney Morning Herald music writer Bruce Elder, who had been generous about my previous albums, wrote of *Dust*: 'The equal of Bogle, Walker and Schumann . . . a cycle of songs that are raw, remarkably honest and suitably ambivalent about the nature of war . . . a collection of songs that offers an intimate perspective on the war in Afghanistan.' Melbourne *Age* reviewer Warwick McFadyen called them '. . . a triumph of poetic journalism and songwriting'.

These reviews were encouraging and gratifying. I was proud of the recording – I had earned these songs not at some artist residency but through eighteen months sweating in my jocks in a difficult place, sifting through a complex and often ugly reality. But also I felt it was a balanced account of things: twelve story-songs, each looking at the war through different eyes, a broad collection of perspectives on a complex situation.

One journalist asked how I managed to handle the conflict between being a diplomat and an artist. I answered that there was no conflict: diplomats try to get a three-dimensional under-standing of a place by talking to everyone, weighing the various perspectives, then reporting. And that's how I went about the album, teasing out a range of perspectives.

TV publicity would also be helpful. I had met Channel 10's Hugh Riminton when he came through Uruzgan in 2010. A classy and principled journalist, he built real relationships with the soldiers he spoke to and honoured those confidences by disclosing in his dispatches only what was fair game. In late July 2011, he was working on a short piece on me for George Negus's evening current affairs show. He thought it would strengthen the story to get Paul Warren's perspective on the song 'Dust of Uruzgan' and asked if I could put him in touch with Paul.

I emailed the new 1 RAR rear details officer, Major Simon Moore-Wilton, asking if he could approach Paul about doing an interview with Hugh. Simon forwarded my request to Paul's platoon sergeant, who replied a couple of days later. 'Sir, I have just spoken with Paul Warren and whilst he is honoured with Fred's song and very happy that something like this has been done, he does not wish to be involved in any interviews or docos. Paul wishes to keep private on this matter.'

Hugh and I could only respect this. My experience with returning soldiers had been that they often turned inwards for a couple years – going into the cave to process the experience. That was understandable, and I now know that Paul was dosed up on painkillers at the time and was generally not on good terms with the world.

That August I hit the road with Liz Frencham on double bass and singing vocals on the songs I had written from a woman's perspective. I built up a suite of photos for each song to give the audience a chance to visualise the place.

The tour itinerary was the best I could do with my cottage industry business model – booking gigs by email at night after a day at work, shooting out on the weekends to play, then scurrying back to Canberra on a Sunday night for work the next day. We played some salubrious venues – the Canberra Playhouse and Notes in Sydney – but mostly it was a down-home affair: house concerts, pubs and folk clubs.

On 19 August 2011, we were playing at the Berwick and District Folk Club out near Ferntree Gully, east of Melbourne. We got the engines going with a duet and a couple of comic tunes before moving into the Afghan material. I was introducing 'Dust of Uruzgan', saying it was about a young guy from this part of Melbourne named Ben Ranaudo, when a woman sitting towards the back of the venue said: 'He's my son!'

The room went silent. Liz looked anxious. All I could do was play the song. I calmed myself with the thought that if Ben's mum had come to hear me play, it was probably because she had heard the song and was okay with it. Liz mightn't have made this leap, and by the time we finished the song she was in tears. I played the Dixi song to lighten the mood, put the guitar down and we broke for intermission.

I went across the room to meet Jenny and her husband, Terry, while Liz sold CDs. Jenny said the song had helped her to understand what actually happened on the morning of 18 July 2009.

She had seen the official report but with all the military language and acronyms couldn't make sense of it. She said the song had set things out in a way she could get her head around. We swapped numbers and promised to stay in touch.

A month later we played a show at the Gaythorne RSL, just up the road from Enoggera Barracks. The crowd was an interesting mix of folk music fans and soldiers I'd served with. We ripped through the first set, finishing with 'Sapper's Lullaby' and 'Niet Swaffelen op de Dixi'. At the interval, a big, fit-looking guy in his early fifties approached me.

'Hi, I'm Rob Moerland,' he said, 'and I'm Dutch!'

It was Snowy Moerland's dad. Again, it stopped me in my tracks to meet the parent of someone whose death I had sung about. It turned out Rob's parents were Dutch and had migrated to Australia – he had that penchant for piss-taking that is shared by both cultures. Initially, I didn't know whether to apologise for the Dixi song or offer condolences for the loss of his son. Neither was necessary. A nurse by trade, he was precious about nothing and happy to talk. Rob thanked me for writing the song and said what mattered to him was that his son's story was being told.

And this was to be my experience with the parents of a number of soldiers who perished in Afghanistan. What struck me about people like Jenny and Rob was their unflinching directness in tackling what had happened to their sons. On meeting them, I'd clam up a bit at first, anxious to say the right thing and not upset them, but soon found they were pretty robust. They had sought to understand the facts and talked openly about their feelings. It was not that everything was okay – their grief was deep and permanent – but they didn't flinch. I'm no expert on grief management, but perhaps this is the value of a song: it helps people to feel their feelings.

The first phase of the *Dust of Uruzgan* tour ended on 30 October with a weekend of shows at the Torquay Bowling Club and the Caravan Music Club in Melbourne. Jenny and Terry showed up to the Melbourne gig, as did Lieutenant Colonel Jason Blain and his family, and my friend Anne Poore, who works as a nurse in the psych ward for repatriated soldiers at Heidelberg Hospital. The evening was pretty charged – on 29 October the second of three 'green-on-blue' incidents had occurred. A rogue Afghan army sergeant had opened fire on Australian soldiers while they were on parade at Shah Wali Kot base in Kandahar Province. Three Australian soldiers were killed: Captain Bryce Duffy, Corporal Ashley Birt and Lance Corporal Luke Gavin. Seven other Australian soldiers were wounded. Losing our soldiers to enemy contrivances was one thing, but having them die at the hand of the people we were trying to help was hard to come to terms with.

I got back to Canberra airport on the Monday afternoon, exhausted from four months of weekend touring and still nursing jetlag from a couple of overseas work trips. Dad met me at the baggage carousel with more bad news: 'Your mate MDK has been killed,' he said. 'He was shot by his own bodyguard in Kabul.'

I shook my head in despair. 'You can't help these people, they just kill each other,' I said. There were email exchanges about it in the office the next day, and a cable from the ambassador entitled 'Vale MDK' lamenting the death of one of the more conciliatory and cooperative figures in Uruzgan. MDK had been stripped of his position as district chief of Chora earlier in the year. He was resting up in Kabul with his Barakzai clansmen, as Uruzgan leaders were wont to do every now and then to get away from the constant security threats in Uruzgan – ironically, as it proved for MDK. It wasn't clear who paid the bodyguard to turn. Suspicion automatically fell on MK, but the new US colonel in Uruzgan had been with MK when he received the first phone call about MDK's death; he reported that MK seemed genuinely surprised and a bit perplexed at the news.

Another suspect was JMK's eldest son, Qasim, as an act of revenge for the death of his father. JMK had been assassinated back in July 2011, also in Kabul, by a team of suicide bombers who hit his compound in a well-coordinated attack that also took out one of JMK's political protégés, MP Hashim Watanwaal. The Popalzai blamed the Barakzai for the job; this might have motivated Qasim to act. Yet it seemed more likely that it was a Taliban initiative, given the complexity of the attack – and they had the motivation. As his obituaries noted, JMK was the Uruzgan lynchpin in the southern pro-Karzai network of warlords. So the Taliban would have seen him as a high-value target. They certainly claimed responsibility.

Interestingly, the obituary for JMK published by the Afghan *Pajhwok* news agency concluded: 'He is survived by four wives, 18 daughters, and 16 sons, the oldest of whom is 30 years old.' Since JMK was well over sixty when he died, this would suggest his love life improved significantly after he quit his job as janitor at Tarin Kowt high school and began a career as a warlord. So we may infer that the rewards for a warlord's work are plentiful, but as they say, he who lives by the sword . . .

I digress. A consequence of JMK's death was that MK was appointed chief of police in Uruzgan. Karzai's general strategy was to have a heavy hitter in each province as a client. With JMK gone, Matiullah Kahn was the obvious choice.

❖

Musically speaking, the pace dropped off for me over the summer of 2011–2012, but then picked up again in the autumn of 2012. I performed at the National Folk Festival, the Port Fairy Folk Festival, the Blue Mountains Music Festival and Western Australia's

Fairbridge Festival, all in the space of about a month and a half. It was a happy and productive time for me, although bad news kept coming from Central Asia. In late March, Luke was enjoying the first few months of a posting in Islamabad when he rolled his vehicle and suffered serious head injuries. Then two officers in our embassy in Kabul were badly burned when a gas oven in their accommodation exploded. Australian OHS standards were hard to maintain in a place like Afghanistan.

But for me the most shocking thing was what happened to David Savage. Dave was a DFAT officer seconded to AusAID, working in the position I had set up at FOB Mirwais in Chora. On the morning of 26 March, he had gone down to the White Compound with his US security detachment, just as I had done twenty or thirty times, to talk business with the district chief. They were on their way back when Dave began to notice suspicious signs. He saw a man sitting beside the road, nursing a teapot, with a small radio in his hand. Dave reached for his camera and asked the man if he could photograph him. The man nodded in agreement, but then covered his face with a scarf as Dave went to take the photo. Then, walking past an AusAID road drainage project as they neared the FOB, he noticed all the workers had left the site, leaving their tools behind. Dave turned back and to his left to see if the man with the teapot had moved just as a young boy dressed in white approached from his right and detonated a suicide vest.

Suicide bombers were usually teenagers, not prepubescent boys, and so the US soldiers had not stopped the boy from entering the security packet. Dave was blown ten metres in the air. Two US soldiers lay bleeding beside him; one, the young medic, tried to help Dave but passed out from blood loss. A team of Australian soldiers came out from FOB Mirwais to evacuate the wounded.

Dave arrived in the Tarin Kowt Role 2 hospital with combat tourniquets on three of his four limbs to stop him bleeding out.

Fortunately, the boy had stumbled just before detonation so most of the shrapnel went downwards; Dave wound up with sixty ball bearings in his legs, torso and left arm, but his head was okay. Though his vital organs were mostly protected by his body armour, some of the shrapnel had found its way into his lungs and spine. After some major medical procedures in Kandahar and at the hospital in Landstuhl, Germany, it looked like he was going to survive. But needless to say, for the small but growing group of Uruzgan alumni in DFAT and AusAID, the attack on Dave was alarming. It could have been any of us.

Notwithstanding all this, as the Canberra winter of 2012 set in, I found myself missing Afghanistan. I longed to go back. A couple of DFAT positions had been advertised in Kandahar and Kabul earlier in the year and I had been tempted. I had even gone as far as to write applications, only to withdraw them at the last minute. I wrote in my diary on 12 June: *I'm bored and frustrated with playing music in Australia and the endless amount of solitary work involved. I miss the variety and interest of Afghanistan.*

The reality of being a self-managed artist in Australia is not that glamorous: I spent a lot of time at home sending emails to venue bookers and writing hyperbole about myself for the media. It's lonely work and also self-referential – the risk of disappearing up one's own jacksy was very real. You can become embittered quickly; many do. It's a pretty small market with slim economic returns. Afghanistan, on the other hand, provided work that was very social, where friendships formed quickly, and it was a job that got me looking intently outwards at a wild and fascinating landscape.

At the same time, I began to wonder if I'd taken the Uruzgan storytelling role as far as it could go; perhaps it was time for me to move on. I felt I was at another crossroads – should I build a proper theatre show to tour the Uruzgan record through regional theatres in Australia, or should I get off the Uruzgan bus, write songs for a new record and start the creative cycle over again? In the end, as usual, I did both. I began putting out feelers regarding the Long Paddock Touring Route of regional theatres – and also started writing another album of songs.

I was sitting at my desk at home on the evening of 23 July when an email popped into my inbox. Its subject line read: 'A quick g'day.' It was from a former soldier from Brisbane-based 6 RAR/ Mentoring Task Force One. He thanked me for the songs I'd written, and for visiting and playing a memorable concert in the summer of 2010. (I guess he didn't realise I was living and working there at the time. Fair enough; PRT business was separate from infantry work and I was up at FOB Mirwais most of that summer.)

He wrote about the summer of 2010, when Australian soldiers seemed to be dying every week. He described the morning of 24 August, when his section had headed west with ANA counterparts, met with colleagues posted to Patrol Base Anar Joy, then turned back east in the direction of the village of Derapet. Then he briefly related the events that led up to the death of Jared MacKinney, whom he described as the epitome of an Australian soldier – a man who'd died helping out his mates when the chips were down. Finally, in a reticent and somewhat embarrassed way, he got to the point. He said he felt Crash's story deserved to be told and asked if I might find time to write a song for his fallen mate.

I wrote straight back.

Thanks for getting in touch and your kind words about my songs. I was at Crash's ramp ceremony and remember hearing a voice in my head telling me that I needed to write a song for him. I'd like to have a go at this, but can't promise anything. All I can do is jam as much relevant information

as I can into my head and see what comes out the other
end ... so please send me more facts. Alternatively, I'll be
in Brisbane for a gig on 4 August; we could catch up then.

I hit send. Months went by with no response and I started to
wonder if I'd been a bit forward in my email.

My Brisbane trip went ahead. From there I travelled up to
Darwin where I 'pitched' a *Dust of Uruzgan* show to about a hundred
theatre bookers at Long Paddock, an annual showcase event.
There was strong and immediate interest. This was promising.
The show was fine to do in folk clubs and pubs with Liz and a
portable projector and a rickety old screen, but to do it justice I
would need to get into proper blackbox theatres with a full band.
This now began to look like a possibility.

Meanwhile, the war went on. On 30 August 2012, there was
another green-on-blue attack – three Australian soldiers, James
Martin, Rick Milosevic and Robert Poate, were shot and killed by
an Afghan soldier as they were chilling out at a patrol base after
a day's work. Robert was a Canberra boy who had gone to the
same boarding house as me, only twenty years later.

By September 2012 it had become clear that Australia would
be withdrawing from Uruzgan in late 2013, in accordance with
the ISAF timetable for handing over authority to the Afghan
government. Around that time, the last DFAT political adviser
position in Tarin Kowt was advertised. In terms of going back to
Uruzgan, it was now or never for me – I devoted two pages of my
diary to 'for and against' arguments. The 'against' column was
pretty full (it always is): I knew Maryanne wasn't too enthusiastic
about me going back, but would support me if I decided to do so.
I sought advice from my dad, whose view was that it's always a bad
idea to go back: 'You can go back to the place but not the time,'
he said, quoting renowned football coach and philosopher Dennis

Cometti. There was wisdom in this, and of course it wouldn't help my professional CV to retrace my steps: I risked being typecast within DFAT as a 'mission junkie'.

In the 'for' column: I loved this kind of work. But more than that, I felt I had something more to offer. The last three years of my life had turned me into a man on a mission – to tell the story of the Australian experience in Uruzgan to the public – and, having come this far, I figured I should go back for this last six months of the mission to see how the story ended. For me, purpose always trumps professional advancement, so I applied.

In early November, Bernard and I were having a drink with Lieutenant Colonel Jason Blain at the Kingston Pub. Jason was in good spirits; one of the soldiers under his command back in 2010, Corporal Daniel Keighran, had been awarded the Victoria Cross for Australia for his actions during what had become known as the Battle of Derapet.

Daniel, in the meantime, had left the army and was working down a mineshaft near Kalgoorlie. One day the foreman came down the shaft looking for him and said, 'Keighran, you just got a call from Canberra. You better call them back.' It was the Chief of Army calling to invite him to Government House to receive the Victoria Cross.

News of the award created an immediate crisis for Daniel Keighran. He had, up until that point, neglected to explain to his wife what he had actually done on the morning of 24 August 2010. And what he had done was quite extraordinary. When Crash MacKinney was struck down by the round, a handful of the guys put down their weapons and began working to revive and evacuate him. But they were in an exposed position and the Taliban, concealed in a tree line about a hundred metres away, began concentrating fire on the guys gathered around Crash.

Keighran realised he needed to do something. So he ran up and down a slope in plain sight of the Taliban shooters not once, but three times, drawing intense fire. The helmet camera footage now available on YouTube shows rounds zipping through the dust all around him. His mad dashes had two effects: they drew fire away from the party working on Crash, enabling the guys to evacuate him. But also, because the Taliban lost fire discipline and shot so many rounds at Keighran, Lieutenant Fanning, commanding the battle in a nearby aqueduct, and other men in the ASLAVs positioned on a hill in overwatch to the north-west, were able to pinpoint the Taliban firing positions in the tree line. The ASLAVs peppered that tree line with 25mm explosive rounds which, as they say in the military, was 'decisive'. Until then, the party had been under significant pressure, pinned down in a well-organised ambush and running out of rounds. So by this one act he probably saved the lives of many Australian and Afghan soldiers and was pivotal in helping friendly forces to regain the initiative.

In a second act of courage and audacity, Daniel somehow managed to explain all this to the satisfaction of his wife, and a few weeks later the couple found themselves celebrity guests at the Governor General's residence. Keighran was by all accounts a level-headed guy and handled it with grace.

Meanwhile, the Fred Smith artistic juggernaut kept rolling in its rickety sort of way. By November I'd written a dozen or so new songs and had begun to record a new album. I had gone to Melbourne to record in the backyard studio of Shane O'Mara, best known as guitar player for artists like Paul Kelly, Tim Rogers and Chris Wilson (I recommend the *Live at the Continental* recording) and also a deft producer. If there was a theme to these songs it was coming home and calming down and the challenges thereof, but in reality I was not ready to do so. We were recording one afternoon when I got a call from DFAT Staffing asking me if I still wanted the job in Tarin Kowt.

'Yes, please,' I replied.

❖

The first quarter of 2013 was a busy time, finishing up work in the International Security Division and preparing to return to Uruzgan. By this stage, the pre-deployment training regimen for DFAT officers had become more sophisticated. As well as the mandatory duty-of-care stuff (first aid, hostile environment training etc.), I did a three-week course in the Pashtun language. I also did the DFAT media course in anticipation of doing a fair bit of media work explaining the Australian mission in Afghanistan to the public. DFAT's media branch and Afghanistan section were supportive. DFAT doesn't get a lot of oxygen in the press, so the general public would be within its rights to assume we were not even in Uruzgan.

In addition, I was still gigging on the weekends. The last of these weekend stints was in Victoria. Maryanne came with me so that we could spend a bit of time together before I departed. On Sunday, 15 April, I was scheduled to play an afternoon concert in the barn of my friend Bonesy in the Dandenongs west of Melbourne. We arrived there to find Ben Ranaudo's mum Jenny and her husband Terry sitting on the deck. They had arrived a little early for the concert. She gave me a hug, I introduced Maryanne and we had a yarn. I told her I was about to go back to Afghanistan. A concerned look came across Jenny's face.

'Fred, are we making a difference there?' she asked.

'Yes, I think so,' I replied, though I was a little unsure. I was out of touch with the place and needed to see it again before I could truly promise this to someone who'd lost a son there.

I changed the subject.

'How's Paul Warren doing?' I asked.

'I think he's doing better,' she said. 'We keep in touch.'

She said that on the anniversary of Ben's death in 2011, Paul and a couple of his mates had travelled to Melbourne and spent the day with her and the rest of Ben's family. She had shown Paul the room where Ben grew up, then they went to the cemetery and visited Ben's grave.

'I think connecting with him and letting him know we were coping helped,' she said.

The gig was quite intense, particularly with Jenny and Terry there in the third row. By this stage, ABC TV's *Australian Story* had decided to do a feature on me; one of the journalists was there with a camera, adding to the sense of occasion in the way that cameras do.

After the concert ended I went to say goodbye to Jenny. She pulled me aside.

'Maryanne is lovely,' she said. 'You should make a video for her, telling her how great you think she is, just in case something happens to you over there and you don't get the chance.'

❖

I was due to go back to Afghanistan at the end of April, and with the gigs done and dusted and a beautiful autumn descending on Canberra, it was a happy time for Maryanne and me. I recorded an interview with the Australian War Memorial for a forthcoming Afghanistan exhibition, and offered to interview a few of my contacts in Uruzgan and record their thoughts on the Australian mission. The AWM people agreed this might be helpful for the exhibition.

In the lead-up to Anzac Day, the Australian media goes looking for war stories. My dad is of the generation who still gets the papers delivered daily – and reads them. I was at his place on Sunday, 21 April, when I noticed Paul Warren's image on the front page of the Fairfax papers. Paul had come out in public, and he'd come out fighting.

He was quoted as saying that the Australian Defence Force had not been prepared for the volume and complexity of injuries resulting from the Afghanistan war. The article began describing the events of 18 July 2009, leading up to the IED strike that killed Ben and blew off Paul's leg. It detailed Paul's difficult journey to rehabilitation. In the article, Chief of Army Lieutenant General Morrison acknowledged that the ADF was playing catch-up on this, learning whatever it could from the Americans. There was now a new soldier rehabilitation centre at Townsville, which Paul was attending.

It was a good article, and significant to me because it revealed that Paul had stepped out into the light. I called Hugh Riminton.

'Paul is in the media,' I said.

'Yes, I know,' Hugh replied. 'I've been spending some time with him and am looking to do a story for Channel 10's *Revealed* program.'

He filled me in: Paul had been through some hard times. From the hospital in Germany he'd been flown to another hospital in Brisbane. The doctors there were so inexperienced with the nature of his injuries they'd had to use the Yellow Pages to find a prosthetic limb supplier. He had only known his girlfriend Dearne for a month before deploying, but she had closed her business in Townsville and travelled down to Brisbane to help him through – all without financial support from the government, since they couldn't prove their de facto status. After a few tough months, they had returned to Townsville together.

Then things got tougher. Paul's whole world unravelled when he got home. He was a champion Muay Thai boxer but he could no longer fight. His prosthetic leg wasn't working properly and was chafing in the tropical heat. He was doped up and more or less addicted to some serious painkillers; he had PTSD and was carrying a heavy load of guilt about Ben's death. Paul went down a tunnel and turned inwards, spending days on the couch in a haze with only the PlayStation for company. Not mild-mannered to start with, he was angry with everything and everyone, including the army. He could see no way forward as a soldier. Unable to cope with all his anger and talk of suicide, Dearne had moved out – though not before falling pregnant.

In August 2010 she gave birth to a little girl they named Kiahni, and this seemed to spark the beginning of a comeback for Paul. He wanted to be a good dad and, by force of will, started putting the pieces of the jigsaw back together. He got off painkillers, acquired a better prosthetic leg, re-engaged in exercise and training young fighters. Eventually, Dearne moved back in and they had another child, a boy, whom they named Jax Benjamin.

'Is Paul still cool with the song?' I asked Hugh. 'I mean, there are inaccuracies – he didn't move in with his mother, he moved in with his girlfriend, and she seems to have been key to his recovery.'

'No, no, he's still okay with the song,' said Hugh, 'except for the verse where you say, "We'd been standing still for hours when I took a quick step back, kicked a small AP mine . . ." He doesn't like the implication that he did something clumsy or sudden. But also, as a matter of fact, he wasn't standing; he had been lying in a prone firing position in that spot for two hours. He just shifted to his right slightly; that's what triggered the mine.'

'Okay, good to know,' I said.

In Nashville, the songwriting capital of the world, they have a saying: 'Never let the facts get in the way of the truth.' But I figure it's worth getting the facts as accurate as I can, particularly when dealing with the story of a living breathing person. So ever since I've sung that line as:

We'd been static there for hours when I shifted slightly back,
My foot tripped an AP mine . . .'

CHAPTER 13

GOING HOME

I don't know how I am going to fit back home
Been out here now so long this is what I know

FRED SMITH, 'GOING HOME'

ON 1 MAY 2013, I WAS BACK WHERE IT ALL STARTED, AT THE RSO&I
course, only now it had been moved from Ali Al Salem to the Aussie
headquarters in the UAE. We were committed to four days of death
by PowerPoint, interspersed with first aid and weapons training. No
one could proceed to Afghanistan until all the boxes were ticked.
I was indignant about doing the mandatory course again, but it was
useful in unexpected ways. For one, it forced me to slow down.
I had been going fast and hard with my self-imposed timetable of
recording, touring and DFAT for the last two and a half years.

This seriousness, anger and impatience from my war on time has
made me antipathetic to company and making friends, I wrote in my
diary, *which takes time. Also, hanging out with the ADF causes you to
let go of your need to be special.*

We were being processed and no amount of attitude was going
to speed it up. 'Cheerful indifference' has always been my approach

to working with the army – it saves your sanity while ensuring no one can accuse you of having an attitude problem.

I also caught up with some familiar faces – people on their way back to Afghanistan for second or third stints, including Padre Al Lavaki, who had done the hard yards through that lethal summer of 2010, overseeing all those ramp ceremonies and carrying the heavy pastoral load that followed. He was on his way back to TK to work with the special forces at Camp Russell.

Next was Kabul, another eye-opener. There were sparrows flitting around in the spring air and the streets were lined with billboards with images of 3G phones and Ahmad Shah Massoud, the Lion of Panjshir, seen by many as the martyr-in-chief, hero and mascot for the anti-Taliban cause.

I went to the embassy and collected the same Nokia phone I'd had three years before, still with the same number, so I was able to dig out my old business cards and save the trouble of a reprint. The morning before I left Kabul I heeded Jenny's advice and filmed a message for Maryanne, lest the worst should happen. It was confronting, but I felt better for doing it.

Later that morning, I landed at the Tarin Kowt airstrip and disembarked to the sight of my beloved mountains to the west. They seemed indifferent to my return. John, the senior AusAID officer in Tarin Kowt, picked me up at the flight line and drove me to the base. We encountered Zia and Rafi Shaheen, the PRT House caretaker, by the side of the road outside the terps' quarters. Now in their mid-twenties, they both looked more mature, manly even, from three years of decent food and time in the gym. We embraced with many *salaam aleikums*.

The civilian contingent on base now had its own accommodation block, Chalet 23, and a shipping container each. I settled in and then called Maryanne on the welfare phone. As soon as she answered, I could tell she was upset.

'What's the matter?'

'I'm pregnant again!'

I nearly fell off the chair.

'That's okay, we can afford to raise a child,' I said, composing myself.

Many things worried her: my response, the impact on her job, but more than anything she feared the heartbreak of another miscarriage.

I walked out into the daylight a little stunned. At the old PRT office block I found my new colleagues packing everything into boxes and throwing the office chairs I had secured back in 2010 into the back of the Hilux. We were all moving into a single office in the centre of the base near Poppy's, as part of what the ADF called 'retrograde' – the incremental process by which the base would shrink to within ever-decreasing circles of razor wire until, by November 2013, we simply disappeared. After seven years in the province, packing up and leaving was a planning and logistical exercise on the scale of Dunkirk; a whole team had been dedicated to making it happen.

In the years I had been away, the Australian civilian contingent, working alongside about a hundred US Navy officers in the PRT, had grown into a well-oiled machine. We were now led by Dave Windsor, an experienced operator with a good political nose who spoke Dari and a little Pashto, so was able to engage our interlocutors in their language. A bright young gun named Sam Allen was all over the tribal stuff and on good terms with various Barakzai leaders, but he was about to leave. My other DFAT colleague, Rohan Titus, had done stints in the Middle East and conflict zones in the Pacific; he had a natural feel for societal complexity and a gentle way with people. We now had a full-time detainee monitoring officer, Penny, and a handful of AusAID officers, including my mate Stacey Greene, whom I'd met through

Luke. It was a nice little team that worked well with the US Navy commander and his soldiers, with wrinkles and problems solved daily by a laconic Australian operations officer we all called 'Pikey'. Pikey worked closely with a lieutenant named Jimmy, who ran the 'OGA Platoon', a team of Australian soldiers dedicated to providing mobility and protection to we civilians from 'Other Government Agencies'.

Over the winter, Australian soldiers had moved back in from the FOBs, part of a strategy of handing security responsibility to the Afghan forces. Zia too had come in from FOB Mirwais, and was now working full time for the PRT in Tarin Kowt. I caught up with him that night. We talked about old friends from Chora. He said no one was really sure who was behind MDK's death, although the shooter was known to be now in MK's employ. He told me that Mohammad Gul, the tango-dancing police chief from Chora, had also perished. His vehicle had hit an IED.

I asked Zia about his family.

'It is hard for the Afghan army to defend the countryside, because the Taliban can threaten people at night. So people are moving to the cities.' His father and brother had left the family home and moved to the city, but were still unemployed, so he was supporting everyone. But there was good news. Zia had finally managed to get married; he and his wife had a bright-eyed little boy named Zalan. I told him Maryanne was pregnant.

'That is wonderful, sir,' he said. 'A child gives you hope.'

The next day we had a small ceremony to mark the departure of US civilians from the Uruzgan PRT. American civilians were being pulled out of the south following an attack in Zabul in which a US diplomat was killed. The guys on the ground, Rob Sipe (from the Department of State) and Bob Mullen (US Agriculture), were a bit embarrassed about going home before we did – they felt they were abandoning us. We assured them we didn't take it personally.

Their departure marked the end of a significant Uruzgan workload completed by US civilians, dating back to 2005.

❖

I spent the rest of the week getting my head around the new reality. The base in Tarin Kowt had completed the transition from Dutch to US control. The Dutch Dixis had been replaced by Sanokil portaloos, and retail opportunities were abundant. There was a bazaar, with shops in shipping containers selling everything from suits to stereos. There was a hair salon run by Turkish barbers who really knew their art; they could trim your nails and burn the little hairs out of your ears without setting fire to your head. Gone were Two and Dick on Arm. There was a coffee shop called Green Beans overlooking the parade ground, on which no one seemed to play volleyball anymore. It did a roaring trade from 7 to 9 am, just like a Starbucks in a working American city.

Karaoke had also blossomed in Tarin Kowt. There was now a full-time entertainment officer, a genial old guy named Mr Lee, who resembled the lead singer from Hot Chocolate. He liked smooth eighties jazz and had been plying his trade at the mega bases in Iraq and Afghanistan over the last ten years. He had resources: a room full of welfare computers, a pool table, TVs linked up to ESPN and, importantly for me, a PA system. A couple of nights a week he would host a karaoke session in a cluster of containers down by the movers shed.

I had changed too. In 2009, I'd taken the low road, hiding my guitar under the bed for the first two months and wearing a brown canvas hat. This time I showed up in my Panama, light and breezy for hot weather, and it had swagger. In my first week on the base a couple of soldiers approached and asked me to sign their *Dust of Uruzgan* CDs, then took selfies with me, before things settled down and I became part of the furniture. By now I had some celebrity. The epitaph I scrawled for myself in my diary in case of an unhappy contingency reflects I was aware of this and a little self-conscious:

Fred Smith, wasn't that the cat
Who went back to war in a Panama hat?

Things had also changed out beyond the wire. The Road to Chora had been completed. Hamidi had managed to negotiate with tribal leaders through the Baluchi and up past Nyazi, giving them a stake in getting the job done. People were now using the road, which cut the commute from Chora to the provincial capital from four hours to thirty minutes. The security situation in the Mirabad Valley was pretty solid and fourteen kilometres of road heading eastwards out of Tarin Kowt had been paved. AusAID had arrangements in place with the UN Development Program to pave a further twenty-six kilometres out there, and had also embarked on a Children of Uruzgan program focused on health and education in the province.

As for security, the Afghan National Army in Uruzgan was now led by Colonel Kandahari, an experienced and robust old war dog. He had been running aggressive independent operations, chasing the Taliban out of the valleys. The police were also becoming more cohesive under the leadership of MK, who, by most accounts had matured since taking up the position in 2011. He now had 5000 men under his command, many staffing checkpoints they had set up throughout the main valleys of the province on the back of years of clearance operations conducted by Australian, American and Dutch forces.

With all these changes, and the prospect of reduced funding from what looked like being a poor poppy season, the Taliban were feeling the pressure. In the past year, coalition counter-leadership operations had taken twenty-one insurgent commanders or facilitators off the battlefield. Increasingly, Taliban leaders were not returning to the province from their winter sojourn in Pakistan, sparking resentment among Taliban foot soldiers resident in Uruzgan.

Nonetheless, with the poppy harvest nearly over, we knew young men would be unemployed and ready for action. It was anticipated that the insurgents would swarm and attack checkpoints in the more vulnerable peripheral districts of the province. With coalition soldiers now in from the FOBs, this would be the first fighting season in which the Afghan National Security Forces would be fending for themselves. Taliban propaganda was telling villagers that the ANSF would collapse without the foreigners' help. We weren't sure what would happen, and were anxiously watching and waiting. The analysts on base saw the resilience of the ANSF checkpoints in the forthcoming fighting season as a kind of litmus test of our mentoring efforts over the years.

Sure enough, on 10 May, the attacks began. Five checkpoints in the Chahar Chineh district in the north-west corner of the province were overrun by Taliban forces, who swarmed across the border from Helmand. These checkpoints were of marginal strategic value, but the Afghan leaders knew the symbolism was everything, so responded fiercely. MK and Kandahari combined resources and sent men up to the district in numbers. Cooperation between them was not exactly seamless – it was a vexed relationship – but by 15 May, the checkpoints were retaken.

Four days later I went down to the governor's compound with Dave for the weekly catch-up. Driving through Tarin Kowt, I peered through the dusty front window of the Bushmaster. The streets seemed busy – there were traffic cops on a couple of the corners. I even saw a few blue burqas walking around the bazaar. Women were shopping.

The governor's compound had been transformed since the last time I was there. There was a three-storey administration building with a large room that hosted a weekly meeting of the twenty-four provincial line directors. The provincial government's allocated staffing roster was now 70 per cent full, up from 30 per cent in 2009.

The former governor, Sherzad, had been replaced by Amir Mohammad Akhundzada. Back in the office we referred to him as AMA, but he was Wali Saab ('Governor, sir') in person. He was from the infamous Helmand Akhundzada family, with connections and influence that enabled him to get things done, even if he did resemble Danny DeVito in a turban. The British, who knew the family from Helmand, described them as energetic, effective but corrupt, and we in the PRT were engaged in an ongoing cat-and-mouse game, progressing our projects while protecting them from his prying fingers. Still, he was genial enough, and seemed to have a good rapport with Dave.

'I think the problem up in Chahar Chineh is not a big one,' he said, and went on simultaneously claiming credit and shifting blame. 'I would like to get up there myself and have a look at the situation. Matiuallah and General Kandahari always cooperate better when I'm around.

'The problem,' he continued, 'is that the border with Helmand is open, so the enemy can simply retreat back to the districts under Taliban control in Helmand. The ANSF have 32,000 in Helmand and yet they can't control the area. I complained to the defence minister about this.'

We raised the matter of the civilian air terminal. The Dutch had finally completed the $14 million terminal building by the Tarin Kowt airstrip and their embassy was keen to hand it over to the provincial government in a ceremony on 5 July.

'That date won't work for me,' said AMA. 'And anyway, they are only promising to support operations of the terminal for six months. This is no use. We can't recruit staff for six months. We need longer-term support.'

Dave suggested he take this up with the Dutch Embassy. In Afghanistan, push usually comes to shove, and we didn't need to be caught up in this one.

This was the kind of work the PRT did – ongoing liaison with the governor or the line directors to keep things moving forward. The governor had an assistant named Abdul, a serious young official in his early thirties who spoke pretty good English from his time working with the Brits in the Helmand PRT. Abdul and I would call each other four or five times a day to solve little problems and refine arrangements on one matter or another.

Dave did the bulk of the direct engagement with the governor and the reporting to the embassy in Kabul. He liked that stuff and was all over it, and in any case, with the mission drawing down, there was less appetite for Uruzgan reporting; we were down to one cable a week unless something serious happened. By this stage, we were attempting to reduce our interaction with the Afghans in the province. Over the years, we had developed a role as mediator, sounding board and, to some extent, shrink for local leaders. They would come and see us to seek help with their problems and grievances. But by mid-2013, we were looking to set our engagement with them on a downward flightpath ahead of our impending departure in late October. Concurrently, the AusAID staff in the office were in the process of wrapping up and closing down various projects.

So apart from the ongoing problem-solving work with Abdul, I had no discrete body of work and therefore time to ponder how I could actually make a positive difference in the coming five months. I locked in on three main tasks.

The first was to put myself in a position to tell the story. I felt the Australian public deserved a good account of what we were doing there and, that with our influence waning, closing up shop and telling the story was all that remained to be done.

One morning, Zia and I went down to the front gate to meet the Uruzgan chief justice. The front gate was always a fascinating scene. There was a constant procession of life: workers coming on and off the base, pedestrians, jingle trucks and military convoys. The Afghan security guards knew me from my concerts at their compound where I'd sung a ridiculous song of mine called 'Tension'. I'd show up and they'd sing 'tension, tension, tension!' at me without knowing what the word meant. We'd joke and chat and I'd watch them going about their work, searching people and vehicles entering the base, or just sitting around. Beyond the gate I could see the rest of Afghanistan going about daily life. It was like a breath of fresh air after the insularity of base life.

Anyway, it was a beautiful Monday morning, a blue sky above and not too hot yet.

I said to Zia, 'Another day in paradise, buddy!'

'Yes, sir,' he replied, 'but it is not very colourful. I do not think God worked very hard when he made Uruzgan.'

Northerners like Zia could be disdainful of Uruzgan. Where we saw bucolic charm, they saw abject poverty. But he had a point. For all that we'd poured into this place, it was still one of the poorest provinces in one of the poorest countries in the world. Which got me thinking about the question Jenny had asked me at the gig in the Dandenongs in April: 'Are we making a difference?'

It was not an easy question to answer. We foreigners tended to stay for a year or so then leave, and our days were filled with managing challenges and setbacks. It always felt like one step forward, one step back. It occurred to me that the people best placed to answer Jenny's question were the older generation of leaders, the ones who'd lived through the Russian era, survived the civil war and the Taliban years, had seen what it was like when the Americans arrived in 2001, then the Dutch and Australians in 2006, and could compare all this with what they could see now.

So with that question and the Australian War Memorial exhibition in mind, I embarked on a project to interview eminent Uruzganis. I cleared my lines with Dave and the embassy, gave the War Memorial a heads-up, took advice from Zia and Hamidi on whom to interview, drew up a list and got Zia on his Nokia making calls.

Over the next two weeks, twelve Uruzgan leaders showed up at the front gate. Zia and I would go down and meet them, drive them up to PRT House, ply them with tea and water, and start asking questions like: 'What has it been like working with the Australians here? Have we made a difference?'

I filmed these interviews on my digicam and had the ADF public affairs guys filming too. By late May, we had twenty hours of footage and about a hundred pages of transcripts.

I sent the footage back to the War Memorial on a hard drive, but didn't have time to reflect on what I'd collected, because by the end of the month things were getting busy. On 27 May, the Taliban overran a couple of checkpoints in the Charmeston area, to the south of the Mirabad Valley. This time we sent special forces, who worked with MK's men stationed in the Mirabad to reclaim the checkpoints. We also received intel that eight suicide vests had been moved in to Tarin Kowt, and were ready to be activated.

On the tribal front, MDK's brother Khoshal had inherited the leadership of the Barakzai tribe. I remembered him as 'Shit Man' from Chora. He was struggling to fill the void left by his father and brother's deaths. He invited me to attend the launch of a shura building we had helped him construct on the Barakzai compound, four kilometres north of Tarin Kowt. It looked like being the final statement in our relationship with the Barakzai and the tribal engagement strategy I had worked on back in 2010.

On the appointed day, we rolled up in a convoy. All the old Barakzai leaders were there, including friendly and familiar faces from my time in Chora. I made a little speech recalling the undertakings I'd made at that same compound when the Dutch were pulling out three years earlier. I spoke of my sadness on hearing the news of MDK's death. I acknowledged that they felt the Popalzai had got more from the coalition presence, but said that their working relationship with us had been good and that, on the whole, most in Uruzgan were better off. It felt like the end of an era for all of us, and they seemed sad to see us go.

Then on 5 June we helped with the Dutch Embassy's launch of the Civilian Air Terminal. To their credit, as with the Road to Chora, the Dutch had seen it through after departing the province in 2010. It was complete with conveyer belts, air-conditioning and a video-monitoring system on a par with Australian regional airports. Some suggested the terminal was a little over-engineered and might be difficult to sustain once we'd left and taken our diesel with us.

Regardless, senior Uruzganis showed up in numbers at the handover ceremony and were proud to be in receipt of such a grand piece of infrastructure. The guests sat through an hour and a half of speeches given by the national Minister for Transport, the Dutch ambassador and the governor. Dave got up and had them all in stitches, starting off in Pashto, switching to Dari when he ran out of Pashto and then English when he ran out of Dari. It was a good day; the Dutch from the embassy were very pleased. We had left the wrangling over dates and ongoing support to the governor and the Dutch Embassy – it was their issue – but the air terminal was part of a bigger problem we would come to see as ours.

That evening in the PRT office we talked about all this. The sustainability of the airfield after our departure mattered to a province defined by its isolation. But there was a lot involved in running an airfield. Everyone in the province had a stake in keeping it going, but as Stacey pointed out, 'Someone needs to take the lead and bring it all together.' I noted her comment and put an asterisk next to it. It was to become my second big project in those final months in Uruzgan.

My third project was of a more extracurricular nature. The base was feeling a bit disjointed to me. People were hanging out in their own workgroups and not really getting together much. The green-on-blue incidents in 2011 and 2012 had made the kind of social get-togethers the Dutch ran difficult. One had to organise 'guardian angels' – basically snipers in overwatch – for any sort of gathering, and it felt like the relationship with the Afghans on base had become more distant. I resolved to put on a concert or two to bring everyone together, perhaps because that's my solution to most problems.

The challenge, as always, was pulling musicians out of the woodwork. On this front, a bit of luck came my way. The IT 'geeks' on base now had their own building; out front was a service counter manned 24/7 by a couple of young privates who could fix problems. I was a regular customer. I was in there one afternoon filling in a form, and they had the stereo going. I overheard a private with *Treasure* written on his nametag say to his mate, 'Aw, listen to the bass line on this track, it's fuggin' awesome!'

I took a punt. 'You a bass player, mate?'

'Yeah,' said Private Glenn Treasure.

'What kinda stuff do you play?'

'Metal,' he said, and I ran a quick risk-benefit analysis in my head. I'd never had a bass player in Tarin Kowt and beggars can't be choosers.

'I'm putting a band together,' I said. 'You keen to play?'

'Yeah, but I don't have a bass here.'

Then a little more luck came my way. There was an American contractor named Jeremy who played covers on his guitar outside Green Beans on Tuesday nights. I recruited him for the band and mentioned I was looking for a bass player. He knew a departing US soldier called Sean who was keen to sell a cheap Fender bass he'd bought in Dubai. Two hundred bucks later, Treasure had his bass and the band had a bassist.

The first rehearsal with Treasure was interesting. He was wobbly and uncertain, trying to make the shift from heavy metal's relentless approach to the bluegrass feel of 'Zeebrugge FOB' and then to the even more spacious waltz feel of 'Sapper's Lullaby'. I suspect he'd never played in three-quarter time in his life. But I got him landing the note just on the one beat and his eyes lit up as he felt the song swing in the space that remained. He was quick to learn and a joy to work with.

On the lookout for backing vocalists, I transcended my ideological aversions and began attending Mr Lee's karaoke nights. A cosy little karaoke community had developed, and included an older American soldier singing Kenny Rogers songs as well as a trio of young African American women who did a rap tune called 'Call Tyrone' by Erykah Badu. The song was written from the point of view of a woman working a tough job while her indolent boyfriend keeps inviting his friend Tyrone around to drink beer and watch sport on TV all day. At the end of the song she tells the boyfriend to 'Call Tyrone!' and go live with him. Compelling stuff – and they sang it with conviction evidently born of experience.

A lovely US contractor by the name of Sunshine often showed up at Mr Lee's, sometimes hanging out with an AusAID officer named Skye. It amused me that these young people, who I presumed by their names to be the progeny of hippies, were out here prosecuting a war.

When it was my turn to sing, I improvised a variation on 'Women in a War' set in TK rather than Kabul.

'Her name was Sunshine, she wore a pistol,' I began, 'with a name like Sunshine, she should have wore a crystal . . .'

In the familiar company of the karaoke community, Sunshine saw the humour in this, as did everyone else.

Three more musicians came on board in the coming weeks: a singer named Kristin Gardiner, a public affairs officer; Steve Burns, an AusAID guy who was competent on Latin guitar; and a US private named Denzel Young who had a great sense of rhythm. Lacking drums and drummer, Chris and Denzel played percussion on the 82mm illumination round cases I found up at the firing range.

We played our first concert outside Green Beans on the evening of the third anniversary of the death of Snowy and Smithy, 7 June. A lot of people showed up and it was pleasant as the sun set over the mountains. 'Sapper's Lullaby' was particularly poignant and we played it well. It was filmed by ABC cameraman Aaron Hollett, who was in for the week with reporter Michael Edwards.

In the days that followed, acting on a request from *Australian Story* producer Ben Cheshire to get footage of me in situ, Aaron filmed me attending a meeting at the governor's compound. I also took him around the base, describing places like Poppy's and the parade ground, telling stories of things that had happened there. It was a melancholy time in a way – like a small town that I'd come to know and love was being shut down. I wanted to tell the stories to somehow preserve them.

By that stage Australian soldiers were not going outside the wire much. This was part of a deliberate strategy to let the Afghans take over, but also because there was no appetite back in Canberra for risking lives that close to the end of the mission.

The special forces from TF66 were still active though, and on 22 June, a highly decorated soldier, Corporal Cameron Baird, led an assault on an insurgent network in Ghawchek village. On his third attempt to storm an enemy position he was shot dead. He was posthumously awarded a Victoria Cross for his actions that day. Corporal Baird was the only Australian soldier killed in 2013. His death took to forty the number of Australian names written on a concrete memorial wall erected outside the dining facility. Alongside them were the names of the twenty-six Dutch, forty-eight Americans and one Frenchman who had perished in the province.

❖

In late June I went back to Australia for a bit of rest and recreation, but didn't get much of either. Maryanne's pregnancy seemed to be going okay, but because she was considered an 'older mum', the doctors had us going from test to test, one of which detected the child would be a girl. We resolved to try to keep the gender of the baby a secret.

Meanwhile, my public role was growing. I did interviews with the *Australian Story* crew as well as Victoria Midwinter-Pitt, who had been commissioned to put together an ABC documentary on Australia's involvement in Afghanistan.

I also took a show called *Peace in the Pacific* to Melbourne, Sydney and Canberra. In the late 1990s and early norties I worked in the Australian-led Peace Monitoring Group in Bougainville and, funnily enough, had written a dozen songs about it, which I released on an album called *Bagarap Empires*. In early 2013, I had collected photographs from colleagues and professional photographers and combined them with the songs in a show that explained the Australian mission in Bougainville.

Australia had a mixed history in Bougainville. The copper mine at the centre of the civil war was Australian run, and we had for a long time supported the Papua New Guinea Defence Forces. The conflict began in 1989 and continued until 1997, when we helped organise peace talks at a military base in New Zealand. At these talks, combatants invited Australia and other regional countries to send peacekeepers to the island, but on the condition they come unarmed. Despite concerns among some in government, we agreed to do it and over the ensuing five years led a regional civil military mission that supported a locally led political process which helped return Bougainville to peace and normalcy.

There's a saying in the media: 'If it bleeds, it leads.' The Bougainville peace process was slow and incremental, and no Australians were killed along the way, so it didn't get a lot of media attention. We conducted that mission with a lot of heart and brains, always leaving the Bougainvilleans in control. This was a rare thing: a good news story about the international community's effort to fix a broken country. It's a story most Australians don't know about, and one I remain passionate about telling.

I got back to Tarin Kowt to find discussions intensifying around how to present the Uruzgan mission to the Australian media. In a meeting on 22 July between the Australian PRT civilians and the ADF media team on the ground, the Defence public affairs major, Haydn Barlow, said they were considering three possible courses of action.

'Whichever way we go, it will be important to get some decent journalists out here at the end of the year to see for themselves.

'Option one is the small target approach – we release just enough information to meet reasonable levels of transparency, and then acknowledge we can't control the future of Uruzgan. Option two is that we claim "mission accomplished" – unworkable at this point. Option three is somewhere in between. The way things are going, Canberra seems inclined towards option one. There's no appetite for explaining complexity in an aggressive media environment, and if things turn to shit after we leave, people are worried any claims of success will be thrown back in our face.'

'AusAID seems to also be leaning towards the minimal approach for the same reasons,' said the AusAID deputy.

'Yeah, but I reckon we shouldn't underestimate the audience,' said Stacey. 'Most Australians are sensible enough to understand we won't be able to control the situation once we leave.'

'And the public are becoming more cynical about the cynicism of the media,' said Dave. 'We owe it to what we have achieved to explain things more fully.'

It was understandable that people in government were worried about the security situation in Uruzgan going forward. MK had become something of a lynchpin in the security architecture – we called him a 'security provider'. His constructive role in this was even being acknowledged by some of his former enemies, and by Dutch academics still keeping an eye on the province. But we couldn't assume he'd live forever. Indeed, on 5 July, while I was away on leave, there had been a brash attempt on his life.

A suicide bomber had somehow made his way into the KAU (Uruzgan Road Police) compound at lunchtime on the Friday before Ramadan. Once inside the dining facility, the bomber couldn't find MK, who had been called up to Kabul at late notice. He was probably contemplating going home for lunch himself and coming back another day when MK's deputy, Dastagir, spotted him.

'What are you doing here?'

The man didn't answer.

Dastagir asked again, this time more insistently. The bomber realised the gig was up and detonated, killing twelve, including some of MK's cousins and senior officers. It was a busy day at the Role 2 hospital.

We learned that the bomber had been wearing a police uniform. Apart from that, and the fact the Taliban claimed responsibility, the backstory to the attack, as usual, never became completely clear. We figured it was someone well enough known to MK to get into the compound, but not close enough to know MK was in Kabul.

We were concerned that MK might use the incident to justify an attack on the Barakzai tribe, but Khoshal was sanguine about this risk when I spoke to him.

'It was an inside job, not us,' he said. 'MK knows who was responsible but isn't telling anyone.'

One evening in late July, I was having dinner with my mate Jim, a smartarse captain in the intelligence cell. I mentioned to him that my wife was pregnant. ADF intelligence officers are trained in highly sophisticated non-violent interrogation techniques.

'Do you know if it's a boy or girl?' he asked.

'Yes, I do, but we're keeping that a secret, Jim.'

'Is it a boy?'

'No,' I blurted out.

'Aha!'

Jim had done a stint three years earlier out at Patrol Base Wali in the Mirabad just as we were inserting into the valley. So we wheeled him out the following night for an Iftar – a meal to break the daily Ramadan fast – that we hosted for Mirabad leaders at PRT House. It was the first in a series of Iftars we hosted to say goodbye to our Afghan interlocutors. About ten leaders from the valley showed up, including Malim Habibullah and Malim Manan, whom I had met back in 2009 when they came in requesting support to rid the Mirabad of Taliban.

These were down-to-earth guys the PRT had got to know well. Habibullah and Jim had been great mates too, and they told stories of the early days when we first moved into the valley – how Habibullah would steal onto the patrol base at night to confer.

Jim showed Habibullah photos of his newborn. The tribal elder asked one of the AusAID officers how many children she had. He was astonished when she replied she had none yet.

'I have eight!' he said.

'Yes, he has eight children, but you know there's not much else to do out in the Mirabad Valley!' Malim Manan chipped in.

The Afghans fell about laughing as the comment was translated.

They said they were happy with the way things were going. The new road had cut the commute to Tarin Kowt down to fifteen minutes, so they could get their vegetables to market much more easily; Habibullah's kids were now coming into town for school. MK had put checkpoints right through the valley and his main commander in the area was liked and trusted, but also aggressive enough to keep the insurgents at bay.

Late July was busy. I spent the evenings preparing for a phone interview with a DFAT promotions committee back in Canberra. Dave and Rohan helped me prepare, but I hate these things at the best of times (who doesn't?), and it was hard to focus with all the Iftars going on and Prime Minister Rudd due to visit on 28 July. These visits always required intensive planning and liaison work, and lining up the local leaders and officials was tricky; for security reasons we couldn't tell anyone outside the wire who was coming.

Afghan leaders could be indignant about this approach – they said it signified a lack of trust. Anyway, I called Abdul in the governor's office and asked if he could arrange for the governor to be at PRT House at 11.30 am on 28 July to meet someone important. I asked him not to bring weapons and explained that he and the governor would be searched. Abdul arced up on all counts, but I promised it would be worthwhile.

On the morning of the 28th, the prime minister's plane arrived at 10 am and he went straight into a series of briefings. Meanwhile, I went down to PRT House to meet the governor and fill him in on the identity of the visitor and what he wanted to talk about.

'So this is not the lady I met last time?'

'No, Wali Saab, she has been replaced by Mr Rudd, whom she replaced a few years ago.'

'Ah, politics,' he said. 'We Afghans are no strangers to politics, but it is unusual for a national leader to still be alive after a successful coup.'

The PM's meeting with the governor went well, and the governor spoke convincingly in a little press conference with the Australian media entourage afterwards.

In October 2012, Australia had agreed to take over the leadership of coalition forces in Uruzgan Province. By early August 2013, Australian Colonel Simon Stuart was finishing up his stint at the helm of the Combined Team Uruzgan and was in the process of handing over to Colonel Wade Stothart, who was taking charge for the last six months of the mission. I set up a meeting for 10 am on 4 August for Simon to farewell the governor and introduce him to Wade. To take advantage of the governor's presence on base, I also scheduled a second meeting an hour later to discuss the airfield. The schedule was a little tight and I was anxious for things to run on time.

At 10.15 am, Wade and Simon were sitting on the couch at PRT House but the governor had not yet showed. I was beginning to worry that I had stuffed up arrangements with Abdul, when he called.

'Abdul, *salaam aleikum*,' I said.

'*Salaam walekum*, Mr Farid,' he said. 'How are you this morning?'

'Very well. And you?'

'I am fine,' he said.

Then he got to the point with one long quick sentence.

'Um, Mr Farid, we were about to leave the governor's compound this morning but there was a suicide bomber waiting for us outside the gate but the police shot him in the face but his friend ran away in the direction of the bazaar but we can't find him so sorry we will be a little late for the meeting this morning.'

'That's fine Abdul,' I said, 'just get here when you can.'

They arrived fifteen minutes later. The governor said the bomber had been waiting outside the compound for him but when he did not emerge had moved towards the adjacent bank building, where Afghan National Police officers were drawing their salaries as they usually did on Sunday mornings. An ANP officer spotted the bomber and quietly alerted two colleagues; one grabbed the bomber's left arm, the other grabbed his right arm (thereby preventing him from touching together the two detonation wires hidden up his sleeves). The third shot the bomber in the face. Not a bad effort; the governor was pleased.

The meeting went well. The governor spoke warmly of the cooperation between himself and Colonel Stuart and was optimistic about the ability of the Afghan Security Forces to protect the province following our withdrawal, citing the morning's events as an example. He did complain about his guests being searched when getting on and off flights into TK, saying this was disrespectful and embarrassing for him. But apart from that, the meeting was positive, and a good opportunity for me to get to know Wade. He was one of a new generation of ADF leaders who had experience working with civilian agencies, and understood how we rolled.

The meeting about the airfield was less promising. There were many players on the Afghan side and it was hard to see how we would bring them all together between now and the end of October. Yet the governor knew it was important.

'It is cheaper to fly from Kabul to Dubai than it is to fly to Uruzgan!' he said. 'This has to change.'

Throughout early August, we continued the Iftars to farewell the various groups in Uruzgan society we'd worked with over the years: provincial government officials, the Chora crew etc. Meanwhile, the retrograde process marched on. Every day I'd see skinny Afghan labourers carrying discarded closets and other furniture on their back – most of which I recognised to be the products of Bunnings nights past – down to the front gate for scrapping or for sale at the TK bazaar.

As part of the retrograde, the American camp on the western corner of MNBTK, Camp Cole, was closed down, and the troops from Task Force Gunfighter moved in with us on Kamp Holland. With Americans came God. Now the chapel was pumping every Sunday and a couple of weeknights with contemporary gospel services, aided by flatscreen TVs displaying lyrics so everyone could sing along. The Camp Cole chapel had a drum kit, which, I noticed, was moved up into our chapel.

And with God came musicians. Some good ones too, from the ranks of Task Force Gunfighter, particularly a singer/guitarist, Sergeant Schaeffer, and a drummer, Lieutenant Alex Tompkins.

I saw them rehearsing in the chapel one night and, feigning interest in church music, wandered in to solicit their services for the band. They were tasteful players.

'Where'd you guys learn your chops?' I asked.

'Church,' they both replied.

The modern American church is DIY when it comes to music; its songbook has a more pop feel to it than the eighteenth-century hymns we butchered of a Sunday at boarding school. That's not to say the songwriting is any good. Indeed, by any objective measure, it is awful. This, paradoxically, makes for better musicianship, since the players cut their teeth polishing turds. (This is just my theory, not the view of the Department of Foreign Affairs and Trade.)

Schaeffer had a hardscrabble sensibility to his playing. He had spent some years in bands in Germany, where he'd had some wild times. He was trying to straighten out; playing in church was part of this. His wife was also deployed in Afghanistan, flying choppers out of Kandahar, while his mother-in-law was looking after their one-year-old daughter back in Iowa. These deployments had become a way of life for many American soldiers and they seemed to accept the sacrifices as par for the course.

Tompkins was a good-looking young lieutenant, well read, politely spoken, and an elegant, lyrical and inventive drummer of the kind one would not expect to meet on a military base in southern Afghanistan. He also spoke of some wild years at college before he had married, straightened up and joined the church. American lives seem to swing a pendulum between oblivion and the path of righteousness, with the church offering a moral emotional safety net to those who can't handle the rigours of sex, drugs and rock 'n' roll.

I got these two together with Private Treasure for a rehearsal one evening in the chapel. At last a full band in TK – and it sounded good, or in Treasure's words, 'fuggin' awesome'. Happily, an excuse for a gig emerged. The end of Ramadan was approaching, and Dave and others in the PRT felt it was important to put on an Eid celebration for the terps. A lot of these young interpreters had given the best years of their lives working for us in Uruzgan. With the end of the mission in sight, some of them were already being sent home with their severance pay. It wouldn't have felt right to let them go without some sort of celebration.

Umary was a de facto organiser among the terps. A selfless guy with a natural talent for organising people, he was the eldest of five children and had paid for the education of his siblings by working for us. We got our heads together and began thinking about how to make this Eid party happen. Mecca had scheduled Eid for 8 August, and this would have been the best date for the party, but Base Command issued an edict banning people from hanging out in non-hardened structures that evening for fear the insurgents would seek to mark the holy day by firing rockets at the base. So we locked in 11 August, but then I found out the drum kit was needed that night for the gospel session in the chapel. (Between the Christians and the Muslims, I was struggling to sort things out. This is what it must be like trying to organise a gig in Jerusalem.) So we went for Monday, 12 August, at PRT House.

I put posters up for that date: TONIGHT WE'RE GOING TO PARTY LIKE IT'S 1389, which it was in the Muslim calendar.

PRT House had a caretaker named Rafi Shaheen, a sweet, cheeky young guy whom we all adored. We gave him cash and he went into town and procured food. Umary rounded up some Afghan musicians from around the base and from Tarin Kowt. I got the band into shape with the core three rhythm section players plus backing vocalists. I lined up the PA system with Mr Lee while the AusAID crew sorted out logistics like decorations, plates and cutlery.

At 5 pm a bunch of terps arrived and, under Umary's super-vision, set up chairs, tables, a barbecue and desk lamps for stage lights. I put together a stage from forklift pallets 'borrowed' late the night before from outside the US Post Office on base.

The evening went right off. I wrote in my diary:

By 7 pm, PRT House was packed. Every terp on Kamp Holland showed up and some from FOB Ripley too. Jeremy played some covers and then a local guy, Wahid, played a set on his harmonium under the neon light. Then we broke for dinner and feasted on the beautiful lamb and rice that Rafi had prepared. We marshalled everyone back into the main room, turned off the lights overhead and kicked off a set of singalong songs. Terps and expats sang along indelicately to some of my more absurd repertoire. My old mates Rassoud and Wali from the front gate security team emerged from out of nowhere so I dragged the lyrics to 'Rassoud be Good' out of my memory banks. The terps all remembered it from those sessions back in March 2010 and sang along with glee, 'Za! Za Rassoud Za Za Za!' before he busted out a solo on his rubab.

By the end of the set, people were getting up and dancing one at a time and then all at once. It was mayhem. We switched from band to iPod and the terps took turns playing their favourite Central Asian dance classics. Soldiers, terps, girls and boys – everybody got into it, dancing on the big rug. Lots of circle dancing and silly dancing and people hugging and taking group selfies on their phones while the older terps sat around watching and nodding approvingly. By the end

of the night, Umary was grinning from ear to ear,
having been stressed about whether the thing would
come together. A totally satisfying evening smashing
the cultures together, and a great relief after all
the frustrations of sorting out the date and venue.

We PRT civilians all showed up at work the next day sporting what felt like hangovers, though no one had touched a drop of alcohol. We went down to PRT House and helped Umary and Rafi clean up, labouring in the afterglow of having done something cool.

❖

Meanwhile, the band kept growing. A couple of really good singers came on board, including an RAAF officer, Debbie Xinos, who had sung in bands in the 1990s before she and her husband had got busy raising six kids.

I was feeling the urge to play another gig, buoyed by the success of the Eid party. I had also just finished writing a new song that seemed to capture the mood of the base. An Aussie major named Mick Spruce had given me a beaten-up, small-body nylon-string guitar that had been handed down from rotation to rotation in Chalet 22. I often get fresh musical ideas when a new guitar lands in my hands – different instruments want to be played differently. I was picking this guitar for the first time one evening when a riff came to me. Words flowed in the week that followed and I had a song called 'Going Home' completed by 20 August. It seemed to capture the zeitgeist of a base in retrograde, in a war wearing to a weary end.

Organising the gig was a struggle from the start, and in hindsight I should have listened to the universe and let it go. Nailing down the date was the usual shitfight. But I felt some urgency since a lot of soldiers were starting to leave. I saw some graffiti in a cubicle in the toilet block adjacent to Chalet 13:

5 Weeks left [crossed out]
10 Days to go [crossed out]
2 days to go [crossed out]
9 minutes left

Next to this someone else had written: *Home is a myth!*

I wanted the departing soldiers to hear the new song and the band before they left, so I resolved to stage a concert out the front of Green Beans before the end of the month. After negotiations on the availability of the PA with Mr Lee and the drum kit with the new US chaplain, I plumped for the evening of Tuesday, 27 August.

Scheduling rehearsals was equally tricky, what with Tompkins' day shifts, Treasure's night shifts and the work patterns of the various singers. I ended up doing seven rehearsals instead of one.

At the same time, my day job was getting busier. The governor had clamped down on the movement of scrap steel off the base. He had the backing of some national government edict saying that all discarded materials from ISAF bases were government property, but we suspected he saw an opportunity; Zia told me a story of a mullah who rose to eminence on the back of revenue he gained selling scrap metal after the Russians left. He became known in Afghanistan as 'Mullah Kabari' – the 'scrap metal priest'.

I was also working to make sense of a series of incidents in the north-east district of Khas Uruzgan relating to Commander Shujoyee. Shujoyee was a local police commander of Hazaran ethnicity, who was playing an important role in keeping this potential Taliban ratline fairly well secure. He had, however, developed a reputation for excessive aggression, and Pashtuns (who coexisted with Hazarans in Khas Uruzgan) held him responsible for many civilian deaths in recent years. There had been an incident on 14 August in which he was alleged to have abused civilians in the village of Kochak. Rumours of this led to national-level protests organised by Pashtun politicians looking to harness anti-Hazara sentiment. The provincial government sent an investigation team to the district and the Ministry of Interior issued an arrest warrant for Shujoyee.

It was difficult to sift the facts from the rumours. Regardless of what had actually happened on and around 14 August, it was an indication that the broader national tribal power struggle might ramp up a notch as the post-NATO era approached. And the Ministry of Interior arrest warrant posed a dilemma for MK – Shujoyee was an effective and indigenous bulwark against insurgents in north-east Uruzgan, and in any case, would prove difficult to catch!

On 23 August, national government ministers came down from Kabul for a meeting of the Base Closure Committee. Then the retrograde people demanded we civilians from Chalet 23 move in with the new US military PRT elements in the two-storey Chalet 21. The result was nice insofar as we had an upstairs balcony, on which American soldiers were playing an endless game of dominoes that languid summer. But the moving and cleaning out of Chalet 23 was time-consuming – and time, for me, was in short supply.

Meanwhile, back in Australia my plans for touring the *Dust of Uruzgan* show in theatres seemed to be falling apart. I got word that the Australia Council had rejected my application for tour support, and with this a number of theatres I'd lined up had withdrawn interest. *Heartbreaking after all the work I've put in*, I wrote in my diary but it was hard to do anything about it from a shipping container in the Afghan desert.

On the evening of 23 August, I managed to get Treasure, Tompkins and Schaeffer together for a rehearsal. We ran through 'Going Home' for the first time. It seemed to hold water and the guys really liked it. This was encouraging.

The following evening, I found Tompkins eating dinner in the DFAC and joined him. I asked how things were shaping up for the concert and whether he could get away from work. He said he could, but that the chaplain seemed reluctant to lend us the drum kit.

'Why?'

'I don't really know,' he said.

This got me worried.

The conversation broadened to politics, and his views were an interesting mix of humanistic sensitivity and National Rifle Association orthodoxy. He was a passionate Republican, which he attributed in part to the moral historical view that the Republican Party had advanced the liberation of the slaves whereas the southern Democrats had resisted it. He acknowledged, though, that people's political views were often a product of their upbringing.

'I guess if I'd grown up white in the south in the nineteenth century I might've felt differently about slaves.'

He spoke of his passions for hunting and guns and his hatred of those 'Nazis in Colorado' who were trying to ban automatic weapons. He said he was training every morning in the grappling techniques used by cage fighters.

'You know, Fred, 85 per cent of fights end up on the ground. You need to be able to neutralise your opponent in this situation, break his arm or whatever it takes.'

As we were emptying our trays, he asked me something. 'Fred, with this concert on Tuesday – would you mind not cussing?'

I said I'd see what I could do. At the same time, I marvelled at this particularly American cosmology – a sensitive and literate soldier who saw shooting deer with automatic weapons and breaking arms as wholesome weekend diversions, but thought 'cussing' beyond the pale.

I was pondering this juxtaposition, walking up towards Green Beans, when out of the corner of my eye I saw Padre Al Lavaki in a close huddle with six soldiers over near the memorial wall. Judging by their beards and baseball caps, these were SF guys from Task Force 66. They were sipping surreptitiously from white plastic cups with about half an inch of brown liquid at the bottom.

I strolled over.

'Hey, Al, what's going on?'

'Anniversary of Crash's death.'

'So it is,' I said, remembering that a number of guys from Crash's Delta Company had gone on to earn 'selection' to the special forces.

I followed them up to Green Beans, hoping to learn more about what had happened on the day of the battle. I said I had been asked to write a song about it, which was probably too direct, and they became tight-lipped; special forces guys are tight-lipped at the best of times.

There was an awkward silence until one of them said, 'There's not much to say, really. Crash was partnered with another soldier who was carrying the section machine gun. The other soldier ran out of steam, Crash grabbed his gun and hauled it up the slope into a firing position. A round went in through his shoulder and into his chest cavity and that was it.'

I wanted to ask a few more questions but was beginning to feel unwelcome. I went back to my shipping container, opened my notebook and made some initial sketches for a song for Crash MacKinney, including:

One man becomes a hero, and others in the grave
the battle scene's a lottery, some die and some are saved.

These words seemed to capture the message of the song I wanted to write, but the golden rule of songwriting was 'show, don't tell'. The song needed to relate the facts in a way that delivered this message implicitly, and to pull it off I needed more facts. So I found the email I had received from the Brisbane soldier back in June 2012 and sent him a gentle poke, saying I had just run into Padre Lavaki and a few of the guys remembering Crash beside the memorial wall.

I went to bed and slept a little but woke up worrying about the bloody drum kit. Thinking it through, I remembered that the chaplain had asked me a couple of times if I'd care to join the band for the church service. I had politely declined, citing busyness rather than atheism. It occurred to me he might be getting Afghan on me and applying some leverage, and that I was on the downslope of a power relationship: in Marxist terms, the chaplain owned the means of production – to wit, the drum kit – and I needed it.

There was only one thing to do: sell my soul to God. That night, I showed up in the chapel and joined the church band for rehearsals.

In the end, it wasn't so bad; almost like a meditation, as the songs were simple. I realised, though, that a ninety-minute service of this music could really hurt, but figured that was the point of a church service: an opportunity for penance. I got to wondering why they didn't reinforce this effect by replacing the pews with pineapples. By the time I'd finished exploring that thought, rehearsal was over.

As we were packing up, I casually asked the chaplain whether it would be okay to borrow the drum kit on Tuesday night.

'Oh, sure,' he said, 'as long as you fill out the 20/62 form.'

The US military bureaucracy has forms for everything; they use the 20/62 form to monitor the whereabouts of drum kits.

After one more band rehearsal we were ready to go for 27 August. I started setting up outside Green Beans late that afternoon. I laid out the US Postal Service forklift pallets for the stage, and waited for Mr Lee to bring up the PA. It turned out he'd forgotten about the gig, so I had to go down to his office and chase it up. I wanted to project photos on the blast wall adjacent to Green Beans. This began to feel ambitious as the gig drew near and even more so when I discovered that the power coming out of Green Beans was US 110V, suitable for Mr Lee's PA system but not for the projector or Treasure's bass amp.

I called Treasure and he found some technical solution for the projector the way people under twenty-five do, but he had to run his bass through the PA system and it made a distorted farting noise every time he struck a note at volume. In a last-minute flurry, I set up the mics and leads as the band and punters began showing up about half an hour before sunset. By downbeat I was stressed to the eyeballs.

It was a rough and ready set-up. I was flying the mixing desk while fronting the band and the evening breeze was bothering the microphones. We knocked out a few of my comic songs, and the band and backing vocalist began to settle as the crowd did the same on the picnic benches in front of us. I had 'Going Home' at song five on the setlist and when the time came swapped guitars with Schaeffer to accommodate tuning differences between our respective axes. His guitar had no pickup, so I had to wrestle a mic into position in front of the sound hole to get it through the PA. We started into the song a little fast, as one tends to do when nervous and trying out a new song in front of an audience after a stressful set-up.

As the song picked up, I could see the audience tune in with the sun going down and the breeze from Kandahar blowing soft and warm on their backs. With each successive verse I could see nods and soft smiles of recognition. The song seemed to nail where we were now in that late summer of 2013 – ready to go home, changed by all we had been through, and uncertain about how we would face home life. After I strummed the last chord, there was a solid round of applause, and all was well in the world.

Going Home

Underneath these northern stars, picking on a mate's guitar
With the breeze from Kandahar blowing soft and warm
See my own is in its case, with the movers just off base
On a pallet down the space 'cause I'm going home

Fighting season got underway after harvest back in May
with attacks in Chahar Chineh and Charmeston
But the checkpoints all have held, it wasn't pretty but oh well
Let them do it all themselves cause we're going home

We don't get out too much these days, with the base in retrograde
This trip hasn't been The Guns of Navarone
Nothing like my first go round, out in the valleys round for round
Forty good men in the ground now we're going home

Now up on Kabul's streets I hear, there are billboards everywhere
of the Lion of Panjshir or a 3G phone
Meanwhile down here in TK, they're banking on MK
And the fighting Fourth Brigade cause we're going home

I don't know how I am going to fit back home
Been out here now so long this is what I know
Brother, thanks for your ear, life is easier out here
It's love and family I fear but I'm going home

Hear the Mullah sing his song, at the rising of the sun
Shares his love for everyone through a megaphone

> By the time he sings again, I'll be on that bird, my friend
> This war is at an end, and I'm going home

In 2012, Michael Balfour, a theatre producer at Griffith University, started work on a production called *The Difficult Return* with actors and ADF personnel. He asked me to write a song for the show. When I realised that 'Going Home' might resemble what he was after, I sent him a rough recording of the rehearsal with Schaeffer, Treasure and Alex. He liked it, so the following month I did a proper recording in New Delhi. I emailed the MP3 to Michael, who forwarded it to Sputnik Productions. They set up a collaboration with Defence public affairs and used some video footage of that first performance of the song in front of Green Beans as the basis for a music video. Ahead of the release of the video on YouTube (it's a nice clip, check it out), we gave the MP3 to Mates4Mates, who then put it on sale on iTunes to raise funds for their ongoing work helping returned soldiers.

Songwriting textbooks say that one exception to the 'show, don't tell' rule is the bridge device, also known as the 'middle eight', since bridges often have eight bars. If you listen to those classic sixties songs, you might notice that they blurt out the message of the song pretty explicitly in the bridge. Some people have commented that the bridge in 'Going Home' is the strongest part of the song and suggested I could have made more of it, maybe repeated it.

> I don't know how I am going to fit back home
> Been out here now so long this is what I know
> Brother, thanks for your ear, life is easier out here
> It's love and family I fear but I'm going home

My friend Anne works as a nurse in the psych ward for returned soldiers at the Heidelberg Repat Hospital in Melbourne. She reckons that the lyrics of this bridge, more than anything else I've written, capture the state of mind of most of her clients when they show up at the door of Ward 17.

CHAPTER 14

ERRORS AND AIRFIELDS

Write with the door closed, edit with the door open.

STEPHEN KING, *ON WRITING*

Neither power nor wealth, only Art and Science will endure.

TYCHO BRAHE (1546-1601), ASTRONOMER

MY APPROACH TO WRITING IS 'SHOOT FIRST, ASK QUESTIONS LATER'; i.e. there are two distinct phases – the shooting, and the asking of questions – and both are important. The shooting phase engages the 'creative mind', the equivalent of Chairman Mao's: 'Let a hundred flowers blossom, and a hundred schools of thought contend.' You follow your whims, write what comes to mind and stay open to 'inspiration' without chasing it into hiding. You become fascinated with your babies, ugly or otherwise, lavish them with attention, and see how they grow.

Then there's a second and equally necessary stage – asking questions, also known as 'editor's mind'. Editing challenges your willingness to 'kill your darlings'. You make judgements about how, or indeed whether, your creations will appear before the outside world. And judgement is the key word, bringing into play both sense and sensibility, and an instinct for how things will or might be perceived.

What happened next reflected a failure to apply this latter process; in other words, a failure of judgement. In the month ahead of the Green Beans concert on 27 August, the Sunshine variation on 'Woman in a War' I had improvised that night at Mr Lee's karaoke session began to grow in the vegie patch at the back of my brain. Setting the song in TK felt interesting, and a character named Sunshine with a pistol on her belt felt like juxtaposition in search of a song. So I began writing more verses. I finished it and rehearsed it, with Debbie singing the female role. Somewhere in the back of my mind, I knew that I really ought to run it past Sunshine to get her okay before giving it a public airing. But I didn't, perhaps because I felt too shy to approach her, perhaps because I was under-slept and overworked, or perhaps because I feared I'd need to edit it – or kill it altogether.

I had it at song six on the setlist for the Green Beans concert, and as the applause ended for 'Going Home', we ripped straight into the first verse.

> I was working down in TK in the last year of the war
> Karzai had decided he didn't love us anymore
> MK ran his checkpoints and construction companies
> And even Akhundzada had an exit strategy.

Then the second verse:

> Her name was Sunshine, she wore a pistol
> With a name like Sunshine, she should have wore a crystal . . .

I followed this with a hammed-up caricature of the male character's salacious thoughts. The fourth verse began:

> A couple of months later, at the Green Beans cafe
> On a hot August night we were sipping our lattes . . .

And on it went to a conclusion similar to the original – the guy propositioning her, then getting slapped down. Debbie really nailed the female character's reproach at the end of the song and the Tarin Kowt references got hearty laughs. It felt like the song really worked, but I did notice some raised eyebrows in the audience. I played out the rest of the concert and it went well — the images looked great projected onto the blast wall after dark.

As we were packing up, Dave asked me if I had run the 'Woman in a War' variation past Sunshine. He reminded me that he had said a few months before that the 'Woman in a War' song wasn't suitable to play on base. The penny began to drop for me – I'd made a mistake. After returning the US Post pallets, I got back to my accommodation container with adrenaline pumping and a bad feeling in my stomach. I wrote in my diary: *In retrospect, perhaps I should have let prudence rule*, but my subconscious knew the matter was serious. I hardly slept that night.

I was working in the office the following afternoon when Dave tapped me on the shoulder.

'Fred, a word?'

We went out to Poppy's and sat facing one another on the picnic benches.

'That new song you sang, "Going Home" – good. The "Woman in a War" song – bad. You're going to have to apologise to Sunshine.'

I could see he was right. To play it in that context without her permission was wrong.

'And I'm going to have to tell the ambassador,' he said.

I felt the blood start pounding in my head. DFAT prizes judgement above all, and this mistake reflected badly on my judgement.

I went around to Sunshine's office. Her office mate read the situation and slipped out the door. I sat down in the chair in front of her desk. Her expression was stern but still.

'I owe you an apology,' I said.

'Yes, you do.'

She said she hadn't been at the gig, but people had been asking her about the song. She was angry but calm and listed the reasons why it had been wrong to include her name in the song.

'I'm a pretty good sport most of the time,' she said, 'but this was a step too far.'

I apologised again and offered to do what I could to make amends.

'I accept your apology,' she said and thanked me for making it. We smiled faintly at each other, I bowed my head slightly, stood up and left the office.

As far as apologies go, it felt right. I was painfully contrite. She'd remained dignified and gracious while speaking her mind. But the matter didn't end there. There were one or two people who felt the performance of the song promoted an unsafe environment for women on the base. They made their concerns known to higher ups and demanded sanctions. News of this shocked me. I'm the only songwriter I know of who has written about gender violence in war. More to the point, the message of the song was, essentially, 'don't make inappropriate advances on women just because you're far from home in a war zone'.

The problem was that the song went about its business subtly and indirectly. It's a cautionary tale that delivers its message through irony and a device Randy Newman calls 'the dubious narrator' — i.e. you are not meant to like the male character. (Cue his 'Short People', for example, or 'Political Science'.) But I could see that this might have been a bit too subtle for a concert on a dusty parade ground on a hot August night in the middle of a war zone.

The following morning, a young ADF captain came up to me outside my office.

'Hey, mate,' he said, 'loved the concert the other night. I like the way you push the boundaries of political correctness.'

When I dropped my washing off at the laundry later that day, an older warrant officer also said he enjoyed the concert but thought the Sunshine references might have been a bit insensitive.

People will interpret a work of art differently, this much I've learned. While an artist probably shouldn't take too much responsibility for that, a public servant should. Singing the Sunshine variation that night was a mistake for which I won't defend myself. But the song, as originally written, I will defend.

Both the US and Australian military take sexual harassment and violence very seriously, and have recently launched campaigns detailing what's appropriate and enforcing clearly stated rules with court-martial sanctions. That's how the military deals with problems – it's a rules-based culture. As an artist, my approach to the problem of sexual harassment would be different. I would take a more subjective approach – to change the way men act by changing the way they think. I would tell a story. Back in the days before TV and the internet, stories were told by old men around the campfire at night to try to influence the younger men of the tribe towards behaviour more conducive to the collective good. Stories are useful for this; they illustrate how one thing leads to another: how attitude leads to behaviour leads to consequences, so they can trigger self-awareness.

On a base like Tarin Kowt, I told a story that began with a familiar landscape like Green Beans, which the male listener could relate to. I set a scene with features they could relate to, through eyes inflamed with the excitement of being in a war zone and intrigued by the beautiful girl getting around with a pistol on her belt. I inserted a couple of jokes, encouraging listeners to open up and invest in a story that made them laugh. I gave voice to the erotic, egotistical thoughts men have in this and every other situation, culminating with the hero cornering the heroine and proposing they consummate what he thought was their inevitable mutual attraction.

Then I threw a switch. I introduced another reality – hers! – which, strangely enough, was different to his. I had her reject his solicitations, mock his war zone chic pretensions and suggest he get back to his wife and family in the suburbs. Suddenly the hero looked like a loser as his delusions crumbled. The listener, having invested his sympathies in a male character he could relate to, suddenly gains a new perspective. He steps back to see the scenario from an alternative perspective, where he can observe that the male character he identified with has behaved like a dick. It is this power to trigger both subjectivity and objectivity that gives storytelling its strength as a moral tool. The listener can be both engaged and detached.

My disposition in all this is not to be judgemental about people's sexual misadventures. These things do happen in both civilian and military worlds, and not just among junior ranks. US Brigadier General Jeffrey Sinclair, who served in both Afghanistan and Iraq, was convicted of military crimes of adultery (a criminal offence in the US military), mistreating his mistress (a young female intelligence captain) and having improper relationships with two other women. He was acquitted of some nastier charges that went beyond sexual harassment.

War is a sexy business and power has an erotic charge. The soul abhors rules. Rules didn't stop Sinclair and others from doing what they did. Self-awareness might have, and everyone would have been saved from the practical consequences – the pain and indignity, the damage to the mission's reputation.

Anyway, it wasn't the time and place for a philosophical discussion about how narrative works. The ADF at the time was in the spotlight with a couple of sexual harassment scandals, so whatever the rights and the wrongs of the situation, justice needed to be done, and be seen to be done. In the office the following morning, I could tell there were deliberations going on around me. Sure enough, Dave suggested we step outside for a chat.

'What's the verdict?' I asked him.

He said it had been decided that I would go up to Kabul to talk to the ambassador. I said I thought that wasn't necessary, but I'd do it if that was what he had decided. He said an all-stations email would be sent to the effect that an inappropriate song had been sung at the concert the other night and that the singer was contrite. I said I'd be happy with that if Sunshine was – and if they added a sentence clarifying the point of the song but acknowledging it could have been misinterpreted.

Dave agreed.

I spent that evening tidying up work matters in the office. Then I headed back to my shipping container to pack. I opened up my laptop and found an email from the Brisbane soldier who had been at Derapet with Crash. He apologised for not responding to my email the year before. He said he'd been through hard times with 'self-medication' and the like, but that his mates were helping him pull through. He told me a little more about what happened on the morning of 24 August 2010. I replied with a few more questions.

The following morning, I went out to the flight line and met up with a couple of Afghan Electoral Commission officials who, as it happened, needed escorting up to Kabul. Sitting next to them on the flight up via Kandahar, I started haemorrhaging verses for the Derapet song in my little field notebook.

Arriving at Kabul, I arranged passage for my wards to the front gate, and then caught a ride to the hostel where the embassy's CPP guys lived. The hostel felt like a kind of monastic bubble, occupied as it was by middle-aged men far from home, living only for work, the gym and meals. It felt like shelter in a storm.

I tried to do some work in the days that followed, meeting with Senator Hanifi, Hamidi and a few other Uruzgan contacts, but I found myself writing furiously, gushing song lyrics like a Texas oil well, processing things through verse. The safety bubble of a hotel room is always good for that, and so is insomnia – I was only sleeping a couple of hours per night. The nervous system won't allow your body to sleep if it apprehends a threat, real or imagined. As a performer, I'd skated on the thin ice of irony most of my life, but this time the ice had cracked, dropping me in freezing water.

My email correspondence with the Brisbane soldier continued, and more verses to the Derapet song tumbled into my notebook. Sunshinegate had cracked me open creatively. It was all phase one stuff, nothing edited or completed, since my critical faculties were shattered by the insomnia and stress.

A couple of days in, I went down to the embassy. I got a few admin things done: arranging a visa for India for my forthcoming leave, and signing up for an embassy trip to the British Military Cemetery where the lyrics to one of my songs were rumoured to be chiselled into a memorial. Then I went upstairs for my appointment with the ambassador. He reprimanded me in reasonable but serious tones and made it clear that this incident would be noted on my file. He said he had read the lyrics of the song and understood its intent, but that I needed to be careful about where my impulses as an entertainer ended and my responsibilities as a government official began.

'Fair cop,' I said.

It was a line I had walked pretty well in the past but I acknowledged I had misjudged it this time.

On an unrelated matter, he asked if I had been interviewed on the recent promotion round. I said I had. He said the list of successful candidates had just come out and that my name was not on it. I thanked him for letting me know.

Leaving the building, I ran into the third secretary, who asked me what the hell was going on down there in Uruzgan.

'The reports you are sending keep spelling Uruzgan leaders' names inconsistently!'

I pointed out that most of our interlocutors were illiterate in their own language and cared not for how we spelled their names in English, but resisted the impulse to quote Ralph Waldo Emerson's 'Consistency is the hobgoblin of little minds, adored by little statesmen and philosophers and divines'.

I went back to the hostel with my tail between my legs, wondering if perhaps I wasn't cut out for the public service.

The following morning, still tender, I went out to the British Military Cemetery. Cemeteries, like stories, can be good for perspective, and perspective was something I needed right now. This cemetery was full of stories. It was located at the site of the Sherpur Cantonment where, in September 1879, Sir Pierre Cavagnari, the British envoy in Kabul, and his escort were massacred by mutinous Afghan troops. In response, a Kabul Field Force was assembled and marched into Kabul, where it set up camp at the Cantonment. In December that year, Afghan forces laid siege, eventually storming the camp. The assault was repelled, but many died on both sides.

The cemetery was now a quiet oasis of gardens and tombstones enclosed by a stone wall in the middle of a frenetic city. There were wooden benches and rose bushes tended by a father-and-son team, funded by the British Embassy. I strolled among the tombstones of soldiers and civilians of various nationalities buried here in Kabre Gora – 'graveyard of foreigners' – as it was known locally. Every headstone told a story.

Set into the southern wall was a stone for Lieutenant John Hearsey, of the 9th Queen's Royal Lancers, shot through the heart in December 1879. Nearby, a mass grave for unnamed infantrymen from the 67th Foot Regiment, mown down by Afghan fire as they tried to storm some hill in a land of many hills. There were other residents from more recent misadventures: a Cossack who fled to Kabul in the aftermath of the 1917 Russian Revolution; the British archaeologist Sir Aurel Stein and the Danish explorer Henning Haslund-Christensen, who both made it this far in the 1940s, only to perish. There were also small headstones marking the resting place of aid workers, journalists and, presumably, hippies from the 1960s. There was the tomb of an American eye surgeon shot in Kabul while trying to do good deeds amid the chaos of the last year of Taliban rule.

Lining the northern wall of the cemetery were memorials from the current NATO intervention, including a section with the names of Australian and New Zealand soldiers killed in Afghanistan since 2001. At the centre of this Anzac Afghan Memorial was a big black marble slate with gold lettering:

> *You give it your all*
> *Knowing if you should fall*
> *That all good things must die.*

Still bruised by recent events, I took some consolation in seeing my words consigned to posterity. I clambered into my body armour and rode back to the hostel with a heart more serene.

❖

A few days later I flew into Delhi International Airport and caught a taxi to the residential compound of the Australian High Commission, where I had spent the first three years of my life. That evening, I played at Friday night drinks at the high commission's Henry Lawson Club. I love Lawson, and used the venue as an excuse to include a rendition of John Schumann's setting of 'Scots of the Riverina'. The granddaddy of Australian war songs, Lawson's poem covers a broad canvas – an unhappy marriage, a struggle between son and father, a pointless tragic war, the perfunctory consolations of the bloodless Presbyterian church and some meagre redemption before death – all in just five verses. Ruthless efficiency.

After-work drinkers' yakking made the gig difficult, but by the end of the second set the listeners prevailed and spirits were high. I was accompanied by New Zealand-born guitarist Cameron Dale, an exceptionally tasteful musician and studio gun who had played for everyone from Katie Noonan to Guy Sebastian. He was living in Delhi with his wife, who was working at the High Commission. An encore was followed by a righteous piss-up, which for me at the time was just what the doctor ordered.

The following morning, slightly hungover, I voted in the Australian federal election at the ballot boxes set up in the chancery building. Then I went over to Cameron's place and recorded 'Going Home' in a little studio set up in his living room. *The Guardian*'s foreign correspondent, Ben Doherty, added some drums to my guitar and vocal tracks. Then Cam laid down an eerie organ-sounding track with a guitar effects pedal and had the song mixed and ready to master by the following afternoon. More ruthless efficiency.

I spent the next week in a hotel room in London, where Maryanne had been sent for work. I walked in St James's Park and worked on my laptop, trying to resurrect the *Dust of Uruzgan* theatre tour, and I wrote a teacher's resource pack (now available for free on my website) at the request of a few chalkie mates who were teaching *Dust of Uruzgan* songs in their literature and Australian Studies classes. It was a productive time, and restful for me – though not for Maryanne, who was exhausted, jetlagged, overworked and six months pregnant.

Tarin Kowt was cooler by the time I returned. There was still no rain, and with all the demolition work, and the Apache helicopter landing zone relocated to just south of the accommodation chalets, the air was dustier than ever. People were complaining of chest infections.

The first few days back felt a bit like the return of the prodigal son; the stress of Sunshinegate still lingered in my body memory. Sunshine herself, like many others, had gone home. There'd been some sort of inquiry, nothing big; apparently, a major had been tasked to interview the people involved. I was given no habeas corpus in the matter. They tried me in my absence, thereby denying me the opportunity to incriminate myself. When asked whether he thought the song was inappropriate, Treasure, apparently, had replied, 'Dunno, sir, I'm just the bass player.' Debbie Xinos was more forthcoming and told the officer she had relished the opportunity to sing her lyrics, expressing as they did defiance towards some of the chauvinist attitudes she had copped in the course of her long career in uniform.

I walked into the DFAC on my second night back and saw the American chaplain and the church band guys sitting there at a table. The chaplain waved me over; they all welcomed me with knowing smiles and pats on the back. The American church does a good line in forgiveness, I'll give it that.

I played in the church band that Sunday, strumming and singing along to the songs, including all seven verses of 'How

Great is My God', a song whose only lyrics were 'how great is my God' repeated ad infinitum. It had limited plot or character development, particularly compared to narrative classics like 'Scots of the Riverina' or 'Call Tyrone'. But it dawned on me that the American church was not a platform for songwriters to show their mettle. Church, rather, was where people went to wash themselves of the heavy burden of their egos, loudly proclaiming their humility to an unknowable God. As I'd come to understand, we could all use a weekly dose of humility.

I went outside the wire the following day for a provincial administration meeting. There was a new mayor in Tarin Kowt – a bright spark appointed by the governor – who proposed a sister city relationship between Tarin Kowt and an Australian metropolis in order to create an 'ongoing symbolic connection'. When asked which city he had in mind, he suggested Sydney. We admired his enterprise and ambition, but counter-offered with Unley, a large suburb on the outskirts of Adelaide, and the hometown of the Aussie PRT sergeant. Privately we thought a sister city relationship would be hard to sustain and might be used by Uruzgan officials to leverage visas. In the end we let the idea drop; thankfully, so did the mayor.

On the Wednesday, I made a final trip to Tarin Kowt prison to visit the last Australian PUC in the Uruzgan justice system. After interviewing the prisoner, I got yarning with the old warden, whom my predecessors had got to know well. He had been working in prisons all his life – with the Russians, with the Taliban, now with the new government. His wizened old face spoke of days, months, years, decades in a compromised system at the coalface of a profession where a good day is a day when nothing happens. I thanked him for his cooperation with us over the years, and we rolled back to base. I suppose I was the last Australian he saw.

❖

On 7 October, the *Australian Story* feature screened around Australia. We had no means of watching it in Tarin Kowt; internet bandwidth was crap, and in any case I was in a meeting with the terps when the show aired. We were sorting out their termination dates and homeward travel plans. In Canberra, a special visa category was being considered for interpreters who had worked with Australians in Afghanistan. They had all filled out visa applications and sent them to a PO Box in Islamabad. The paperwork was an inch thick. There's a general distrust of Pakistan in Afghanistan, so I don't think any of them truly believed the Pakistan postal service would deliver their applications to the high commission, let alone that they would ever make it to Australia.

I called Maryanne afterwards. She said the *Australian Story* piece was beautifully put together and made me look like 'Mahatma Gandhi with a harmonica'. She said it was a nice summary of all that I'd been up to over the last fifteen years, and that I should let myself be happy.

This was gratifying, but nothing changed for me on the ground and the workload began to accelerate towards the closure of the mission. On the morning of 8 October we hosted the final meeting between the governor and the senior civilian representative from Kandahar in PRT House. The governor was generally upbeat, though he complained of the difficulty of getting good staff to Uruzgan. He explained that the first female students would graduate from Uruzgan high schools in the next year and would be eligible to attend university.

'Education is the solution to all the problems,' he said.

I recalled the many meetings Kate Elliott had endured in that room four years earlier, trying to secure land for the Malalai Girls' School.

Meanwhile, Rafi was packing up his PRT House caretaker's office; I spent a couple of hours with him preparing the place for handover. It was a melancholy task, taking the wooden plaques off the wall from the eight rotations of Dutch, who had built PRT House in 2007. I pondered the thousands of meetings, and the millions of pages of notes that the building must've generated, with rotation after rotation of earnest foreigners leaning their shoulder to the boulder to try to move Uruzgan 'two yards down the field' (as Russ put it). I also remembered the concerts and good times we'd had in PRT House. It was a place where two worlds had met.

Abdul seemed oblivious to all this history when he came in to take receipt of the keys. He was focused on ensuring the generator still worked, and getting back to the governor's compound, where the governor was on his back about some problem.

The following afternoon, I wrote references for Rafi Shaheen and our three remaining terps Sadat, Zia and Umary. Then we cordoned off the back corner of the DFAC and had a farewell dinner for Rafi and Sadat. Sadat spoke the most fluent English of all our interpreters and made a nice speech in which he thanked me for the role I had played in bringing him and the others into the PRT terps pool.

Rafi was too shy to speak but was very happy; his father had just laid down 50,000 Afghanis by way of a deposit on a wife, with another 200,000 to be paid on delivery at a wedding date to be determined. We took him and Sadat out to the flight line and sent them off to an uncertain future. Zia and Umary, who remained with us, waving them goodbye.

❖

The following day, we got word that 28 October had been set as the date for a Transfer of Authority ceremony marking the closure of the Australian mission. The first job for Dave and me was to make sure the governor would be there, although Canberra was insisting, for operational security reasons, we hold off telling anyone outside the wire of the ceremony's timing. This was awkward; we knew the governor was making travel plans. Big Eid was scheduled for 15 October and most provincial government officials would be heading home. We called Abdul; he confirmed that the governor planned to be away towards the end of the month. The situation called for some massaging, so we invited Abdul in for dinner that evening.

He arrived at six thirty and we went into the DFAC. From his time with the Helmand PRT, he knew his way around a bain-marie, and stacked his tray with meat, fruit and vegetables. 'Where's the Pepsi?' he inquired.

We let him know what was planned for 28 October and gave him a broad idea of the calibre of people who would be showing up. He said he would need to do some work to persuade the governor to stay in town. He seemed a bit anxious about it. Dave changed the topic, mentioning that I was a musician.

'Oh really?' he said. 'I play the flute.'

'You must come and play with Fred sometime,' said Dave.

'Oh no. People in the provincial government must not know I play flute. You know – actors, musicians, movie people . . . What do you call them?'

'Artists?'

'Yes, artists — they are not respected in Afghanistan. Of course everyone loves music but artists are not respected. They will play at weddings and that is very good. But you must not arrange for your daughter to marry one.'

'Sound advice,' I said.

❖

Meanwhile, out in the province, the fighting season was winding down with the weather cooling and the holiday season approaching. The security forces had done pretty well over the summer. MK and his guys had successfully interdicted five suicide vests from a compound in Tarin Kowt. The American police mentors were pleased that the entire operation had been handled by MK's police, from intelligence to search to arrests to forensics, without help from ISAF.

Earlier in the month, in the far north of the province, the Taliban had launched an attack on the Gizab District centre, amassing around fifty men for the job. But the local police fought them off, killing at least a dozen, and pushing them twelve kilometres back with the help of '8SOK' (Special Operations Kandak), now resident in the province. 8SOK were thought particularly useful as they were all Hazarans and so had no compunction about killing Pashtuns. Most Taliban are Pashtuns; the Taliban, more a state of mind than a military structure, has been described as an extreme extension of Pashtun nationalism.

Big Eid provided a welcome lull. A mate of mine up at the special forces camp managed to burn the *Australian Story* feature onto a thumb drive and I sat in my Drehtainer watching it. It was indeed a beautifully edited piece, and emotional for me. It seemed to explain to anyone who cared all that I'd been up to for the last fifteen years, and why I'd strayed from the straighter path of a diplomatic career. the doco was also about more than just me. It shed light on the journeys of the families of soldiers I sang about, and on the kind of work DFAT does in complicated parts of the world.

The following morning I was walking to the PRT office when the regimental sergeant major, 'Squirrel' Tyrell, buttonholed me.

'What are you doing on the second of November?'

'Dunno,' I said. 'Probably sitting by the pool of a Dubai hotel.'

'We're putting on a Commemoration Ceremony out by the memorial wall for family members of soldiers KIA in Afghanistan. Keen to have you play a couple of songs.'

'I'd be honoured,' I said. 'Let me ask the boss if I can stick around.'

This Commemoration Ceremony was an interesting proposition. The Canadians had hosted such a ceremony when they pulled out of Kandahar in 2011, flying in parents and spouses for the day. They reported it had offered family members a bit of closure. I understand the idea had been debated internally with Defence at some length. DFAT supported it. Eventually, the Chief of Defence Force, General Hurley, decided to go ahead, and sent letters to the wives and biological parents of all forty Australian soldiers who had been killed in Afghanistan, offering them the opportunity to fly to Tarin Kowt and participate.

It was a courageous project and I wanted to be involved. I asked Dave whether I might be allowed to stick around. The embassy's plan had been to get us out immediately after the Transfer of Authority, but he was supportive and forwarded the request up the line. Then I checked with Treasure and Tompkins. Treasure said he was available to play, but Tompkins said the US chaplain had packed up the drum kit and sent it back to the States. It was never easy organising a gig in TK.

❖

After Big Eid, Canberra became tighter in the sphincter about approving our movement requests – I don't think we went outside the wire again. Risk management was the new religion, and I guess they weighed the potential risks with the potential benefits and decided there wasn't much left to gain.

We'd had one more planned trip to the governor's compound to discuss the results of the Uruzgan Monitoring and Evaluation Program (UMEP), but ended up hosting the session on base.

UMEP was a survey-based initiative to try to quantify the impact of international development work on the province. We had an in-house think-fest the day before. The senior AusAID officer acknowledged that trying to do development work in an ongoing conflict zone was always going to be hard. World Bank statistics showed that a country affected by conflict usually took thirty years to get back to the development stage it had been at when the conflict started. We knew we couldn't fix Uruzgan in eight years.

Someone worked out that the Dutch had put $300 million into the province since 2006, the US $210 million and Australia $120 million. Surveys showed education, health and roads were what people cared most about and that in terms of numbers of schools, hospitals and roads built, the progress had been significant. This was appreciated by most Uruzganis, but many were anxious as to whether the momentum could be maintained.

A deterioration of security after our departure was seen by Uruzganis as the main risk to future progress. Colonel Wade Stothart said we had to assume there would be some degradation of security when we left. Connectivity was another concern. If government and NGO workers couldn't get here, progress would grind to a halt. So the airfield remained critical. In a province defined by its isolation, the ongoing viability of the provincial government, development work and much of the economy depended on the airfield.

The airfield also affected the sustainability of our main project in the province – the ANA. Australia had invested a lot in the Fourth Brigade of the Afghan National Army in Uruzgan; their leave arrangements and much of their resupply came via the airfield. If the airfield stopped working, it would jeopardise their continuing operations in the province.

There was a lot involved in running an airfield: the US Army Corps of Engineers had laid down a pretty solid slab of concrete, but concrete alone does not an airfield maketh. You needed maintenance, baggage handling, trained air traffic controllers in the tower, mobile stairs to get people off the plane, safe and reliable aviation fuel, a fire fighting crew and, especially in Afghanistan, security.

All these elements had to come together to persuade a commercial air carrier, in this case KamAir, to continue flying to the strip. International forces had made all this stuff work for the last eight years, but it was not clear how or whether the Afghans would do it. Lack of resources was part of the problem; coordinating the various Afghan government and business stakeholders another.

We figured the chances of keeping the airfield running into 2014 would be pretty slim unless we brought it all together into a functioning system before we left. But for this, a lot would need to happen quickly. The ADF airfield engineers were struggling with the language barrier to convey to local officials what was needed, and were starting to think they would have to just throw the keys to the Ministry of Transport and Civil Aviation and leave.

The situation called for a hero to pull it all together. Apart from some early experimentation with paper planes, I knew nothing about matters aeronautical, so it wasn't going to be me. Flying Officer Samad 'Sam' Ali Reza of the Royal Australian Air Force seemed a better candidate. He spoke Pashto and Dari, as well as Hazara and English, and he knew a lot about aeroplanes and airfields. Either by dumb luck or brilliant management, the RAAF had sent this junior officer out to Tarin Kowt earlier in the summer in some functional role, but Dave and I and a few others began to see that he was the only person who could 'unfuck' the airfield situation (as they say in the ADF). Like the heroes of antiquity, though, he had a flaw and, we figured, was in need of the services of a diplomat.

On the afternoon of 18 October, I drove out to the airfield with a guardian angel. Sam was rumoured to be out there somewhere doing a survey of the airstrip with the provincial government Ministry of Transport representative. I came across a group of Aussie soldiers mentoring a platoon of Afghan soldiers on some drill. I asked their terps if they had seen Flying Officer Samad.

'Who?' one asked.

'You know, Sam – the Hazara guy in the Aussie uniform who plays chess with the older terps every night.'

'Oh, you mean the short guy, the arrogant one?'

'Yeah, that's the one,' I said, and they pointed towards a cluster of buildings on the other side of the airfield.

I would have said 'imperious' rather than 'arrogant', but either way, he had earned it. At the age of fourteen, at the height of Taliban excesses, he had escaped Afghanistan and made his way alone to Australia by boat. He had lived in a foster home and attended an Adelaide public school, blitzed his matriculation exams and gone on to Swinburne University to pursue his passion for aeronautical engineering. From there he had been recruited as an officer into the RAAF.

I found Sam over near the ANA aircraft hangar talking to, or rather at, a young man in a shalwar kameez and a sparkly red skullcap. Sam introduced me to Asmatullah, the provincial Ministry of Transport rep. With big almond-shaped eyes, hirsute knuckles and full lips, Asmatullah was a more sensual entity than transport officials I had met in Australia, with their clipboards and blue King Gee shorts. In conversation, he held not so much one's hand as one's finger, stroking one's hair with his other hand to ensure one was relaxed and comfortable.

Time was short. By now, most of the PRT civilians had left – bar Dave, Rohan, Stacey and me – so there were plenty of Nokias left behind. I gave one to Sam. I got Asmatullah a base pass and put my chauffeur skills and the PRT Hilux at their disposal. Sam brought his chess player's mind to bear on the big picture of the airfield while his fingers did some walking, making calls in Dari, Pashto and English, lining up meetings.

He persuaded the US firefighters on base to train some local ministry officers in airfield safety and leave their truck behind. He talked Base Command into gifting the air tower and generator to the Afghan authorities. He arranged for the base security guys to train the local police in search procedures. He spoke to ANA General Kandahari and his Aussie mentors about Fourth Brigade leave rosters and their ability to provide overall security to the base.

By the end of the week, the local elements were coming together. But some key suppliers and decision-makers were headquartered in Kabul; we needed to go up there for meetings but, short of a convoy of armoured vehicles, the ADF had no platform for running a junior officer like Sam around the capital. The Australian Embassy, however, did. So Sam lined up the appointments on the phone and I made arrangements with the embassy for transport and logistics.

On the morning of 21 October, we picked up Asmatullah and went to the flight line.

On that shaky little plane, I wrote a scratchy diary entry:

Asmatullah is up the front of the small white Beechcraft plane of the kind that 1950s rockers made a habit of dying in. He is trying to communicate to me with a series of smiles, winks and hand gestures that I can only pretend to understand. Sam is down the back, fast asleep. He sleeps the sleep of the self-possessed, like Napoleon on his horse. Anyway, here we are, three unlikely musketeers off on a mission to save Uruzgan from oblivion.

On landing, we dropped Asmatullah off in town, then went to the embassy's CPP hostel. Over dinner, Sam described how he had become fascinated with aircraft as a boy, watching the Russian helicopters circling Kabul. I tried to draw him on how he got to Australia, but he seemed reluctant to talk about it. We retired early. It had been a big week already.

Settling into my room that night, I felt the urge to launch into another creative binge and finish off the Derapet song I had started during my last stay at the hostel. But I knew from experience that getting lost in artistic revelry would cost me too much – to write you need to turn inward and let worldly commitments slide. I had too many balls in the air and I couldn't let them drop. Two weeks to go and a lot to do; there'd be time for writing when I got home.

The meetings came thick and fast the following morning, and Sam was brilliant throughout. We met with US Captain Clason, who was running an entity called Personnel Movements Concept. Their job was to fund flights to sustain the ANA. They had signed an arrangement with KamAir through the Ministry of Defence and were looking to get runs on the board and birds in the sky. Sam produced the ANA leave rosters and convinced them the airfield would be functional throughout November. Clason got excited and agreed to talk to KamAir about using Uruzgan in the first trial run for the program.

Then we met with KamAir. Sam talked them through the security procedures and fuel supply arrangements currently in place in Tarin Kowt; they were satisfied. He asked if KamAir might be in a position to support the Ministry of Transport and Civil Aviation with additional personnel on the ground. They said this should be possible if everything else was in alignment, and agreed to join us in a meeting with Personnel Movements Concept on Saturday.

In the afternoon we met with Dawi Oil. Sam outlined the potential business opportunities in Uruzgan. He offered to do a survey of the fuel supply farm and forward them the results.

The Dawi rep was keen to get involved, but asked if there were any potentially disruptive unresolved landownership issues. Dawi had had problems in other locations – different ministries had sought to charge rent for the same piece of land.

'We have been able to resolve these issues in the past by going to Karzai. Very small things go up to Karzai, you know!' he said.

Sam assured them ownership of the airfield and other parts of the base had been clarified. Dawi agreed to send a team down in early November.

Next stop was the Ministry of Transport. Initial signs were good: they said they were willing to provide administrative oversight, firefighters and technical personnel for the airfield. But there was a problem with money. The ministry was willing to send trained recruits to run the airfield, but had no budget for paying them until the Afghan New Year, 21 March 2014. They needed five months' worth of funds for wages and supplies. The Dutch had US$2.5 million allocated through development agency GIZ for 'capacity building' around the Civil Air Terminal that we helped launch back in June. They had written to GIZ, asking that these funds be allocated towards wages and ongoing costs, but the GIZ had declined, saying this was 'outside the scope of the program design'.

I called the Dutch embassy and persuaded them to set up a meeting the following day with GIZ. We needed to talk them both into showing some flexibility, and we were only going to get one crack at it. The situation called for a strategy, so I called Hamidi. He was now working in Kabul on a part-time contract with the embassy, but knew the Dutch well from four years in their employ. I asked him to come in the following morning to discuss a plan of attack, and join Sam and me in the meeting.

Hamidi arrived at nine. We explained the situation with the ministry and the Dutch, and he offered some strategic advice. The Dutch, he said, were very focused on 'capacity building', and had an aversion to paying anything that looked like ongoing wages. We should reframe the ministry request for funds as covering 'on-the-job training' and supplies rather than salaries; this would be more palatable in The Hague.

The meeting was intense. The Dutch were indeed fixated on 'capacity building', and only for the Civilian Air Terminal, not the airstrip as a whole. We argued 'capacity building' meant nothing without staff to capacity build, and that the air terminal would be a pretty sad place if the planes weren't flying to the airstrip. It took all four of us to get our points across, but in the end, they saw the logic of our arguments. The GIZ rep suggested Asmatullah redraft the Ministry's letter of request and resubmit.

We drove back to the hostel triumphant. I looked out the window at the old houses that covered the Kabul hillsides.

'Beautiful city,' I said, pointing up at the hills.

'Horrible houses,' said Sam. 'The only way to get water up there is to carry it. The city is overcrowded; it used to hold 200,000 people, now there are five million. It's the biggest city in the world without sanitation!'

Over lunch with Hamidi, Sam opened up a little more, confiding that, at the age of twenty-nine, he felt financially established and ready to get married. He was talking to his cousins in Kabul about a particular girl he knew of.

❖

The following day was Friday, the day of prayer and rest in Afghanistan. Sam took the opportunity to track down a long-lost cousin. That evening I found him on the landing outside his room. He was looking pale and smoking a cigarette.

'I just threw up!' he said. 'The food here is dangerous.'

'The staff are good, though,' I said, nodding in the direction of one of the receptionists who was cleaning up the mess in Sam's bathroom. 'I leave them tips and they look after me.'

'Yes, he is a good guy,' said Sam. 'He is trying to get an education but has to do this work to feed his family. He is the eldest son. I gave him a USB stick full of books and told him, 'You don't need to go to school, you can educate yourself.' I have books on everything: politics, engineering, maths. There are hundreds of educational institutions here in Kabul. In ten years, this place will be a long way ahead of Pakistan.'

He drew on his cigarette, then continued, 'My cousin came and visited today. We'd never met before. I have a lot of cousins. My aunt had eleven kids, another aunt had nine, the other seven. My cousin said I look like my grandfather. My grandfather owned land here in Kabul. He was a great guy. He was seventy-five when the Taliban killed him. They took him into prison and tortured him until he died. Unbelievable.'

'They are pigs,' I said.

'Worse than pigs.' Sam shook his head. 'My cousin said I looked young for a guy of twenty-nine. It was awkward. I couldn't say the same to him. He is forty-nine but he looks sixty. He is a qualified doctor but had to sell potatoes and tomatoes to survive during the Taliban years. Anyway, it was great to meet him – and my aunt is coming tomorrow.'

'The one with nine kids?'

'No, the one with seven.'

'How many brothers and sisters do you have?' I asked.

'I had six but two died. The four that survived are living in Australia now.'

'They followed you out?'

'Yes. When the Taliban came for us, my family dispersed – some went to Pakistan, some to Herat, some to Mazar-e-Sharif. I went to Mazar but they came after us.'

He showed me a scar where he'd been shot in the foot.

'It's better now, I've had surgery. A French doctor at the refugee camp gave me a letter, and that's how I got out of Afghanistan.'

The chundering seemed to have loosened his tongue, and he went on.

'I flew to Thailand, took a bus through Malaysia, then a boat to Indonesia. I was lucky at the Indonesian border. I made some good quick decisions.'

He told me that on the tiny, crowded boat from Indonesia to Australia, everyone thought they'd die.

'That's when I learned how strong the human instinct for survival is.'

'I don't think people in Australia know how lucky we are,' I said.

'No, they don't, and values are important. Teaching the young to understand community values – to make a better society – that's important.'

❖

On Saturday, 26 October, we got KamAir and the Personnel Movements Concept guys together for a meeting and agreed to test run an ANA sustainment flight in mid-November. Hallelujah!

The following morning, Sam rested up, recovering from a big week and his food poisoning. I went in to the embassy, where they were flat out preparing for the incoming delegation for the Transfer of Authority ceremony. Visits are hard work for embassies at the best of times, and this one was big: Prime Minister Tony Abbott, Opposition Leader Bill Shorten, their advisers, Afghan ministers, senior officers from AusAID, ambassadors from Australia, the US and the Netherlands, plus a big Australian media contingent – all about to descend on the base in Tarin Kowt. Accordingly, there was a flight going south to TK that evening with half a dozen embassy staff on the manifest, plus me, Sam, Asmatullah and Hamidi.

I went from the embassy to ISAF headquarters and had lunch with a US diplomat named Joe Relk. He'd prepared a forty-page brief for his ambassador ahead of the visit. I had asked him if the US Embassy had a spare snare drum for the Commemoration Ceremony on 2 November. He brought one in a bag with some sticks for Tompkins to use, as well as a book of photographs he'd taken during an earlier stint in Afghanistan. (Diplomatic services the world over are full of artistic types!)

The flight south was beautiful on that late autumn afternoon. The Hindu Kush mountains were browner than I'd seen them, with an early dusting of snow that caught the light of the sinking sun. Nearing Tarin Kowt, I looked down for the last time over the Chora Valley and identified the contours and features I'd walked with Zia and Willie and the team three years before.

We arrived in Tarin Kowt to find Rohan, Dave and Stacey tired and feeling the pressure of the imminent visit. We all met after dinner in the PRT office. Rohan laid out the plan, explaining to each of us what our roles would be in the proceedings. It took me a while to figure out how I was going to pull off my task. My job was to go to the front gate, meet the governor, bring him up to meet the prime minister, then fang it back down to the front gate to meet the provincial line directors and return them to the parade ground. It sounded straightforward enough, but I sensed there would be wrinkles.

'Okay,' I said, 'but I think I'll need Hamidi. He knows the directors well and can iron out any kinks.'

'You've got him,' said Rohan.

The following morning after breakfast, Hamidi and I did a reconnaissance of the parade ground; it had been graded and swept so smoothly you could have staged the French Open on it. We identified the chairs allocated for the governor and the provincial directors, then set out for the front gate in a minivan.

We didn't get far before I noticed that things were not as they had been described the night before. A new entry control point (ECP) had been set up on the road between the front gate and the parade ground, comprising a 'shoot' – a forty-metre stretch of road, surrounded by concrete T-walls and guarded by a machine-gun post, and a couple of Connex containers. Between the ECP and the parade ground, a temporary barbed-wire fence had been stretched across the road along which the governor was supposed to drive to meet the prime minister.

I asked the corporal in the ECP to have the fence moved. He called Base Command, who told him to leave it where it was – it could only be moved for ISAF vehicles. There had been a breakdown in communication. The PRT were all about the visit; Base Command were all about security, and they weren't going to budge.

I spoke with the corporal in charge.

'If the governor has to walk from here to the parade ground, he isn't going to be happy.'

'My orders are to let no cars in except for the authorised minibus. And we're going to have to search him.'

'What?!' I said. 'He's the provincial governor! We've never searched the governor. He's got a red pass; he doesn't need to be searched. He hates it when his staff are searched, let alone himself.'

'We've been told to search everyone.'

'Oh, for fuck's sake,' I said and called Rohan.

'Sorry, mate, can't help you,' he said. 'You're going to have to improvise. Good luck.'

Hamidi looked worried as we went to the front gate. He carefully explained the situation to the governor, who didn't take it well. I got thinking about the worst-case scenario: MK and the governor hated each other; they were rivals in the province. What would I do if MK showed up at the ECP at the same time – and got in without being searched?

Sure enough, as soon as we arrived at the ECP, MK showed up with his US police mentor. I explained the situation to the American soldier, while MK waited in his armoured SUV with its tinted windows. The soldier relayed the problem to MK. A couple of minutes passed but it felt like an hour.

He finally came back.

'Okay.'

When the governor understood that MK would accept being searched, he agreed to the procedure. They left their vehicles, were searched and walked together to the parade ground. Afghans could be cool sometimes.

By this stage, Hamidi and I were late picking up the line directors. We hurried back to the front gate and found them filing into the minibus, having already been searched at the gate. As they were getting settled into the minivan, Hamidi explained that they would need to be searched again. They began to click their tongues and shake their heads. I stood up and made a little speech apologising humbly for the excessive security measures. Hamidi translated.

By the time we got to the ECP they had calmed down. But not me; it took half an hour to process them and we arrived at the parade ground just as the ceremony was about to begin. In the front row seats were everyone who was anyone: the Australian ambassador, the Dutch ambassador in his orange tie, the US ambassador, MK, the governor, the Uruzgan chief justice sitting next to Mr Shorten, Mr Abbott sitting next to Colonel Kandahari.

It was a solemn ceremony. The prime minister made a speech. 'Australia's longest war is ending,' he said, 'not with victory, not with defeat, but with, we hope, an Afghanistan that is better for our presence here.'

He spoke about the progress that had been made in the province, with a particular emphasis on roads, health and education. He and Mr Shorten laid wreaths in front of the memorial wall. Then the Australian flag was lowered and the Afghan flag went up.

After the ceremony, everyone went to Poppy's for a barbecue. There was a comic moment when I saw the Uruzgan chief justice and a couple of line directors eating lamb chops while leaning up against the bar; a wooden sign above their turbaned heads read OUTBACK BAR. A neat juxtaposition of cultures; I had to take a photo.

Mr Abbott made another speech thanking the soldiers on behalf of the Australian public, and invited Mr Shorten to do the same. Soldiers and Afghan guests then posed for photos with both leaders. Cake was eaten and the delegation piled into the minivans and back to the flight line. Hamidi and I escorted the line directors back to the front gate and, for the very last time, waved them goodbye.

Later that afternoon, we took Hamidi and the embassy staff out to the flight line. When their bird took off for Kabul, the world went quiet.

CHAPTER 15

DERAPET

That's why he was where he was when
the round burst through his chest

FRED SMITH, 'DERAPET'

I WAS SITTING ALONE IN THE OFFICE THE NEXT MORNING WHEN A couple of 'geeks' showed up to take our laptops away.

'Wait a minute,' I said, 'we've still got business to do!'

'It says here you're scheduled to move out today,' said the young private, looking at his clipboard.

'Plans have changed.'

We agreed we'd have everything packed and sorted by the end of the day.

Soon after, Dave, Rohan and Stacey drifted in looking exhausted but relaxed. The plan had been for Rohan and Stacey to leave on 30 October, and for Dave and me to stick around, me to play at the Commemoration Ceremony, and Dave to speak to the families about the work the PRT had done in the province. But we'd heard Canberra was getting edgy for the usual duty of care/

risk management-type reasons and seemed inclined to yank us out as soon as possible.

So I woke up on 30 October not knowing whether it would be my last day in town. By mid-morning we got word that Dave was to fly back that afternoon but the embassy had managed to negotiate dispensation for me to remain on the grounds that there'd been a formal request from the ADF.

Dave sat me down.

'Here's what you gotta do – four things,' he said. 'Look after the ambassador when he gets here; deliver a presentation before the ceremony to the parents; play your songs at the ceremony; then steal the OUTBACK BAR sign and bring it up to Kabul for the embassy bar when you leave on the ambassador's flight. You'll have to loosen the nuts the night before.'

He gave me a list of statistics about the PRT's achievements and a spanner for removing the sign. I sensed he'd done this sort of thing before.

Late in the afternoon, Dave, Rohan and Stacey, along with Zia and Umary, chucked their bags into the back of the PRT Hiluxs, and Sam and I chauffeured them out to the flight line. As we drove past the PRT sergeant and the Other Government Agencies protection platoon, they hurled abuse, shouting: 'The hat, the hat!' Apparently there had been some running joke between Dave and the sergeant, who was so appalled by the condition of my Panama that he'd been agitating for permission to put it out on the range and blow it up.

It was true; the hat was stuffed, beaten to a shadow of its former self not so much by the rigours of war, but as a consequence of an ADF rule prescribing the wearing of hats in the DFAC, which meant I had to fold the hat and stuff it down the back of my pants every time I went for a meal. (The hat had seen dark places no Panama should.)

Anyway, laughs were had at my expense, and when we got out to the flight line there were hugs and handshakes and some nice group photos. It'd been a sweet little team that had worked well with the military headquarters on base. We all felt the end of an era as the Beechcraft set off into the sunset.

❖

The staff in the headquarters were nervous about this Commemoration Ceremony, certainly more than they had been for the Transfer of Authority ceremony. Having never done anything like this before, they didn't know how the parents would respond. Emotions were hard to predict.

There's an ADF joke about a private who comes in one morning to see his platoon sergeant. He was having a few problems at home and wanted to talk about it. The platoon sergeant replies, 'Emotional problem? See the padre!'

This joke is the ADF parodying itself, but there is truth in it. The padres are the emotional safety valve of the ADF machine. It's not so much their connection with God that facilitates this role as their mandate for discretion. In a competitive 'get on with it' culture, you can tell the padre anything. It struck me, though, that the padres had no one they could download to, so I kept an eye out for them. When I saw the Aussie padre that night at dinner, he looked burdened. I dropped into his office after dinner.

'Mate, we just don't know how this is going to break,' he said. 'We've never done this before. The family members will be tired, jetlagged, emotional. Every padre in the ADF is going to be on that plane, but who's going to look after the parents when they get back home?'

I told him I thought things would work out, then went back to the office, which was empty and quiet. It felt a bit lonely but reminded me that this was how it all started, Farid on his Pat

Malone in a sea of green uniforms. Contrary to Dave's instructions, I set up the office again in preparation for the biggest task he had given me: telling the story of our time here – and not just to anyone, but to the parents and wives of soldiers killed in the province. I felt a weight of responsibility. But I also felt that this was my purpose, the reason I'd come back to Afghanistan. I had the history, and I had met some of these parents and I knew they would prefer straight talk.

I started by considering a fundamental question worth asking when making any presentation: Who am I talking to? Fifty-seven family members had accepted General Hurley's invitation. The majority were parents rather than wives, and on the list were some familiar names, including Jenny Ward, Ben Ranaudo's mother, whom I had last seen back in April in the Dandenongs. Rob Moerland, Snowy's dad, who by now was a mate of mine, was also coming. Most of the others I didn't know, but their surnames were familiar to me from the memorial wall beside the DFAC. I was also familiar with the circumstances of each of their son's deaths.

The second fundamental question was a more internal one: What do I want to say? I opened up my notebook to a blank page and started scribbling. Not surprisingly, I found there was a lot I wanted to say.

By early afternoon on 31 October, the Adjutant was hassling me to get a copy of my intended speech for Colonel Wade Stothart to scrutinise. I suppose I could have been indignant at this, but I knew Wade had good judgement. I also knew that there was too much I wanted to say, and not enough time to say it. The text would benefit from the application of an 'editor's mind', and I was too close to it myself to step back and wield the blade. By 1700 hours I had a first draft ready. I emailed it to Wade, then set up a packing-crate stages at Poppy's for one last gig.

Given how much I had on my plate, it probably wasn't a great idea to play another gig. But people had been asking if I was going to play again and I wanted to get Treasure and Tompkins warmed up for the ceremony. Perhaps, too, I wanted to finish my TK concert career on a good note after Sunshinegate. It was a quieter gig than the previous two, with Tompkins playing the snare drum I'd borrowed from the US Embassy rather than a full drum kit. Debbie and a couple of other backing singers came along and it all sounded good. A small but high-quality audience showed up and the whole thing had a lot of heart, and a nice sense of closure for the little band that had come together over the final months of the mission.

I got back to my Drehtainer that night with one more problem on my mind. I had met with Wade and the RSM the day before and suggested we get some of my mates in from the valleys to talk to the parents – wise old guys like Malim Habibullah or Haji Zahir Barakzai, who would know what to say and set them at ease. But the headquarters team felt it might be too confronting for the parents to meet with Afghans. In any case, the schedule was tight and unpredictable with the flight timings, and talking properly with Afghans always took time.

I was in the shower thinking about arguing the toss on this when I had an idea. I went back to my container, dried off and began poring through the transcripts Zia and Umary had written up from the interviews I had done back in May.

Reading the transcripts was interesting. There was a lot to go through, and a range of perspectives, both positive and negative, on a range of topics. Colonel Haneef, the fierce and inscrutable chief prosecutor, had praised the aggression of the Australian soldiers, as a result of which there were far fewer places in the province where insurgents could hide.

He said Australians and Dutch had done well to promote balance between tribes in the province, although the Afghan government had not always been helpful in this.

Engineer Hashim said the provincial administration during the Taliban years had comprised only a governor and four line directors supervising a handful of staff.

'Now there are twenty-three line directorates. Some have five or six staff, while others have forty or fifty.'

Haji Rahmatullah, Popalzai tribal leader and former director of education, said that during the Taliban times all schools were inactive; only madrassas (Islamic religious schools) were operating and they were a breeding ground for young radicals. He spoke of a number of the schools Australians had built, including the Malalai Girls' School, which now had 700 students and was the first opportunity girls had had to go to school in Uruzgan.

Rahmatullah also offered some interesting big picture perspectives. He listed the five main things the international community had achieved in Afghanistan: highways and roads; a viable education department; the development of systematic and organised government after years of chaos; a vast improvement in security; and the establishment of basic elements of a modern economy – a stable currency, a mobile phone system and the introduction of the internet to Afghanistan. All of these were big achievements after forty years of war.

Rahmatullah said ISAF's main mistakes were civilian casualty incidents: airstrikes gone wrong and situations where innocent people had been attacked 'based on wrong information'.

'People understand that these sorts of mistakes happen in war, but this has been the main cause of loss of support for ISAF among Afghans.'

Rahmatullah said people did not view ISAF in the same light as the Russians or the British invasions of the nineteenth century.

'The US and NATO forces came to Afghanistan with the agreement and support of the international community and stayed at the request of the Afghan government. People understand that the goals of the mission are removing terrorism and bringing peace to Afghanistan.' He, like others interviewed, pleaded for ongoing support for Afghanistan from the international community.

Of most interest to me was the transcript of the very last interview I had done at the end of May with Khaksar, the old poet, historian and pharmacist from Chora. I had opened the interview offering fond recollections of the beauty of the Chora Valley and the exquisite quality of light up there. He agreed it was indeed a land of abundance and launched into an abridged history of the district.

'You see, Chora was originally inhabited by Hazara tribes, but they were driven northwards by Pashtuns from the Barakzai sub-tribe 115 years ago. We have lived there ever since.

'I was born in Chora but went to high school in Paktia then graduated from the political faculty of Kabul University. I was teaching in Tarin Kowt, but when the civil war broke out it became too dangerous and I had to go back to Chora. Then, when the Taliban took over, it became difficult for an intellectual person to live anywhere in Afghanistan, so I migrated to Pakistan and stayed there for eight years. I returned to Chora when international forces kicked the Taliban out.

'I have been writing poetry and small novels and chronicling daily events for forty years. I published my first book when I was a refugee in Quetta, Pakistan. My fifth book on Uruzgan will be published soon, and I have twenty other books that I am hoping to find the money to print.'

I think in the back of my mind I had always been a little dismissive of Khaksar. Perhaps I'd absorbed the attitude of the soldiers in the FOB Mirwais 2 Shop who took the views of warriors like Malim Sadiq more seriously. But now I marvelled at his productivity, toiling for little worldly reward in the barren soil of an obscure little province. Some people are pathological storytellers – I guess there's one in every village!

'Five books about Uruzgan! That's a lot to write about a small province,' I had responded.

'It is a small province,' he said, 'but an important one in Afghanistan's political history. The Taliban leader Mullah Omar came from Deh Rawud, you know, and of course Karzai began his rise to power here in Uruzgan.'

'I've heard this but never understood what actually happened,' I said.

'Well, when international forces first came to Afghanistan, they got together with the Northern Alliance and drove the Taliban out of the north of the country. This wasn't too hard because no one up there really liked the Taliban in the first place. But here in the Pashtun south, it was harder to get rid of them. The West was looking for a Pashtun leader for the new Afghanistan because we are the biggest tribe. So Karzai saw an opportunity. He travelled by motorbike from Pakistan to Tarin Kowt and tried to rally local leaders against the Taliban governor. He got some support, but the Taliban soldiers came after him and he fled into the mountains near Deh Rawud. He was about to be captured when he called a CIA contact on the satellite phone they had given him, and a helicopter was sent just in time to save his life.

'A few weeks later, Karzai returned to Uruzgan, this time with a team of twelve US special forces soldiers. They began training and arming local militias out in Deh Rawud. They were aiming to build up a big force, but when they got word that locals had driven the Taliban governor out of Tarin Kowt, they realised it was now or never, so they moved down to the town with the small group of men they had and took over the governor's compound.

'When Taliban headquarters in Kandahar found out about this, they sent a big convoy up the road to deal with this little band of troublemakers. The convoy left Kandahar late in the afternoon, but it was Ramadan, so at nightfall they stopped in a village half way to eat. They decided to camp there overnight rather than drive through the night and attack at dawn. This delay gave the US soldiers time to organise their airforce. The next morning, as the convoy drove in broad daylight across the open plains to the south of Tarin Kowt, American fighter planes and bombers attacked and destroyed the whole convoy in fifteen minutes. There were smoking wrecks all over the desert. This changed everything. The Taliban guys in Kandahar saw they couldn't win and started heading for the Pakistan border. Tribal leaders rallied behind Karzai as he swept south and took Kandahar. Two months later he was elected interim president.'

The transcript shows the conversation moved on to more local matters. I asked about a matter close to my heart, the suicide attack on David Savage. Khaksar repeated basic details I already knew without saying who was behind the attack. I remember sensing at the time that he knew more than he was letting on. Even a poet is not free in Uruzgan.

He was more forthcoming about the death of Malim Sadiq.

'The enemy damaged many things with one arrow that day. They deceive our mullahs with jihad and play with the minds of our teenagers to persuade them to kill our leaders. They kill Afghans and they kill themselves with this political nonsense. Every night I pray to avenge Malim Sadiq, to punish whoever organised his death. I would do it myself if I could.'

They say history is written by the victors. That's not quite right, the victors are generally too busy being victorious – and, in any case, are only marginally literate, Ulysses Grant and Churchill excepted. It's the poets and writers who write history. Not fighters by nature, they tend to see all perspectives, but in the end must choose sides, life being as it is.

I stayed up till 3 am reading the 100 pages of transcripts. All these stories and perspectives were fascinating, but not what I was after. I was looking for words I felt the parents should hear; of course, in the end, there were too many. I ended up grabbing just a handful of paragraphs from four of the Uruzgan leaders, setting them out in a Word document with annotations identifying the related time code on the video. I awoke at 0800 and took the document and video files in to bandmate and public affairs officer Kristin Gardiner, who had video editing skills. I explained the job to him and his boss Haydn, who gave him the green light to get stuck in to it; Kristin set to work compiling a single MP4 of the various Afghan leaders speaking.

I went back to bed and woke at midday needing to piss. Opening the door of the container, I stepped into the corridor in the flamboyant dressing gown my mother had sent, looking like a dishevelled pimp emerging from his mistress's boudoir. I bumped right into a line of thirty US soldiers standing to attention in the corridor. They were about to move into the containers the PRT guys had just vacated. I mumbled 'at ease' and shuffled past them down the stairs to the washrooms, aware that in one single moment I had confirmed all their prejudices about civilians.

That evening I went in to see Wade about the speech. Initially, he was conspicuously diplomatic, flattering me, saying I was a very powerful storyteller, before suggesting we might need to prune a bit. I guess he figured I was a red-head and an artist, precious and volatile, and, having fielded the complaint after Sunshinegate, probably suspected I was also a loose cannon. I made it clear that I was neither, that I was here to serve, and we rolled up our sleeves and began wielding the knife.

I had included a couple of paragraphs addressing the question: 'Was it worth it?' Wade suggested that this was neither the time nor place to ask that question so directly – it was too early to say, too hard to answer and too tender an audience. I heeded that advice and am glad I did, cutting this text and more until we had about ten minutes of speech.

On my way back to the accommodation lines I dropped in on Kristin. He had got Sam in to overdub translations, a job a bit below Sam's pay grade, but all our interpreters had left by now. I found them sitting together at Kristin's desk, speaking the last translation into a microphone. At 2300 hours, he gave me an MP4 on a thumb drive. I took it back to my container and stuck it on my laptop, then stayed up another couple of hours packing all my stuff for my flight to Kabul.

The next morning, I hauled my bags into the PRT office. I then went to Poppy's and connected my laptop to the same projector through which the Dutch had watched the World Cup soccer final back in 2010. I was testing the audio when my little Nokia rang; it was the ambassador calling from the airport in Kabul. He said his chartered plane had been assessed unserviceable and he wouldn't be able to make it. He wished me good luck, asked me to pass on his apologies and lay a wreath on behalf of the embassy.

At 1100, a C-17 from Al Minhad Air Base with the fifty-seven parents and wives, along with Chief of Defence Force General Hurley, Major General Orme from headquarters in UAE, and every padre in the ADF landed on the TK airstrip. The parents were brought onto base in minivans, then drifted into Poppy's looking, to me, like a folk club audience: somewhere between middle-aged and elderly, in no great hurry, dressed in cardigans and light jackets, with an air of vulnerability about them. As the padre had predicted, their journey had been a long one. They had all flown from their respective hometowns to Perth then to the UAE and finally here. But of course, they were all at different stages of a more profound journey: a journey of grief that had begun on the day the notifying officer had knocked on their door. For some it would never end.

When they were all seated at Poppy's, Wade got up, welcomed them, outlined arrangements for the day, and thanked them for coming so far.

'It's like a small country town out here,' he said, 'or a family, and we think of you all as part of our family. I realise today could be very emotional for you; it'll certainly be emotional for us. We've got a few things programmed for you and we want you to have a chance to have a wander around the base and look out at the countryside. But first I am going to turn you over to Fred Smith from the Provincial Reconstruction Team. He is going to talk to you about what they've been up to out here for the last seven years.'

I stood up and smiled.

'Welcome to Uruzgan. I appreciate you coming here. I realise it's a bit out of the way. And you've come at a bad time – Movember – and there are some nasty moustaches around.' I nodded in the direction of a few of the soldiers who were sporting shockers.

'As you can tell by the condition of my hat, I've been here a long time. I first got here in July 2009 and worked for eighteen months through to January 2011. Then, in May this year, I decided to come back for a second stint, I suppose because this is a mission that I believe in, but also . . . I like it out here!

'I mean, it is not without its challenges,' I added. 'Day to day, it's cramped accommodation with communal ablutions, heat, dust – the dust gets into the laptops, which don't talk to each other because we're working on three or four mutually incompatible computer systems. And when we're not struggling to communicate with each other, we are trying to talk through interpreters to people from a profoundly different cultural background who themselves are struggling to survive in a fiercely competitive tribal environment while dodging incoming rounds and rockets from a violent syndicate of foreign-funded religious extremist wackos too small to take on Afghan security forces directly but big enough to harass and intimidate with roadside bombs, assassinations and rude letters. But apart from that, it's all pretty straightforward.'

They laughed.

'In April, just before I came back, I was playing a gig in the Dandenong Ranges out to the west of Melbourne. Jenny showed up at the gig' – I nodded towards her at one of the tables – 'and when I told her I was about to go back to Afghanistan, she looked me in the eye and asked, "Are we making a difference there?"'

'I said something like, "Well, yes, I think so . . ." But I wasn't sure, you know. We come here for short stints, eight months to a year, and only see the difficulties, not the progress. It feels to me like the people best placed to answer that question are the older Afghans. They were here when we came, and they'll be here after we've gone. I could bang on for hours about all that we've done here, but why would you believe me? I'm a Canberra bureaucrat with a message to sell. But please, listen to some of my mates from the valleys.'

With that I nodded to Haydn to start the video on the laptop. He pressed the mousepad but it didn't work; the MP4 had jammed. I improvised, quoting John Lennon.

'Life's what happens when you're making other plans! But it's like that out here, things often don't work – the dust you know, gets into everything. Actually, I've written a song about it . . .' and all of a sudden the video started and the governor's voice came booming through the speaker.

'*The Australian Army, military and special forces have tirelessly served in this province. Security is the backbone of a province; if there is no security there will be no development, no schools, and no hospital. So security is very important, and the Australian Army, side by side with ANSF, have brought security to Uruzgan Province. When they first came to the province, the security in Uruzgan was limited from Tarin Kowt to the Garmab Bridge, but now it has been extended to the borders of all the districts of Uruzgan.*'

Next, the less officious tones of Malim Habibullah.

'*People were in huge trouble with the insurgents – parts of their bodies were being cut off, their ears and noses – people died while being tortured by insurgents with sticks and stones. Now people can relax; people can now feed their families through work, and our children have a very good life now we have a very secure environment. Children saw the very bad times we had in the valley, now they do not have worries about their security.*'

Then old Haji Zahir Barakzai, the bespectacled Dorafshan tribal leader, spoke.

'*Since Australians came to our land – Afghanistan and Uruzgan – it is like we were sitting before in darkness and now we are sitting in the light. More construction has happened in our province, our roads asphalted, ditches have been made, our agriculture is improved. Australia has lost many sons in our province and we are very sad for them because they were guests in Afghanistan and were not supposed to die here.*'

Next on screen was Dr Myakil, the hard-working provincial director for health.

'*When I came at the end of 2001 to Uruzgan Province, there were only two health facilities . . . But now there are twenty-nine health facilities available in Uruzgan Province, as well as three hundred and eight-five health posts.*'

Then Habibullah spoke again.

'Now the Afghan National Security Forces have replaced the Australians in the patrol bases, people in the villages feel happy about this. They understand that the international forces cannot stay here in Afghanistan forever, and that therefore it is important to have Afghan security forces for the future of the country.

'I appreciate the work of international forces in Afghanistan who helped the people emerge from disaster to prosperity, particularly here in Uruzgan, where I appreciate the efforts of the coalition, as a consequence of which we now have a better environment. The blood that has been sacrificed by coalition forces here for the poor people of this province will not be forgotten.'

My speech as originally written had me then regaling the families with some of the statistics Dave had given me. But as the MP4 ended, I looked at the faces of the families and felt instinctively that there was no need to plough on and inflict statistics on them. My Afghan friends had made their point at a heart level, and it had been received at a heart level.

So, after a pause, I began to improvise.

'I wish you could have met some of these men. We were hoping to get some of them to come in and talk to you, but the program looked too tight – and believe me, there is no such thing as a short conversation with these guys. Afghans are very conversational people, courteous, funny, and with a deep tradition of hospitality.

'They look and sound so different to us, but maybe it won't surprise you to know we are similar. They want the same things we do: a safe home, to be able to water their gardens, go to hospital when they need to, drive on safe roads, to look after their children, send them to school, and have something to hope for. The problem with ongoing conflict is all these simple things become impossible and there is nothing to hope for. And that's why we are here, to help a peaceful majority defend themselves from a violent minority.

'The feedback we've got is that our soldiers created security out in the valleys, and on the back of that, we in the PRT have been able to provide people with some basic services. I'm not saying the situation is perfect; I could talk for hours about the problems here. We haven't turned the province into Switzerland, nor rolled out the NBN. But they don't want the NBN here, just security and basic services, and the provincial government has been able to deliver some of these.

'I was going to hit you with a whole list of statistics, but I'll spare you!' They laughed with relief. 'You came here to feel and experience. To see the digs, and the mess, and the gym where your boys lived and played. To look out to the valleys where they fought and died. It must've taken a lot of courage to decide to come and spend time with us. I thank you for doing so.'

I finished there. A gentle pattering of applause followed, then the parents milled around a bit. Haydn gave me a quiet thumbs-up. He knew I'd put a lot into it. Sapper Jamie Larcombe's dad came up to me and said, 'Thanks, I needed to hear that.'

General Hurley thanked me and asked if there was anything he could do. I explained that the cancellation of the ambassador's flight had left me without a ride home.

'How about a lift to Dubai?'

He turned to his adjutant and asked her to make it so.

Nice. I could go out in style.

The family members were taken on a tour of the base followed by lunch. With the ceremony due to start at 1300 hours, I went from Poppy's straight down to the parade ground to sort out the PA. Tompkins showed up at 1230 and set up the snare drum. I hadn't had time to fully explain to him or Treasure what the ceremony was about. He was gobsmacked.

'Man, the US Army could never do something like this!'

He was right. They had lost too many soldiers in too many provinces to contemplate staging such ceremonies. In Uruzgan alone they'd lost forty-eight.

At 1255, the parents shuffled out from lunch in the DFAC and onto the parade ground, where they began to take their seats. Private Treasure emerged from the direction of the accommodation blocks, bleary eyed and blinking in the sun, bass in hand. Having pulled another nightshift in the Geek shop, he had clearly been deep in REM when his mate woke him. I explained what was going on as he plugged his bass in to the PA. Then we slipped behind the concrete memorial 'T-wall' which afforded some shade and a kind of backstage Green Room, out of view of the family members, who were mostly seated by now. With all the Australian soldiers standing in ranks behind them and to the side, it felt as if the parents were being embraced and protected by those who had remained for those last months of the mission.

It was hot and bright when the RSM gave us the cue to start the ceremony with a rendition of 'Dust of Uruzgan'. It wasn't appropriate to wear sunglasses, and my beat-up Panama didn't afford much shade. Squinting in the blinding daylight, I could see Jenny and Angelo, Ben Ranaudo's father, sitting in the front row. They were both in tears and holding hands, although they had been separated for some time.

A dignified and solemn ceremony followed, much in the style of an Anzac Day ceremony. There was a catafalque party, Bible readings, and a recording of 'Abide with Me'. General Hurley made a short speech, and wreaths were laid at the base of the memorial. Then the band and I came out again and brought the ceremony to a close with 'Sapper's Lullaby', with Debbie Xinos and Mark Correa, an American soldier, chiming in on backing vocals. Again, I could see Snowy's dad sitting right in front of us, holding hands with his former wife, Snowy's mother.

As I strummed the last chord, there was silence across the parade ground. Eventually, the padre stepped up to the podium and invited the family members to come up and place poppies by the memorial wall. I unplugged my guitar, slipped behind the T-wall and, leaning against it, took a deep breath, exhaling really slowly. The band were emotional too. There was a quick round of hugs and handshakes and farewells before they went back to work, or in Treasure's case, to bed. The parents were milling around the memorial wall.

I was still leaning on the wall thinking about what to do next when a rough-looking bloke in his fifties rounded the corner, clasped my hand and burst into tears. He apologised.

'I didn't want those cunts to see me crying.'

He introduced himself; by his surname I knew him to be the father of one of the sappers in 'Sapper's Lullaby'.

'That was the first time I've heard the song,' he said. 'A mate sent me the CD a couple of years ago but I haven't been able to bring myself to play it. Glad I didn't. Mate, that was moving.'

Everyone drifted up to Poppy's, where there was cake and speeches and bouyant conversation. I could hear it all going on through the walls of the PRT office where I had all my stuff spread out. I was frantically repacking for my flight, moving things from one bag to another, chucking things in the bin. The change of flight arrangements called for a different pack: I had to rearrange my bags so I could fit the snare drum and the civilian body armour into a bag that the movers at Al Minhad Air Base could send back to Kabul. Then I chucked my bags in the tray of the PRT's last Hilux and fanged it out to the flight line, hoping to make bag-drag in time for the 1600 flight with General Hurley and the parents.

I pulled up and ran into the movers' shed, found a corporal with a clipboard, and told her I thought that I was on the manifest for the next outbound flight.

'We've got you on a second freight flight at 1750. You'll be the only passenger.'

I suppose I had my heart set on the symbolic nicety of leaving Uruzgan in the same plane as the families. For a moment, I considered whether to take being shunted onto a freight flight personally. But I figured that there might've been practical reasons and that, in any case, it was a better option than walking. I was in good humour from the day's events, so I went with my 'cheerful indifference' motto and shrugged it off. I handed over my bags and strolled out to the tarmac, where the families were saying their goodbyes in preparation for boarding.

When the loadmaster signalled 'time to go', all fifty-seven family members, along with their assigned ADF hosts, arranged themselves for a group photo in front of the C-17. I happened to be standing beside General Hurley watching. Someone called on him to join the group pose and he stepped forward. I was considering whether I ought to do the same, when one of the parents waved me in. I stepped forward and was about to pivot towards the camera when I heard a senior ADF officer from the visiting party call out, 'Get out of the way, Fred!'

I scurried back to where I had been standing, embarrassed to have presumed that my role in the day's proceedings, my friendship with some of the family members and two years of service in the province had earned me a place in this photograph.

As the C-17 took off, I stood there on the tarmac with Wade and Squirrel, who were glowing with quiet satisfaction and relief at the way things had gone. They thanked me for sticking around. I hadn't eaten all day, so I headed back to the DFAC to grab a bite before the flight. I found Sam sitting with Haydn and Kristin. I thanked him for doing the overdub translation on the video but he didn't seem to take it on board – he had better things on his mind.

'It's done,' he said. 'Decided! Her mother in Kabul has agreed!'

'Oh, the girl,' I said, remembering he was hoping to marry. 'That's fantastic, Sam.'

I joined them for one last meal in the DFAC, then Haydn and Kristin drove me out to the movers' shed for the 1730 flight.

When we got there, I slipped around the back of the shed for a pee and I found, to my wonder and amazement, a Dixi, a genuine Dutch Dixi, certainly the last on base. The Dutch must've left it behind. After all these years it had the mystical presence of a unicorn. I was so pleased, I asked Haydn to photograph me and Kristin standing beside it before they waved me off.

I walked across the tarmac in my body armour and helmet with the sun setting over Deh Rawud. Reaching the plane, I turned and took one more look at my beloved mountains, then climbed the ramp into the back of the C-17.

C-17s are the second-biggest military aircraft in the world. I'm not usually a sucker for 'the beauty of our weapons' because I know how much they cost. But the C-17 is what Treasure would call 'awesome'. They don't just saunter down the runway and putter up into the sky. The pilot throws a switch, four jet engines explode and the muscular frame launches from 0 to 500 in about two seconds.

I was sitting in the belly of this beast, on the webbing seats against the side bulkhead of the plane, leaning forty-five degrees to my left to compensate for this sudden thrust of speed as the bird screamed and shuddered down the runway and up over the mountains. It felt like a poet's exit, alone in the cavernous cargo hold with four homeward-bound Bushmasters chained down like bulls for company.

Three hours later, as we closed in on UAE, I was made to feel like a prince. The pilots invited me up into the cockpit of this magnificent aircraft as it cruised in over the lights of Dubai and landed at Al Minhad Air Base as if on a cushion of air.

❖

In the days that followed, my soft landing from the war got softer. I checked into a hotel in Dubai, and the following night dined with Dave and Rohan, who were passing through on their way home. We sipped gin and tonics on a warm night and Dave forgave me my failure to nick the OUTBACK BAR sign in the circumstances; I understand it eventually made its way to the embassy rec room as a result of more formal liaisons between Wade and the ambassador.

On return to Australia, I didn't slow down; I went on tour. In the arts you're only fashionable for fifteen minutes a decade. In the wake of the *Australian Story* feature, I felt the need to make hay while the sun shone out of my arse (pardon the mixed metaphor). I gigged with Liz every weekend through November and December, only really stopping in early January when the baby was due.

The thing about stopping and staying still is that you can actually get things done. It had been on my mind to finish the Derapet song I had promised the Brisbane soldier. So one morning in early January, I cleared the crap off my desk, opened up my notebook from that last week of August and started punching verses into the computer from pages of handwritten scrawls. I find handwriting useful for 'creative mind' phase; indeed, I've handwritten most of this book. But computers are useful for 'editor's mind'. You can set things out clearly, step back, cut things, paste things, shift things around. There was a lot of that to do – this song, like 'Dust' of Uruzgan', was going to be long.

Computers are also good for research. I knew most of what I needed to know from my email exchanges with the Brisbane soldier. But songwriting is a scavenger's profession and everything is useful – you can never have enough details on your palette, even if you don't end up using them all. A Google search on 'Battle of Derapet' yielded links to maps, interviews and photos, including a series of shots from Crash's funeral: a grey morning at Ashgrove Baptist Church in Brisbane, the pallbearers, the catafalque party, and shots of Prime Minister Gillard standing beside Mr Abbott, Air Chief Marshal Angus Houston, the Chief of Defence Force, and Lieutenant General Ken Gillespie, the Chief of Army, their faces racked with sorrow and the gravity of the occasion. There was also a photo of a heavily pregnant young woman in a black dress, sitting in the front row at the church service, her infant daughter by her side, being consoled by an older couple, perhaps her parents. It was Crash's wife Beckie. The *Courier Mail* article reported she had given birth to a son, Noah, later that day.

Our baby was due on 8 January. The day arrived but the baby didn't. This did not surprise me. My wife has never been on time in her life. Her father was a Greek jeweller and watchmaker. Greeks love nice watches but only use them for ornamental purposes. The doctor at the hospital recommended we induce, given the statistically proven risks with 'older mothers'. Maryanne said 'no'. Negotiations ensued and we agreed that if the baby didn't arrive within a week, we'd come in for the procedure.

By the late afternoon of 15 January, nothing had happened, so with trepidation we chucked our bags in the car and went to the hospital. Maryanne's waters broke on the linoleum floor of the foyer as we walked into the hospital that evening. At six thirty the following morning, Olympia was born. I felt like I'd been hit in the bum by a rainbow, and I've been happy ever since.

Now in the evenings after work I roll around on the living room floor with a two-year-old Oly and she says, 'I lub you my daddy,' and I feel blessed. I came home from Afghanistan better – freer, clearer, more grateful. The war was good to me, and good for me. But I was one of the lucky ones.

I often think about the guys who found themselves in the wrong place at the wrong time, like Ben Ranaudo, Snowy Moerland or Robbie Poate, who died too young; or like Dave Savage and Paul Warren, whose lives and limbs were changed forever; or Crash MacKinney, who never made it home for the birth of his child. And I think I owe it to them to be happy here in this land of plenty. And I owe it to them to tell their stories. What else can you do?

Derapet

You're looking hungry, cobber, here, plant your arse down, mate
Would you like some mashed potatoes with that burger on
    your plate?
It's been another long shift here at the Coober Pedy mess
But if you've got a minute I've got something on my chest

The twenty-fourth of August back in 2010
I was working out of Tarin Kowt with a squad of twenty men
The Dutch had pulled the pin leaving Uruzgan for good
It fell to us to fill the void to the west in Deh Rawud

It had been a lethal summer, starting back in June
We'd lost Smithy, Snowy, Aplin, Palmer, Chucky and then Bewes
August took down Jason Brown, then Kirbs and Tomas Dale
On the morning of their service, we set out on Route Whale

I was carrying the Maximi it was a thumping belt-fed gun
With an action like a jackhammer, the weapon weighed a tonne
We drove south of the Tangi to an RV where we met
With two bricks of boys from Anar Joy and we turned for Derapet

Lance jack MacKinney – the boys all called him 'Crash'
He was the fastest bastard we all knew for distance or for dash
A soldier's bloody soldier and the fittest man I've met
I was proud to march beside him on approach to Derapet

Sixty clicks out in the sticks to the west of Tarin Kowt
The sappers saw the FAMs move in and the women all clear out
A TIC was what we wanted, a TIC was what we'd get
It was only a matter of when and where in the fields of Derapet

Me and Crash were partnered in reserve back at the rear
Although we weren't at point that day I felt and smelt the fear
The boys kept probing forward through the aqueduct and sluice
Till from a nearby tree line I could see all hell break loose

They'd hit a complex ambush of about a hundred men
There was the chattering of AKs and the thud of PKMs
The rounds were whistling around them but we couldn't tell
    where from
'Cause the Taliban had concealment in the tree line and the corn

A call came on the Icom to come forward from the back
They needed my machine gun up at the front of the attack
So me and Crash we hoofed it as the rounds around us cracked
Running with that weapon and my armour and my pack

We'd come 600 metres through the muddy aqueduct
By the time we reached the front line, frankly I was fucked
My mind said 'Keep going' but my body just said, 'Nope'
And I collapsed back on my pack at the bottom of the slope

Crash grabbed my Maximi and hauled it up to the crest
That's why he was where he was when the round burst through
    his chest
I looked up in that instant and I never will forget

As he spun around and crashed face down in the dust of Derapet

Woolley called for dust off, we were too far from the cars
We worked on Crash for an hour taking turns on CPR
The chopper came and medivaced him back in to TK
Where the doctor at the Role 2 declared him DOA

Meanwhile, Keighran broke cover, dancing dangerous and strange
A hundred Taliban muzzles flashed until the ASLAVs found
    their range
Between those gun cars, the Apache and the M777
Many Talibs became martyrs with their virgins up in heaven

The battle soon was over they had lost their will to fight
They left their dead and dying, they'd pick 'em up that night
We walked back to the ASLAVs and crawled into the FOB
I remember sitting quietly with Langer, Sean and Rob

Fanners ran the section through an after-action brief
I tuned in, though exhausted I was numb with shame and grief
The BDA said by the way there's thirty of them dead
and so they say we won the day and the Battle of Derapet.

Beckie's waters broke at the crematorium
Just a few hours later, she gave birth to a son
The boys help out with mowing and she got some compo cash
Helps pay the bills but it won't fill the hole where once was Crash

Langers won selection, Daniel Keighran got a gong
Abbott won the election, and Fred Smith got his song
Those who get these accolades deserve all that they get
But Crash did not deserve to die at the Battle of Derapet

I came back to Brisbane and got out on civvy street
Now I'm working in this mine, mate, in this mess where miners eat

I'm married now with children to a woman named Regret
It's the price you pay for a summer's day in the fields of Derapet

The Brisbane soldier was in bad shape for a while there, but when we last spoke he seemed to be coming good; he said he'd had a kid with his gal and they'd bought a house. These things take time, I suppose, and outfits like Mates4Mates and Soldier On play an important role in helping returned soldiers make it through the tunnel.

THE TREMBLING SKY

Never say die to the trembling sky

FRED SMITH, 'TREMBLING SKY'

I'M IN ROOM 12 OF THE COUNTRY ROADS INN IN WEST WYALONG ON the Friday night of a five-date tour of the Riverina. The decor is somewhere between grey and brown, and there's that sweet chemical smell of industrial carpet cleaner. Most of the other guests showed up in hi-vis.

We played tonight in the Soldiers' Memorial Hall, its lime green walls and timber floors reminiscent of its halcyon days as the town's dance hall. About twenty-five people showed up, most of them in their early eighties, apart from the local cop and a handful of farmers who sat in the back row sipping beer from sixpacks they had stashed in plastic shopping bags. The gig went nicely and the old timber hall sounded great, although the trucks rumbling past the front door every five minutes were a distraction.

As with the previous night's show, a couple of saints from the town arts council helped with the pack-up (bless them). The deputy mayor, Mrs McGlynn, said she loved the show but just wished more people had come to see it. 'It's a hard show to sell,' she said. 'People are always looking for the feel-good factor, and it was hard to explain to them what it is with this show!'

Now, sitting on the bed in the motel, I cruise Facebook to slow my mind down for sleep. I 'like' a photo posted by an Uruzgan colleague currently working in New York, and wonder how it is I came to be in West Wyalong. The short answer is that I've been touring a show called *Dust of Uruzgan* on and off since I got back from Afghanistan.

I stopped gigging for a couple of months after Oly was born and went back to work. As usual, good things happen when I stay still.

At work one morning in February 2014, I was walking out of the elevator when I got a call on my mobile phone.

'Fred, it's Brendan . . .' said the caller.

'Brendan, how's it hanging buddy?!' I said. (The only Brendan I knew was my self-identified 'yobbo' mate from Queensland.)

'. . . from the Australian War Memorial,' the caller finished.

'Dr Nelson,' I said, adjusting my tone.

Dr Nelson said he had been talking to Lee Kernaghan, who was keen to get in touch with me. He asked if it would be okay to pass on my number to the country music star.

I said that would probably be all right, and an hour later Lee called. He said he had heard the song 'Dust of Uruzgan' and loved it. He asked me how I came to write it, and said he was keen to record it for an album called *Spirit of the Anzacs* he was working on.

We ended up recording the song as a duet, working with producer Garth Porter, the former keyboard player from Sherbet. Lee and his team don't muck around and they had the best session guns in Sydney in there, bearing down on the song with the intensity of special forces hunting a target. It was awesome to watch them roll, and we ended up with a searing rendition of the song; it's fierce and it works. The *Spirit of the Anzacs* album topped the Australian charts for three consecutive weeks, the first time that had happened since INXS. The album was even available at the post office!

Meanwhile, my dream to tour an Uruzgan show to proper theatres was coming together. Working independently and with regional touring bodies, I had organised a fifty-date itinerary for the winter of 2014. Now all I had to do was write the show!

It wasn't hard to do. Most of the building blocks were already there from the gigs I had played at Poppy's and from touring the album in 2011–12. And that second stint in Uruzgan had given me what I needed to finish the story – a vantage point from which to reflect on the overall arc of the mission, and two new songs, 'Derapet' and 'Going Home', to round out the show. I could offer a fairly complete account of the Australian experience in Uruzgan: how we came to be there, what the challenges were, what we might have achieved and all that we'd lost.

I debuted this full and final incarnation of the *Dust of Uruzgan* show at the Shoalhaven Entertainment Centre on Anzac eve, Thursday, 24 April 2014, taking the stage with Liz Frencham on double bass and Carl Pannuzzo on keyboards and percussion. It worked. In the quiet dark space of that well-appointed theatre, I felt the magic of song, story and images all weaving together to transport the audience back to Uruzgan Province.

The following morning, I played 'Sapper's Lullaby' at the dawn service at the School of Military Engineering at Steele Barracks in Moorebank, then drove across town to Allianz Stadium to perform at the NRL's annual Anzac Day Cup. The next day, Saturday, 26 April, we flew up to Cairns and played a show at the Centre of Contemporary Arts before driving south for a Monday night date at the Townsville Entertainment Centre.

I hadn't attempted to make contact with Paul Warren since 2011, figuring his general preference was to be left alone. But from the media he'd received in 2013, I knew he had come out of the cave, and with some velocity! So I'd sent him an email inviting him and his wife Dee to the concert.

I arrived at the Townsville Civic Theatre with a gnawing sense of dread. I had always worried that I might have invaded Paul's privacy by writing the song. And what do you say to a man whose story you've been singing for the last four years? As we sound-checked, Liz and Carl sensed I was on edge. I explained to them that Paul Warren would be at the concert, which then made them a bit edgy too. To make matters worse, by the time we walked out to perform, there were only about sixty people in a 600-seat auditorium. I could see Paul sitting there in the second row right in front of me. There was nowhere to hide.

To stand up in front of a guy and pretend to be him describing the day he stepped on a mine and lost his mate was . . . well, confronting. As the song began, thoughts were running through my head: *Who am I to be doing this? How is he feeling about this?* But sometimes on stage you just have to throw a switch, turn off the thousand variables you've been juggling in your mind to make the gig come together, get inside the song and deliver it, knowing you can't control how people respond. That's where I went in the end, and we finished the song, and then the set, and broke for intermission.

It was in the foyer at half-time that I first met Paul. I quickly felt at ease with him, but not because he carried himself in a particularly relaxed manner. He was an intense guy with eyes wide open, rocking back and forth on his prosthetic leg. There was a direct, no-bullshit energy about him that I trusted immediately. And with Dee there by his side emanating strength and good sense, we managed to have a decent conversation in that hectic foyer environment with people thrusting CDs at me to sign.

Paul said he was really enjoying the show, that it had given him a bigger-picture sense of the Afghan situation and what we were doing there, the stuff they didn't explain to diggers in any detail. He said a few of his mates who had got out of the army had, like Paul, found work as security guards on Nauru and Manus Island. The fly-in-fly-out lifestyle and work environment was not particularly healthy psychologically. Many former army mates were struggling and he suspected more guys would end up taking their own lives after returning than had perished over in the 'sandpit'. He wanted to do something about this and had a few ideas. I had the sense of a man beginning to find his purpose. I found him inspiring and returned to Canberra the following day with my own sense of purpose renewed. I applied for a chunk of recreation I'd accrued from DFAT, and prepared myself for a long winter on the road.

❖

The second leg of the tour took me to the Northern Territory. The budget was tight, so I played it solo. Maryanne and Oly came along for the trip, the former sitting at the side of the stage clicking through the images on a laptop with the latter, now five months old, strapped to her mother's chest, sleeping. We played Olive Pink Gardens in Alice Springs and the Tennant Creek RSL before heading up the road to Katherine. After a couple of gigs in Darwin, at which I pulled Private Treasure out of Robinson Barracks to play bass, I rejoined the band for the third leg of the tour in regional Victoria. The audiences weren't always huge, but the reviews were generous:

That was one of the best shows I've seen in my life. It was informative, intelligent, insightful, it had humour, emotion and restraint. A story well told.

Sharon Hope, Ballarat (email)

A great tribute to the young soldiers and also enlightening about why we were there.

Dave Jenkins, Kyneton on Facebook

The stories told help us to form an understanding of the people on all sides of the story.

Eleanor Dempster, Fargum Pastoral Co., Tooborac (email)

Not all the responses have been positive. Sometimes I am misunderstood. On a *Dust of Uruzgan* poster I'd stuck above a urinal at the National Folk Festival, someone scribbled: *Warmonger! Come and see Fred Smith defend war.* Following a performance at the Yackandandah Folk Festival, an audience member wrote an email to the organisers complaining that the show was 'racist', particularly the song 'Live Like an Afghan'. I've always thought of 'Live Like an Afghan' as my own little homage to the resilience and courage of the Afghan people, balanced with some gentle pokes at a few of the contradictions in the culture, which the Afghans themselves acknowledge are manifold.

I still take to the stage with nuance and irony in the kitbag. This leaves one open to the possibility of being misconstrued by the mischievous or misunderstood by the pathologically self-righteous. But I'll persist, though it's not safe, because the truth has many versions, and I can't think of a better way of explaining this. I'm not going to tell people what to think. That's a politician's job.

Duke Ellington once said, 'Never underestimate your audience.' While the *Dust of Uruzgan* show covers tough terrain, people do seem to 'feel good' when they walk out. Perhaps this is because they haven't had their intelligence insulted. Perhaps it's because they've been given the opportunity to use their imagination, draw some inferences and sit with the complexities. I can understand though how Mrs McGlynn might have struggled to convey this to the good burghers of West Wyalong.

I got back from the Victorian tour in late June 2014 and was killing time on Facebook one evening when I saw a post from Paul Warren:

> Thanks to my wife Dearne Acland for keeping me honest,
> my book manuscript is done. Let's get this bad boy published.

In 2013, I had received emails from a couple of publishers about writing a book, including Jane Palfreyman at Allen & Unwin. I had got back to Jane saying I was keen and had even written an outline, but simply hadn't got around to writing the damn thing. I was intimidated by the task. A song I could knock off in an afternoon, but a book . . . that could annoy me for years. So here was me, with two university degrees, eight albums under my belt, offers from publishers and twenty-seven diary notebooks from my time in Afghanistan, procrastinating about writing a book. Meanwhile, this kickboxing private soldier from Townsville had just planted his arse in a chair and smashed one out. Like the people who make the sneakers say: 'Just do it!' Paul had. And good on him! I replied to Paul's post, offering to put him in touch with Jane Palfreyman.

Jane liked Paul's book proposal and engaged one Jeff Apter to work with him on his manuscript. The book, *The Fighter*, published by Allen & Unwin in 2015, is a fascinating account of a guy coming back from the brink, and offers hope to soldiers struggling with 'the difficult return'.

I suppose I did Paul a favour putting him in touch with Jane, but it felt like the least I could do for a guy whose story I'd been singing for three years. What goes around comes around and good things came back to me pretty quickly: Jeff contacted me and asked me to write an afterword. I agreed, and knocked out 6000 words in a week. I enjoyed the writing, and felt there was a story I was uniquely placed to tell, not just about the heroics of our soldiers, but also about the political and tribal dimensions of our work in Uruzgan – we weren't just there playing shoot-'em-ups. So I got in touch with Jane and said, 'Let's do it,' and give or take the odd gig and weekly turns behind a desk at the Department of Foreign Affairs and Trade, I've had my bum in a chair ever since.

The tour went on. In August 2014, we worked with Country Arts WA to take the *Dust of Uruzgan* show right through the state, starting up in Broome and dropping south. In every town people would come up to us after the show, keen to talk about their particular connection to the story we were telling: sons, cousins, nephews and nieces who had served in Afghanistan, fathers who had fought in Vietnam, grandfathers in World War II. Many said they felt a need to reach an understanding of the Afghanistan mission that twelve years of media coverage had failed to provide.

One Afghanistan vet posted on Facebook:

> Thank you for a very enjoyable and memorable show at Exmouth Yacht Club last night. As a veteran of two tours to Afghanistan, I think you produced a very accurate portrayal of the country, the people, and the Australian men and women who have all experienced 'time' over there. I took my wife with me to your show, and she commented that it

gave her a better understanding of what I couldn't tell her about my experiences.

Shane Cheney

In Perth's State Theatre I did a variation on the *Dust of Uruzgan* show, more a lecture than a theatre piece, as part of a series of events to launch *Afghanistan: Hidden Treasures*. This exhibition had an extraordinary backstory. In the mid-1990s, as chaos reigned in Kabul and with the Taliban circling the city, a handful of curators at the National Museum of Afghanistan saw the writing on the wall and moved millions of dollars worth of artwork and antiquities into a vault in the country's Central Bank. They sealed the vault with bricks and mortar, swearing an oath of silence before going their separate ways. Some of the curators perished while others fled as refugees to Pakistan, the United States and Melbourne. When the Taliban fell, the vault was reopened and the contents were toured, with DFAT support, as the *Hidden Treasures* exhibition.

I had written the text of the lecture in a grimy motel room in Cue two nights beforehand. (I get a lot of writing done in grimy motel rooms.) The more academic format was a new challenge and gave me the opportunity to delve into the history and politics of Afghanistan, as well as to trot out some of the statistics I'd spared the parents that morning at Poppy's on 2 November 2013:

By the time we left Uruzgan, we estimated there were 200 schools in the province, including thirty-eight girls' schools, six times more than there were in 2006. There were thirty-two health clinics around the province and 70 per cent of pregnant women were getting at least one prenatal healthcare visit.

And we built bridges and fixed up more than 200 kilo-metres of roads. This made a big difference to people's lives in a province defined by its isolation.

Beyond Uruzgan, Australia played a role in an international mission that fundamentally changed life in Afghanistan.

There is now a network of passable roads, including a national ring road and other access roads. Thirty-six TV stations and more than 100 radio stations are broadcasting, and there are several newspapers. Twelve million mobile phones are in use!

Eight million children are at school, including some 2.7 million girls. Back in 2001 there were only 900,000 kids at school, very few of them girls.

There is also a lively parliament, including forty women; and there are the makings, at least, of a vibrant civil society. And last year Afghanistan held elections which led to the first non-violent political transition in Afghan history.

In short, the lights have been switched back on in Afghanistan, and they can't readily be switched off. Whatever happens after 2014, the country will not go back to what it was in 2001.

The lecture I delivered wasn't all statistics and politics. I played a handful of songs, and I took great delight in introducing a special guest: Rafi! The terps' visa applications had not only made it through the post to Islamabad, they had been processed. With a week's notice, Rafi had found himself on a plane to Australia. Others followed, including Zia and Umary. The single guys were settled in Perth, while the married guys and their families went to Newcastle.

I took advantage of Rafi's presence in the audience to make some comedy, drawing him up on stage to demonstrate the alacrity with which Afghans greet one another in the street: the series of hugs, kisses, and *Salaam aleikums*.

That evening, me and the band and a few staff from Country Arts WA went to the house in the northern suburbs of Perth that Rafi was sharing with a couple of our former terps. They had set up a mini shura space in one of the rooms, with cushions on the floor. Rafi was prospering. He'd got a job as a forklift driver in a warehouse and had bought a car. Needless to say, he and his mates laid on the hospitality – delicious lamb stew and Afghan saffron-and-sultana-infused rice. They told stories about life in Afghanistan and the funny things that happened in Uruzgan, which gave the band a fresh take on the place they'd heard me banging on about on stage.

Their observations about Australia were interesting and of course the adjustment to living here was not easy. They were amazed by the absence of guns here, and pretty bloody happy about it. They were finding our suburban streets a bit quiet and lonely, and were puzzled as to why the people who picked the fruit for the supermarkets didn't wait till it was ripe. In common with most Afghans encountering the Western world, they were finding Australia stupidly busy. Most of them were working jobs in petrol stations and studying at TAFE, while running around trying to sort out various bits of paperwork like driver's licences, bank accounts, medical procedures and Centrelink forms. Rafi said the guys in Newcastle with wives and kids were struggling without grandparents at hand to help out, which would be the norm in most households in Afghanistan.

So the winter of 2014 was all about touring *Dust of Uruzgan*. Come the spring, it was time to move on. On my return from Western Australia, I put the finishing touches on the album I had begun with Shane O'Mara in November 2012, the recording sessions for which had been interrupted when DFAT called, offering me the job back in Afghanistan. I had trouble deciding whether to include 'Going Home' and 'Derapet' on the new album, or to stick them on a reissued version of *Dust of Uruzgan*. In the end, it made sense thematically to put the new Afghanistan songs on the new record, which I called 'Home', as it was broadly about the challenges of coming home and calming down.

While the new album was thematically about coming home, promoting it of course involved getting out on the road again – a paradox not lost on my wife. Still, it was nice to be playing gentler material after the tough terrain of the *Uruzgan* album and I made it through to the end of the year with my marriage intact.

Maryanne went back to work in February 2015. I resolved to spend more time at home looking after the baby, watering the plants and contemplating whether to shave off the beard I'd grown for Afghanistan. I was doing all three on an early autumn afternoon in March 2015 when news came on the radio of the death of Matiullah Khan. I whispered under my breath, 'Faaark,' or words to that effect. I was never a great fan of MK, but understood his importance to security in Uruzgan.

As always, it never became clear what happened. Like JMK and MDK before him, he perished in Kabul, this much we know. The 'official' version was that he was walking down a street in the city's sixth police district when a person wearing a burqa approached and detonated a suicide vest. The Taliban claimed responsibility; they always do. But according to a friend and confidante of MK – quoted by *The Sydney Morning Herald* – when he washed Matiullah's's body he found a bullet entry wound on the left side of his neck, another on his left shoulder, and bruising on his wrists consistent with MK having fought to free himself from handcuffs. MK security's detachment simply said he had gone walkabout alone that evening, which was very much out of character, and that his body turned up in the morgue eight hours later.

MK's death left the Afghan government with a dilemma: who to appoint as Uruzgan chief of police. The obvious choice was Matiullah's younger brother, but it took some time to resolve the decision in his favour. In the meantime, media reporting suggested the Taliban took advantage of the vacuum and had a fairly successful crack at police checkpoints in Deh Rawud and the peripheral districts.

In the months that followed, articles appeared in *The Sydney Morning Herald* and *The Canberra Times* essentially blaming the Australian mission for the situation in Uruzgan. One *Herald* article by Paul McGeough from 26 June 2013, with the headline 'Who killed Australia's warlord in Afghanistan?', began by describing MK as 'the corrupt millionaire police chief effectively installed by Australia as overlord' and sponsored and funded 'mainly by Australia'. The article concludes:

> The Australian and US military failed in a critical aspect of counterinsurgency doctrine enunciated by the former US commander in Afghanistan, General Stanley McChrystal, who demanded protection for 'all local populations'. In relying on warlord power in the form of Matiullah Khan, Australia put a floor under the local patronage machine run by a man who became a provincial dictator. Those who were Popalzai were looked after; those who weren't, said Juma Gul [former Uruzgan police chief], 'were treated cruelly'.

I didn't write this book to engage in history wars, and for most of my time in Tarin Kowt I was in the Matiullah-skeptic camp. But I'll set the record straight, because if I don't, no one else will. I won't tell you what to think, but I'll tell you what I think, and what I know: we didn't install MK as chief of police; President Karzai appointed him. Indeed, we advocated in favour of keeping his predecessor in the job, and had concerns about MK's appointment to the position.

While we weren't entirely innocent of his ascension, Matiullah was certainly not sponsored and funded 'mainly by Australia'; he accumulated a critical mass of wealth and power between 2006 and 2010, when we were relatively minor players on the base. By the time we took over the PRT in 2010, and the Combined Team Uruzgan in 2012, the horse had bolted and he was a fact of life. We could have tried to work *against* him, I suppose, but then the British tried that with Sher Mohammad Akhundzada in 2006, unleashing chaos that killed hundreds of their men and played right into the hands of the Taliban. We could have tried to work *around* him as the Dutch did, tying ourselves in knots pretending there was no elephant in the room. So we chose to work *with* him – an option which, of the choices available, was the best one, and realistically the only one open to us given he was the government-appointed chief of police. And in the end, he was a constructive player and recognised as such by some of his former enemies.

To say that we looked after the Popalzai and treated the rest cruelly is simply inaccurate. Soldiers at the forward operating bases in Ghilzai, Noorzai, Barakzai and Achekzai country worked closely with tribal leaders like Malim Sadiq and Malim Habibullah to protect their people. The PRT, meanwhile, went out of its way to ensure that leaders of those tribes got a share of the projects.

To say we relied on warlord power to provide security in the province is inaccurate. Most of the ADF's time and energy in Uruzgan was invested squarely in the Fourth Brigade of the Afghan National Army, and they remain there and still use the airfield for resupply and leave. The theory of working in fragile and conflict-affected states is that international actors should invest in building institutions, not individuals. We worked hard on building the institutional capacity of the ANA Fourth Brigade, but in Afghanistan, 'big man culture' prevails; personalities dominate over institutions. Like my interlocutor from Dawi Oil said: 'Even little things go up to President Karzai.' It's called a patronage system. If we'd been prepared to stick around another couple of hundred years, perhaps we might have been able to make a dent in that. In the meantime, we could only do what we could, with what we had.

The broader problem alluded to in the *Herald* article is an important one though. It's a problem the international community is only now starting to wrestle with, and is well articulated by Sarah Chayes in her recent and aptly titled book *Thieves of State*. The West is now, more than ever, confronted by the question of what to do about fragile and conflict-affected states like Afghanistan. We swing on a pendulum between intervening and not intervening. We go in to Afghanistan and Iraq and struggle, making us reluctant to wade into places like Syria.

Doing nothing does not seem to be an option: the humanitarian costs of conflict are too awful to ignore. But also, the problems that brew in these 'failed states' become our problems – terrorism and narcotics to start with, as well as mass migration. Syria, Iraq and Afghanistan are currently the leading sources of refugees to Europe, and there are over seventeen million people displaced by conflicts in Africa looking for somewhere to live.

So the question is not whether we need to do something about conflict affected states, but what to do. The orthodoxy in recent decades has been to invest in building institutions. This makes sense, since fragile and conflict-affected states are the way they are because they lack these institutions. So we put money into programs to strengthen the capacity of governments to achieve legitimacy in the eyes of their people. We invest in their security forces, court systems, financial accountability and capacity to deliver services people really want, like health and education.

But what if the institutions we are trying to build are commandeered by elites who are corrupt or tribally partisan, or worse, use those institutions to persecute their enemies? When the state becomes criminalised in these ways, supporting those institutions causes resentment among those missing out or copping the rough end of the pineapple. This is how insurgencies are made. In a country full of bullets, there are no silver ones available; the latest wisdom is that the best we can do is to engage with the range of non-state actors who are actually influential in these contexts, and do the best we can to distribute power and wealth evenly within the society. In retrospect, these two pillars were the guts of the PRT's political strategy in Uruzgan post-2010.

Speaking of political strategies, the other thing we know about conflict-affected states is that, in the long run, the solution needs to be a political one. If there is a pathway to a political accord, there can be peace. That's why we succeeded in Bougainville. If there is no pathway to a political accord, war will continue. That's why the international community has been reluctant to go into Syria; at this stage, we can't see a way through.

In his book *Cables from Kabul*, former UK ambassador Sir Sherard Cowper-Coles laments the lack of a coherent political strategy throughout the international community's mission in Afghanistan. After returning from Kabul in 2010, Cowper-Coles became the UK special envoy for Afghanistan, working with my dad and counterparts from other coalition countries for three years to try to create a shared strategy for promoting a viable political accord in Afghanistan, central to which had to be some dialogue with the Taliban. In the end they failed, thwarted by the multiple tyrannies of complexity involved. The mission was ultimately controlled by the US, and there were many in the competitive Washington policy circles who felt negotiating with the Taliban was akin to negotiating with terrorists. And many in Kabul felt the same way, arguing the Taliban were so fractured that they were impossible to negotiate with, and in any case were untrustworthy and needed to be pursued to the hilt.

Of course, this absence of a clear winning political strategy is felt by soldiers on the ground, and in the recent ABC TV documentary series, *Afghanistan: Inside Australia's War*, retired generals speak critically of the failure of Australian political leaders to give the ADF a strategy for success in Uruzgan. In fairness, such a strategy was not an Australian leader's gift to give; no strategy for success in Uruzgan was possible without a strategy for success in Afghanistan, and for the reasons cited above, this never eventuated. Perhaps, after around 2003, such a strategy was not even available. Professor William Maley argues Afghanistan post-2001 was like a broken leg – we didn't set it right to start with, so it never healed. The line from the Bush administration at the time was 'We don't do nation building'; but, then, as Colin Powell famously said: 'You break it, you own it!'

Australian political leaders had a strategy. It was as simple as 'send troops in order to meet alliance and coalition commitments' and 'fight terrorism by strengthening the Afghan Government against entities that harbour terrorists'. In that sense, our soldiers achieved the government's first strategic objective the moment their boots hit the TK airstrip. They could have continued to achieve that objective if they had sat on the base in TK playing horseshoes. But the second objective was always going to be harder, and in any case, sitting passively is not how Australian soldiers roll, nor DFAT officers for that matter. We wanted to make a difference, so we got out there in the valleys and took our chances. Lives and limbs were lost, and for a while there we did make a difference. We took the ball 'two yards down the field'. Now the ball looks to have moved back a yard, but we did what we could, with what we had, while we were there.

❖

These thoughts are big thoughts to be thinking before bedtime in the Apple Inn in Batlow on a Sunday night after a five-date tour. I think about all this stuff during my day job in the Civil Military and Stabilisation Section of the Humanitarian Division of the Department of Foreign Affairs and Trade. Then I get out on the weekends and sing about it. It's a living, okay?!

The gig tonight in the Batlow Literary Institute was nice. Actually, the whole tour has been long on heart if a little short on glamour. As usual, in every town we meet people with some connection to the Afghanistan story. In Wagga a couple of RAAF pilots came out from the air force base; they had been involved in flying caskets home after ramp ceremonies. An Iraq veteran who suffered permanent damage in an IED strike also came out with his wife. In Coolamon, the mother of one of Sapper Snowy Moerland's close mates showed up. She said her son was only just starting to get over the death. In Temora, a Vietnam vet told me the show reminded him of patrolling the jungles of Vietnam. He was a big fit-looking bloke with an Order of Australia pin on his sports jacket, but I could hear the quiver in his voice when he recounted the work sappers did probing the jungles for mines and booby traps out the front of those patrols, and the ever present fear of being killed by something you didn't see.

Before the Batlow gig tonight, a quietly spoken well-dressed woman approached me and introduced herself as the aunt of one of the young men shot dead by an Afghan soldier in the 'green-on-blue' incident in 2012.

I could see her sitting in the third row of seats, and feel the intensity of her concentration during the first half of the show as we played through some of the tougher songs – 'Dust of Uruzgan' and 'Sapper's Lullaby' in particular. Towards the end of intermission, after I had sold a few CDs, she came up to me and we talked a little more.

'All those young lives ruined,' she said. 'Such a waste, and what for? The Taliban seem to be taking over again.'

I wasn't of a mind to argue. Her second point is partly right. According to a recent article in *The Economist*, 'the Taliban currently contest more territory than at any point since 2001'. It goes on to say: 'Yet the Taliban are not on the verge of victory. Government forces still control all the main towns and cities. Big advances by the Taliban have usually been reversed within a few days . . . Defeating the Taliban proved impossible; preventing them from winning is probably easier.'

The coming fighting season is going to be tough, particularly in the south. Insurgents in any civil war have an advantage in that their enemy, the government, is obliged to hold all territory, whereas they are free to swarm and attack one place. Taking a city or town for them is possible and creates media excitement. Holding territory is harder. While the government forces can hold the cities, the Taliban business model suits rural areas, where the syndicate can intimidate people. Afghans are survivalists and it's easier to spread fear than hope. The Afghan security forces number 300,000. The Taliban are estimated to have about 30,000. If we continue to support the Afghan government and security forces, the most likely scenario is an ongoing stalemate, with the Taliban chipping away at people's sense of personal security, the fabric of society and prospects for growth and progress. Most Afghans would consider this stalemate better than the alternative – a reversion to the chaos of the civil war years, or to the horrors of the Taliban era. So they plead with the international community for ongoing support.

I could have offered some response to her first proposition – that it was all such a waste – but it was time for the second set to start. We kicked in upbeat with 'Taliban Fighting Man', then took things down with 'August 20', and even lower with 'Derapet'. At that low ebb, my monologue asked Ben Ranaudo's mum Jenny's question, 'Did we make a difference?', then I ran two minutes of footage of the Uruzgan elders speaking to that topic. As the MP4 ended, we went straight into 'Going Home', the last chord of which always feels like the end of the show but isn't – it's a false bottom of sorts.

After 'Going Home', I generally loosen up a bit and say whatever comes to mind. Tonight, at the Batlow Literary Institute, I opened up and addressed the question that Wade counselled me to avoid in front of the parents back in November 2013 . . .

> Thanks for coming along tonight to hear my songs and stories. I appreciate this is not exactly a 'feel good' show, and that some of the songs are a bit heavy going. Still, 25,000 Australians have served in Afghanistan in the past fifteen years and I think it's important that we understand their experiences so they don't walk the land as strangers in the way that a generation of Vietnam veterans did.
>
> People out here in the bush tend to speak their minds, and throughout this Riverina tour people have been asking me questions you shouldn't ask a diplomat, like 'Was it worth it?' I'm not going tell you what to think, you can come to your own conclusions about that and I'm sure you will. The political calculus of war is always an ugly thing to look at too closely. And even a single soldier's death is a tragedy, and a failure of diplomacy, but maybe

the cost–benefit analysis looks something like this . . . The costs are easy to measure: we lost forty soldiers in southern Afghanistan and many have taken their lives since; 260 soldiers were wounded and a couple of diplomats too; and our mission there was expensive – probably around $7.5 billion. In terms of benefits, well, they are not as easy to put a figure on: certainly Afghanistan hasn't been a launching pad for terrorism since 2001 and we did make a difference while we were there. We gave the younger generation a glimpse of something better.

All this calculus is confused by the consideration that, for a nation of our size, values, alliances and allegiances, perhaps we had no choice but to be in Afghanistan. It was not just about honouring the alliance commitments to the US; it was a fifty-nation international coalition acting on a UN mandate. The Canadians, the Brits, all the western European nations, Singapore, New Zealand, Tonga were there. Then you look at the countries that weren't: Iran, Iraq, Syria, Russia. Who are we as a nation? What company do we want to be in? From this high strategic perspective, our elected leaders felt we had to be involved. That was the way the Liberal–National Party saw it, and that was the way Labor saw it. Bob Brown argued against our involvement for reasons I can respect, but other Greens were conflicted: they don't like war, they don't like the US alliance, but they don't like the Taliban either.

And at a moral level, the decision to go in to Afghanistan was made in the context of the time – in the immediate aftermath of 9/11, of course, but also the international community had just witnessed five years of Taliban rule. When the Talibs came to power in 1996, there was hope that they might at least bring some order after the chaos of the civil war years. But they turned out to be violent anti-modern thugs and the country went backwards in every way. The economy went to scratch and millions starved. Meanwhile, they introduced bizarre rules: women were forbidden from walking the streets without a male relative, men were forced to grow beards as long as the width of their fists, homosexuals were stoned to death, dancing was banned, music was banned, kite flying was banned, poetry was banned – Afghans love poetry and will travel miles and take risks to attend a poetry meet. All these rules were enforced by sham trials, public beatings and executions at half-time in the goal squares of football stadiums. As a consequence of all this, by 2001, there were over three million Afghan refugees outside the borders of Afghanistan. Most fled to the mountains of western Pakistan, but some made it out here to the Riverina.

This last song is written from the point of view of one of those refugees; it's called 'Trembling Sky'.

Trembling Sky

For Khaksar

For my homeland I am pining
I will keep this letter rhyming, they can decode, what is written
　　in prose

So they tried me in my absence, when I heard about my sentence
I had to smile, here in exile
For you know from your excursions if the truth has many versions
Then what is a lie, to the trembling sky?

As our nation looked for heroes we both fell in with the weirdos
All of our peers, artists and queers

As I recall we still were kissing, as our friends were going missing
Spit in the eye of the trembling sky!

If you are taken for correction, they will ask about connection
Just play the game, slander my name
And don't ask them for a reason, or they'll have you tried for treason
Never ask why of the trembling sky

As our countrymen all hardened, Esmat found me in my garden
Gave me the cue, time to slip through
So I hope you understand there was no time to touch your hand
When I had to fly from the trembling sky
Never say die to the trembling sky

ACKNOWLEDGEMENTS

THANKS ARE DUE TO MANY PEOPLE, BEGINNING WITH THOSE WHO shared this journey with me. To colleagues from Australian, Dutch and US foreign ministries, your camaraderie, decency and good humour made working in Afghanistan a pleasure. We've gone our separate ways, but I treasure our friendships and the unguarded collegiate way we put our heads together to make sense of Uruzgan.

Likewise to the many soldiers I worked with – deep respect for your commitment to task and calm common sense in a difficult place. I particularly thank the sappers and infantrymen who protected me outside the wire, and others I worked closely with: headquarters staff; the two shop collectors and analysts; PRT personnel; OGA Platoon; and the public affairs officers.

I would like to highlight the work of Defence photographers who took their chances downrange to capture so many great images, some of which appear in this book and in the *Dust of Uruzgan* show. Among them are Doc Doran, Rachel Ingram, Paul Berry, Mick Davis and Haydn Barlow.

Special thanks to the interpreters and cultural advisers – particularly Zia, Hamidi, Willem, Umary and Rafi Shaheen – without whom I would have been deaf and dumb over there.

Thanks go to the members of various iterations of the Tarin Kowt Musicians Union, including Bainesy, Glenn Treasure, Alex Tompkins, Jeff Schaeffer, Debbie Xinos, Johnno, Amy, Jeremy Goodnight, Carola, Wali, Rassoud and George.

Special thanks to Liz Frencham, Carl Pannuzzo and Steve Vella for their egoless commitment to delivering the *Dust of Uruzgan* show here in Australia. And my publicist Christine Taylor for her work on the *Dust of Uruzgan* album. Also to the staff at Regional Arts Victoria, Country Arts WA, Artback NT, ArTour Queensland and Eastern Riverina Arts for getting the show on the road.

In the production of this book, there have been many editors, and I am grateful for their close attention to this text: Jeff Apter has been with me from the start as mentor, cheerleader, sounding board and editor of first call. Without him, this book would be longer. Then Ali Lavau, in her comprehending and comprehensive way, brought her sensibilities to bear.

A number of colleagues from DFAT have read all or parts of the text, particularly Rohan Titus, Bernard Philip, Alan Sweetman, Paul Foley, Kate Elliot, David Savage and David Windsor. Likewise from Defence: Jason Blain, Justin R and others, and my mate Bruce Ryan at no fixed address. My dad, Ric Smith, has read it two or three times. I've valued your suggestions, editorial and prudential. That said, any mistakes and all the judgements in this manuscript are my responsibility alone. Every one of us experienced a different Afghanistan, and this is only my account of what I saw.

I am grateful for the prompt and sensible way the DFAT and Defence media units have handled the clearance of this book. I won't name names but appreciate those of you who took time from busy schedules to scrutinise the text.

And thanks to the team at Allen & Unwin – my publisher Jane Palfreyman, who approached me out of the blue about *The Dust of Uruzgan*, and editor Sarah Baker for her meticulous work in seeing the project through to completion.

ArtsACT have supported me in the writing of this book, and at a number of other important junctures in my artistic career.

Families of those who perished in Afghanistan, or who have succumbed since, deserve special acknowledgement: those I've written about herein, and the many I haven't. I wish you courage, strength and peace. And to those still feeling the psychological and emotional effects of service in Afghanistan, you are not alone.

Finally, much love and thanks to my family, especially Mum, Dad, Oly and Maryanne for their support and their tolerance of my absences, physical and emotional, while in the field, on the road, and in the writing of this book. I'm home now.